This was really great. Finally we were getting to shoot at targets we could see instead of colored smoke rising up through the trees. My elation was interrupted by a huge explosion inside the building, and it appeared that the roof had come off in one complete section, rocketing straight up. Beneath the roof was an ominous black-and-red fireball. For a split second, it looked like something out of a Saturday-morning cartoon. Then reality set in and I thought that my life had ended. I didn't see how we were going to miss all that flying roof, now directly in front of us and only seconds away from flying through my windshield.

I felt my whole body being pushed into the seat with unbelievable force as Zeroth pulled the Cobra into a near-vertical climb. "Too late," I whispered, and closed my eyes as I felt and heard the terrifying sounds of debris impacting on the Cobra's bottom.

APACHE SUNRISE

Jerome M. Boyle

IVY BOOKS • NEW YORK

Ivy Books
Published by Ballantine Books
Copyright © 1994 by Jerome M. Boyle

Map copyright © 1994 by Bob Rosenburgh

Library of Congress Catalog Card Number: 94-96131

ISBN 0-8041-1069-7

Manufactured in the United States of America

First Edition: December 1994

10 9 8 7 6 5 4 3

DEDICATION

This book is dedicated to Sonny and Dusty Jones, of Muleshoe, Texas, and their children, Kyle and Bonny. Also Clay, Mary, and Jan Kellenberger of Oceanside, California. Their advice, letters, tapes, and care packages, provided the love and support so needed during my eighteen months in Vietnam.

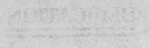

IN MEMORY OF

All those who gave their lives doing what they loved the most, flying helicopters, especially;

RICHARD HENKE, my classmate and good friend, who gave his life when his helicopter disintegrated in flight in May 1970, over Vietnam.

NORMAN R. "RED" COONS, my platoon leader and teacher who taught me and so many other pilots how to survive and how to protect those who depended on us. Norm lost his life when his civilian helicopter disintegrated in flight over south Texas in July 1980.

ACKNOWLEDGMENTS

When this project was begun, I had no idea how many people would become involved in assisting me to write it. I would like to thank Marc, Eric, and Ernest Hermann of Channel Coast Yacht Service for their moral and financial support and the use of their office equipment. Tom and J. T. Taylor, Ada County sheriff's officers, Boise, Idaho, for their invaluable assistance with research. Art Docktor, for initially suggesting that I write my story. Richard Horne for making my dream a reality. David Boyle for his misguided admiration. Walt "Buff" Kenyon for his twenty years of being my mentor, which, thank God, has been far superior to his ability as a navigator or duck hunter. A very very special thanks to Sonny, Dusty, Kyle, and Bonny Jones, of Muleshoe, Texas, who, for over thirty years, have treated me as part of their family and had the foresight to save all the letters, tapes, pictures, and maps that I sent them from Vietnam; without them, this project would never have gotten off the ground. My beautiful wife, Andrea, who, for the last twenty years, has guided my life through thick and thin, and without whom there would be no life. James, Kevin, and Jennifer, my children, and Mike Kenyon, who always wanted to read the page not yet written. And Brent and Matt Mikesell, my stepsons. Carl Rosapepe for being my copilot while I learned to become a better pilot, and for being the best map reader Apache Troop ever had, a fellow aircraft commander, and my roommate and—despite that—remaining one of my closest friends over the last twenty-three years. Thanks to the guys on Ventura police department, Tom Burke, Herb Dynge, Marv Houghton, Larry Lotton, and Bill Strickland who resisted Blue Boy and supported me while in Vietnam and well after my return. Thanks also to the Ventura County Footprinters for their support, and to the owners of North Star Escrow of Ojai, California, for all their help and for the use of their office equipment and supplies. Thanks also to James Edward Thompson, for being my best buddy since fourth grade and introducing my book to Mace Neufeld of Neufeld/Rehme Productions, and his assistant, Kathy Day, who liked what they read. To John R. Siperly, Illinois Department of Veteran's Affairs, and his beautiful assistant Ava, who worked for days to locate many of the people mentioned in this book. To John and Sue Farrell, Terry and Lois Farrar, Ed and Opal Clinkenbeard, and Dave Vadnais for their constant kicks to my rear end. To Ansel Schoonover and Brian Swopes, my aviation flight instructors, who are two of the greatest pilots I know, and to all the Apache Troop pilots who refreshed my memory, especially John Bartlett.

I would also like to thank Owen Lock, my editor. Himself a veteran, he guided me, advised me, and did not pressure me, even though it took me a lot longer to complete the book than first thought. Without him, obviously, this story and the people mentioned and their story, would have faded to dull memories.

I would like to thank Kregg P. J. Jorgenson, author of *Acceptable Loss* (Ivy Books) and *Necessary Battles* (Ivy Books, forthcoming), who, while a sergeant in the Blue Platoon, on two occasions I'm sure of, but probably more, was responsible for getting me out of a crash site alive, at the risk of his own life, and then, twenty-two years later, provided the inspiration, guidance, and unyielding prompting and encouragement to start, continue, and complete this book.

Finally, I would like to acknowledge and thank the great people of the San Carlos Apache Reservation and the Apache fire fighters at Point of Pines, especially Gary and "Bear," who taught me the true meaning of "Apache."

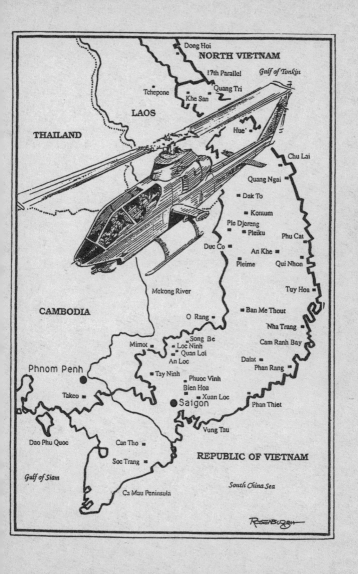

PROLOGUE

1960

I felt the sharp jolt as the chute deployed above me. I looked up to check the panels, as I always did, and finding everything okay, looked toward the sandy beach where ten or so friends were waiting to pick me up. But it became clear that the wind was no longer as strong as when I had measured it two hours earlier; instead of being blown toward the beach, I was heading straight down toward the ocean. Everything seemed to be going by in slow motion except the realization that I was going into the water approximately a half mile offshore.

It was early September, and I was performing a demonstration jump for some of my coworkers and friends. The pilot, Ansel Schoonover, who was also my fixed-wing instructor, had put me out at forty-five hundred feet after advising the local airport control tower to disregard calls about a crazy parachutist.

I was twenty-two years old, in very good shape, was reasonably sane, and wasn't too worried about swimming to the beach. Of course, I knew that I would have to get my heavy jacket and boots off before starting for the beach. But what seemed like a simple task, turned into a nightmare when, while I was taking off my jacket and treading water, the shroud lines of the chute wrapped around my ankles. I had unstrapped my helmet on the way down and dropped it, and now wished I had done the same with my boots. To complicate matters, when I contacted the water, my reserve chute had popped open, which meant I had two chutes and fifty-six shroud lines around me. I felt like a fly in a spider's web. The main chute sank first, then the reserve, and with my ankles bound together by shroud lines, I quickly followed. Each time I attempted to get the lines

1

off my ankles, I sank and had to flail with my arms to get back to the surface.

What happened next was to change my life forever, although it would not become apparent for nine years. This single incident allowed me to go to army flight school, Vietnam, and Apache Troop, 1st of the 9th Air Cavalry—and with the exception of my wife and children, those three things were and are the most important things in my life.

After sinking and beating my way to the surface, five or six times, I could no longer move my arms, and I resigned myself to the fact that I was going to die. As I was sinking, I remember the pressure changes in my ears, wondering how long I had before I could no longer hold my breath. Raised Catholic, but not very religious, I was thinking to myself, If there is really a God, I need your help now. Needless to say, I was more than merely surprised when the lines fell away from my ankles, and I started toward the surface. The next thing I remember is being dragged onto something and a young voice asking if I was okay, then being told not to worry, that his friend had picked up my helmet.

The young voice belonged to Richard Horne, then fourteen years old. I was spread across his paddle board, a thicker, longer surf board. Dick told me to hold on as we went down the front of a wave and slid up onto the beach. There I was lifted to my feet by my friends and taken to my apartment. Later that same afternoon, I went to a local gun store and bought a new .22 magnum rifle and gave it to Dick the following day.

Nine years later, and six months' worth of back-and-forth paperwork between Dick and Washington, D.C., including a waiver of my age (I was, by then, thirty-one; the age limit was twenty-nine), and an approved flight physical by the surgeon general himself, Dick, a first lieutenant in the army and in charge of the Los Angeles recruiting station, had me raise my right hand and swear to serve the U.S. Army until dead or discharged. This was four months prior to my thirty-second birthday. Now, thirty-one years later, I still have the helmet, Dick still has the rifle, and on the thirtieth anniversary of his saving my life, I gave Dick the rip cord which I had managed to hang onto throughout my rescue and the next thirty years.

We all have a skeleton or two in our closet. It is my intention to tell the whole story, regardless of how much it may hurt, and as well as my memory will allow.

From the onset of this project, I would like to make perfectly clear that I have a great deal of love for the army; not its bureaucracy. Because of the war in Vietnam the army provided a new occupation for me and gave itself the opportunity to learn a lot of lessons. Thank God, some of those lessons about what works and what doesn't didn't fall on deaf ears and blind eyes. The biggest proof that those lessons were learned was in General Schwartzkopf's actions during DESERT STORM.

The Apache Troop I served in wasn't part of the army; the army was part of Apache Troop! We were mavericks, but the kind of team that any commander with hair on his ass would want his unit to be like. If we couldn't get what we needed to accomplish the mission through normal channels, we begged, borrowed, or stole it, usually the latter. With few exceptions, I'd follow the men of Apache Troop into hell, knowing full well that sooner or later someone from the Blues, Whites, Reds, Lift, or Mess Sections would emerge from a smoking hole dragging the dead, smoldering ass of the Devil.

CHAPTER ONE

Driving down the winding mountain road from the police pistol range, I couldn't help but notice the fogbank that still engulfed the city. It was August 1968, and normally the fog would have been gone before ten in the morning. I had no idea that this cold chilling fog was about to wrap itself around my entire life and change it forever.

My wife was out of town, visiting her sister, and as I walked through the door, the phone was ringing. The call was from a girl I'd been seeing on and off for two years or so. Mostly I'd get on and then get off. As I had not heard from her in almost six months, I was caught a little off guard by the call, but nowhere near as much as by what she had to tell me. She said that she and her present boyfriend had been arrested for the sale of marijuana. The charge was later reduced to possession, but that wasn't much help to me and the five or six other police officers who, during the last year, had been observed in the lady's company.

"For actions unbecoming a police officer," I was fired after eight years on the department. None of the officers, including myself, had any involvement with her narcotics activity, but all were suspended or fired—depending on their relationship with their particular chief of police. Mine was about as bad as it could be, so I found myself on the outside looking in.

I attempted to find employment with other police departments, but even with glowing letters of recommendation from my commanding officers, I was turned down. Blue Boy, as we all called the chief, had given orders that all inquiries be directed through his office. He was out to make an example of us and, as some said, a political career as well.

I decided to turn to my second love, flying. The decision

was made easier by a saying that kept running through my head, "There is nothing worse than an ex-cop!" For the most part, the older guys treated me well, as they knew what the real story was. It was the younger officers who were giving me the cold shoulder. With money running short, I contacted my mother, who lived in North Hollywood, and asked if I could move myself and the family in with her.

My father had died three years earlier, so room at my mom's house was not a problem, and she loved my year-old son, Jamie, very much. Once the housing problem was solved, I again began to seek employment. Not only had I been frozen out of other police departments, but judging from the expressions I got from prospective employers when they read on my application that I had been fired from a police department, the winter of my discontent would be a long, cold one.

My world was looking about as inviting as one of those black holes in space, but a command-detonated Viet Cong mine would provide the key that opened the door for my entrance into flight school.

For six of my eight years on the police department, I was also a member of the Army Reserve; I had joined in 1961 to keep from being drafted. My unit was, at the time, an army field hospital, which meant that we operated in and out of tents as opposed to a shiny white building. But that was then. Seven years later, in 1968, I thought back to my first exposure to the army's way of doing things. In June 1961, I was sent to Fort Ord, California, for basic training, and then to Fort Sam Houston, Texas. In the four months that I spent in Texas, the army trained me as a combat medic. Vietnam, at that time, was only a place on the world map, but everyone knew where Cuba was. Army Reserve units were being activated, and everyone around me was hoping that his unit wouldn't be one of them; we all suspected that a war with Cuba meant a war with Russia, and this time it wouldn't be a police action like the one in Korea.

I don't think I'll ever forget the expression on Phil Eberle's face when he received word that his unit had been activated, and he would be remaining in the army for an additional year. I've kept in touch with Phil who is now a successful pharmacist in Merrillville, Indiana. I was one of the lucky ones who, on December 22, 1961, departed for good old California. Within three months of my return, I was back at Fort Ord serving forty-five days active duty for missing too many reserve meetings—it was the policy of the army at that time that if you missed more than four meetings in one year, you were ordered back to active duty for forty-five days.

Upon reporting to Fort Ord, with Bill Tudor, another reservist from my unit, I was asked by the CO what my duties were in my reserve unit. As I started to say, "Medic, sir," I was jammed in the ribs by Bill Tudor's elbow, and at the same time, I heard Bill say, "He was in my mess section, sir." From that day on, and even upon my return to my reserve unit, I was a cook.

I wasn't a strong believer in destiny at that time, but am now. The above incident seemed unimportant at the time; nine years later, that single incident was to play a major part in my Vietnam adventure.

It was now late September 1968. Martin Luther King had been killed, and Bobby Kennedy had been assassinated two months earlier. Hap Dittman, a good friend and my old scoutmaster, called me one morning and told me that he had arranged for an interview with the chief of police of Warner Brothers Studios. They had their own police department and thought that there might be a place there for me. The thought of my becoming a rent-a-cop didn't set too well, but I was broke by then and needed to do something, anything, to make money. I went to the interview, and the chief listened to my explanation without sign of belief or disbelief. At the end of the interview, we both stood up, and he looked me in the eye and said, "I believe you, son, and I'll get back to you." I left his office with more hope than I'd had in months.

But two weeks passed, and no word came from Warner Brothers. So I got in my car and drove north to Ventura to see a recruiting sergeant whom I had met a couple of times while on the police department. I told him that I wanted to get back into the army and go to flight school. He had a lot of really nice things to say, including, "you are too old and very out of shape." I left his office depressed, and drove around for hours. Suicide had entered my mind a few times, but I thought to myself, things are about as low as they can get, they can only get better.

Eventually I found myself sitting in front of the Army Reserve center. I really didn't know what I was doing there, but I thought that maybe good ol' Command Sergeant Major Book might be in a position to give me some advice. We talked for about an hour, but he didn't have much to offer. He did say that he would be more than happy to write a letter of recommendation for me whenever I wanted it.

In 1966, while still in the Reserve, I had applied for army flight school. The program allowed you to attend flight school on active duty and then revert back into the Reserve. I'd had the necessary college degree, but was turned down because there were no helicopter Reserve units within a reasonable distance of my Reserve unit.

As with a lot of things happening in my life at the time, chance played a big part in it. While I was sitting in Command Sergeant Major Book's office, waiting for him to get through doing some paperwork, I picked up an old copy of a newspaper. On the front page was a picture of Dick Horne. As I recall, he was in a hospital bed, with his wife, Julie, standing next to him. The article described how he had been "blown away" by a Viet Cong command-detonated mine* in the village of My Lai on July 7, 1968. Four months earlier, a lieutenant by the name of Calley had made a name for himself in the same village. Of course, it was the same Dick Horne who had saved my life some eight years earlier. I had lost contact with him upon his entry into the army.

The article indicated that Lieutenant Horne would be in Letterman Army Hospital for a little while longer and then would be reporting for recruiting duty in Los Angeles.

I drove down to the beach where Dick's mother lived and waited for her to get home from teaching school. I told her where I was staying and asked her to tell Dick I said hello and that I would really like to get together.

A few weeks later, while I was watering the front lawn, a car drove into the driveway and out stepped Dick. He didn't look like the Dick Horne that I'd known before he went to Nam. He was skinny, pale, and really looked like shit. I figured he had escaped from the hospital.

My mom had met Dick many times before and was as surprised as I was at his appearance. Army doctors had done a really good job patching him up, but even the best doctors in the world couldn't cover up all the scars. Dick's right ear had

---

*In most cases, such Viet Cong mines were not mines at all, but dud one hundred- or five hundred-pound U. S. bombs in which the Viet Cong had replaced the fuse with an electrical blasting cap. After that was done, they placed the new mine under a trail, waited until you were in the right position, then exploded it.

been blown off, but enough remained for the docs to sew it back on. But he would never hear out of that ear again. From head to toe, his right side had been filled with small sharp fragments of steel.

Dick and his wife had moved into an apartment in Canoga Park, at the west end of the San Fernando Valley. This put him about twenty minutes away from my house and about fifty minutes from the downtown Los Angeles recruiting station.

We sat in the living room for what seemed like hours, talking about Nam and what it was really like, and me telling him about my own little Vietnam right at home. Dick never did anything by halves. I think the army saw that also, because they took him directly from advanced infantry training (AIT) and sent him to officer candidate school (OCS). To this day, I don't know if what Dick said next was prompted by our close friendship, or because he was just being a good recruiting officer, but he looked me in the eye and said, "You know, Jerry, the army doesn't require that you list previous employers."

So began four very long months of paperwork. I told Dick that I was over the age limit. He replied, "Let me work on it," a saying that I've heard from him at least a few hundred times over the last thirty-one years. I pointed out to Dick that it was an old Indian tradition that if you saved someone's life that you were responsible for that life from then on. Dick has been doing his best to get me killed ever since just to get rid of that responsibility!

About a week after our meeting at my mom's house, Dick called. He suggested that I come down to Los Angeles and meet his commanding officer (CO) and executive officer ("exec"). We went to lunch together, and I had a chance to tell them what I wanted to do, why, and what I thought I had to offer the army. I told them of my six years in the Army Reserve, that I had a private pilot's license, and that I didn't think it would take a lot to transition into helicopters. I had no idea how dumb that sort of thinking was, but they listened and didn't laugh. And provided I could pass all the other preentrance exams, they agreed to help me try to secure a waiver of age. And with just one little catch, I did pass them all. On the day of my eye test, the enlisted medic administering the exam told me that the machine was showing that I had twenty–sixty eyesight. I understood enough about the army to know that if I continued the test and failed, that would be my last chance at it. So I got up, walked out, and drove home.

Dick called me that night and wanted to know how the test went. He was a little upset when I told him what I'd done, but in his typical way said, "Let me work on it." Within a few days he called me back and said that they had checked the machine and found it was defective, and that I should come back down and retake the test. The second test went considerably better.

With the testing behind me, we submitted the complete package to the Department of the Army, better known as DA, requesting a waiver of age. It took almost a month for DA to deny the request. Back to the black hole again.

As expected, Dick told me not to worry, that he was "working on it." He suggested that I go up to Ventura and see Sergeant Book and my former commanding officer and get some glowing letters of recommendation. He also said that he would send along a copy of my pilot's license when we resubmitted the request for waiver of age. I had no trouble getting the letters from Sergeant Book and Colonel Maguire (the latter just happened to be my personal doctor). Along with my pilot's license and letters, we resubmitted the request, and then waited for another month. I was beginning to think that the war would be over before I ever got through the damn paperwork.

In mid-December the request for waiver was approved, and I'm sure Dick was relieved. He would finally be getting rid of this pain in the ass! But, I still had one thing I wanted to do before I signed on the dotted line. I wanted to take and pass a military flight physical—there was no sense in joining up before I knew I was physically qualified to attend the school I wanted.

I don't know to this day how he did it, but Dick arranged for me to travel to Norton Air Force Base and take a class-one flight physical. That piece of paperwork then had to be submitted to the surgeon general for flight school approval. We were again in for a month-long wait. During that time, I started trying to get back into shape because I had a pretty good idea what was awaiting me. After all that paperwork crap, I wasn't about to flunk out because I couldn't do push-ups or double-time with the rest of the kids. I had told myself that, if told to, I'd get down and eat dog crap before I gave up and quit. That resolve was to be tested on more than one occasion, before flight school and during the forty weeks that I was learning how to become a warrant officer and a pilot, in that order.

On February 7, 1969, I raised my right hand, and the kid

who had saved my life nine years earlier swore me into the army. As I got on the bus that was to take me and the other recruits to the airport and from there to Fort Polk, Louisiana, I felt like a little boy entering school for the first time. I looked back at where Dick was standing, and the big grin on his face said it all. He had said he would see what he could do; now it was up to me to do the same.

CHAPTER TWO

The plane landed in a freezing rainstorm and almost skidded off the runway. As could be expected, I was the oldest recruit of the group, and the word had gotten around that I was "prior service." For most of the flight, I had been asked all the usual questions about what the candidates could expect. The questions continued while we waited for the bus from Fort Polk. I remember telling them to listen, not to ask questions, and not to volunteer for anything. I also told them that upon arrival, we would most likely be met by the biggest, blackest, meanest drill sergeant that they most likely would ever encounter. Unfortunately, my prediction came true. We were up all night and half the next day going through the routine. When we were finally shown a barracks and issued sheets and blankets, I was about dead. But I had to show the guys how to make their bunks so we wouldn't get our butts chewed out when the big, mean sergeant came back.

Within a few days of arrival, we all had to pull guard duty. Demeaning hardly describes the feeling I had, standing in a pouring rain with a clipboard hanging from a chain around my neck. The clipboard contained all my general orders. I really felt very stupid, and I was beginning to wonder what the hell I was doing there and why Dick had gone out of his way to make my life so miserable.

On one of those cold guard-duty nights, I went into a phone booth and called Dick—collect—just to tell him what a miserable son of a bitch I thought he was for letting me get myself into this position. He laughed good naturedly and told me to "hang in there."

On the fifth day, we were going through more processing

11

when an extremely nice first sergeant called me over to his desk and said, "Boyle, what the hell are you doing here?"

I said, "Sergeant, I'm here because I have orders to be here. Is there something wrong?" He informed me that whoever drew up my paperwork had screwed up big time. He went on to explain that because I had been out of the Reserves less than two years, that I was not, I say again, not, required to repeat basic training. I really can't explain my elation; it was better than a dream-come-true story. He had me sit down in his office, got me a cup of coffee, and said he would see what he could do about cutting me some orders. He took me off all recruit duty rosters and told me to go back to the barracks and wait for orders. I didn't have to pull guard duty that night; I could just sleep and hope that all the hair that they had cut off would grow back soon.

The next day I was assigned to Headquarters Company to await my flight-school class, which was to begin in May. Back into my black hole, headfirst. What the hell was I going to do for three and half months!

I reported into Headquarters Company the next morning and showed my orders to the spec four sitting at the desk. He told me where I'd be staying and to check the board at the end of the room for assignments. That afternoon, the paper was posted on the board, and my name had "KP" next to it for the next week, which meant cleaning pots and pans, peeling potatoes, and a sixteen-hour day. I called Dick again that night and told him what had happened and that I still thought he was an asshole for getting me into this. The following morning, I asked, and was granted, permission to speak to the first sergeant. As I walked into his office, he was talking to a bird in a cage next to his desk. He told me to sit down and seemed very friendly, possibly because, at thirty-one, I was probably the oldest recruit he had ever seen. I handed him a copy of my orders and asked if there was any way of moving the date for my flight-school class up a little—like three months? He turned his chair around so that his back was toward me and read the orders. He then stood up and showed the orders to the damn bird in the cage and asked the bird what he thought, and "could we help this poor recruit out?" It was then, prompted by the laughs of another sergeant, that I noticed the goddamn bird was stuffed. The Headquarters Company first sergeant explained to me that his company was full of grunts awaiting courts-martial, and all he could assign them to was KP. He gave me the name of a spec four at the adjutant general's office who he thought might be able to help me out. As I started to leave his office, the crazy sergeant said, "Hey, Recruit, be prepared to pay!"

I still had to pull KP that night, but I was at the personnel office first thing the next morning. I found the spec four and explained what I wanted to do. He indicated that he thought he could help me, but asked what I was willing to pay. At that point, I think I would have given him my first born to be on my way to flight school. He indicated that he really enjoyed whiskey and that a fifth would be enough. He further stated that I would have to get by the lady at the other end of the room who really liked flowers and candy. I told him that I'd be back with the stuff as soon as the PX opened. That afternoon I walked out of the AG's office with a huge smile on my face and fresh orders in my hand. Behind me in the AG's office was a spec four with two quarts of whiskey, and a middle-aged secretary with a dozen roses and two boxes of candy.

I almost ran back to the company area and into the first sergeant's office. I showed him the orders, and after he finished reading, he looked up and said, "You learn fast, Recruit. How much did all this cost you?"

What he had just read were orders allowing me to catch a plane for home that very night, a ten-day "delay enroute," authorization to drive my own car to flight school, starting in three weeks, and enough advance pay to get it all done. I was in hog heaven. And with any luck, might even get laid that same night. Well, two out of three wasn't bad!

The morning following my arrival home from Fort Polk, I received a call from the police chief at Warner Brothers. He offered me a great job at the studio, and I almost regretted having to tell him that he had waited just a little too long. He seemed honestly happy for me when I told him about army flight school, and he assured me a position in his department when I got back from Nam. He wished me luck.

Ten days later, I reported in to Fort Wolters, Texas, and was assigned to a "snowbird" company—a snowbird was a warrant-officer candidate not yet assigned to a flight class. I went into the black hole of depression again when I found out that some of the men in the company had been waiting for over a month to get into a class; it didn't take a lot of deep thought to figure what I'd be doing for the next month or so. I was getting real good at policing up parking lots, front lawns, and flight lines.

Two days after my arrival, we were bused to a building for

more processing. Upon arrival, in a pouring rain, a warrant officer told us to get off the bus and line up on the lawn in front of the building. After we'd stood in the rain for thirty minutes, a major came to the door, took one look and hurried back inside. Within seconds, what I first thought was an elf ran out the door and told us to get back on the bus. The elf was addressed as "Mr. Hampton." He was a chief warrant officer. Once we were back on the bus, he asked if anyone already had an approved flight physical. I was already standing, so I just came to attention and said, "Sir, Candidate Boyle. Yes, sir, I do."

Mr. Hampton took me into the building and told someone sitting at a table to process me into his flight. I was later to find out that it was a new, experimental flight, something called an "accelerated" flight. That meant we got out of doing most of the PT, but had to go to classes for more hours, fly more hours, and had only Sundays off.

Just about everyone used Sunday to sleep. Every second of every day was planned. If you weren't with the program, you were out and gone quicker than you could blink. We lost about one third of our class prior to graduation in July, 1969.

A few important incidents took place during my tour at Fort Wolters that should be mentioned. The army is now and was then very down on drugs, but in flight school, it was the kiss of death to be caught with any type of medication that was not issued by the flight surgeon. So it was no surprise when we had a very unannounced inspection and the candidate across the hall from me was found with a kilo of marijuana. No surprise because the guy was a real dud and apparently had well-placed friends in the army. We all felt relieved when he was booted out of flight school and probably the army. In the army's view of life, learning to fly came second to learning how to be a good officer.

I had been led to believe that because I already knew how to pilot an airplane that learning how to fly a helicopter would be no problem at all. Instead I had to unlearn and break a lot of habits used in flying airplanes that are not used when flying helicopters. Controlling the movement of a helicopter is something that a diamond cutter or a Swiss watchmaker might find easy, but to the average klutz like myself, and to just about everyone else, it is probably the hardest thing we ever had to master. Every student was given the same demonstration of how to hover by his instructor. He would first bring the helicopter to a three-foot hover, hold it there, steady as a rock, for a minute, and then tell you to take the controls. I sat there and watched my instructor hold the helicopter steady for almost a minute, with no noticeable movement of the controls. His left hand was on the collective which, by moving it up or down, controls the pitch in the main rotor blades. His left hand also controlled the twist-grip throttle, which controlled the engine's RPM. His right arm rested on his right leg, and his right hand controlled the cyclic stick, which stuck out of the floor like a broomstick with a pistol grip on the end. The cyclic controlled the movement of the rotor plane and the direction of the helicopter. Finally, his feet rested on two pedals that controlled the pitch in the tail rotor. As hard as I tried, I could not detect any movement of any of the controls by my instructor.

"You've got the helicopter, Candidate," he said.

Almost immediately, without my moving a damn muscle, the helicopter began to drift right. I corrected with a little left cyclic. The helicopter then shot to the left and started to sink. I added right cyclic and pulled up on the collective. The helicopter shot to the right, began to climb and spun to the right because I had not added any left pedal to compensate for the additional torque when I pulled up on the collective. The RPM also started to bleed off as I had not twisted the throttle to give the engine more gas. Within fifteen seconds I was performing an action well known to all new helicopter pilots: it's called "wiping out the cockpit." This is a reference to the rapid flailing of the arms and legs of the would-be pilot in a futile attempt to hover a helicopter. What really made the new student pilot feel like a pile of hammered dog doo was the action of the instructor when he finally had had enough and said, "I've got it," and the helicopter immediately resumed its three-foot, motionless hover.

Mr. Hampton who, with the grace of God, guided us through the first twenty weeks of flight school, had one little quirk that we all came to know and hate. My car had been put off-limits to me except when I had Mr. Hampton's permission to use it. He allowed me to start it on Sundays to charge the battery. After ten weeks I got to wash it. But he called me into his office about 6:30 one Friday night and asked me if my car was running. I said, "Sir, Candidate Boyle. Yes, sir."

He told me that he had a navy artillery shell at his house off-post and wanted me to go get it. He told me it was heavy and to take another candidate to help lift it. There was no reward offered for doing the deed as he knew that just getting off the post and being allowed to drive my car would be reward enough.

I got Richard Henke to go along with me, and we drove to Mr. Hampton's house. He had said that the shell was in his garage and that the door would be unlocked. What he had failed to tell me was that the shell was actually a defused warhead. And from the size of it, I would guess that it came off a battleship. It was two and a half or three feet tall with a lifting ring in the nose. Toward the base of the huge bullet were copper or brass bands that I assume were gas checks. There was no way in hell that we could lift the damn thing.

Dick and I sat down on the floor of the garage and finally figured out that the job must be one of Mr. Hampton's little tests. We also figured that everyone else had failed in their attempt to return the shell to the barracks. We made up our minds that we weren't going to fail.

As Dick and I rolled the shell down the driveway toward the street, I looked over at Dick and said, "If a cop drives by, we're in deep shit!"

We moved my car as close to the curb as possible and just rolled the thing onto the front floorboard. I should point out that my car was a 1966 Sunbeam Tiger, a small, V-8–powered, British sports car. With a lot of struggling, we managed to get the warhead into the car, but now we had an additional problem. The weight of the shell was so great that the open door of my beautiful little car became imbedded in the front lawn, so we could not get the door closed. Fortunately, the curb sloped, so the problem was solved by opening the driver's door, and with Dick sitting on the end of it to counteract the warhead's weight on the other side, we were able to get the right door dislodged from the lawn by driving ahead a few feet.

What a sight we must have been when we drove back on to the base. Dick, being six feet four, was wrapped up like a snake in the front seat, and the car looked and drove like it had two flat tires on the right side.

As we rolled the shell into his office and stood it up in front of his desk, the expression on Mr. Hampton's face was a mix of surprise and shock, but he quickly regained his composure and informed us that we had taken too much time.

"What did you guys do, stop and have a beer or something?"

We tried to explain all the trouble we'd had and that it had taken over an hour just getting the warhead up the three flights of stairs to his office. But we were informed that we would now be responsible for polishing the damn thing each and every day for the remainder of our training. After a week or so, Dick and

I were let off the hook, and everyone else got a shot at polishing the shell. It became a focal point of hatred for everyone in the flight, and looking back, I think Mr. Hampton had designed it that way. We had been taught to act as a team in whatever we did. This had been pounded into every candidate who went through flight school, and it was good. With the shell, we had something that we could hate as a team. Many times during the remaining weeks at Fort Wolters, each of the warrant officer candidates had wished that he could sit Mr. Hampton on that shell and pound on his head until the lifting ring became an inverted filling. Toward our last few weeks at Fort Wolters, I think most of us in the class began to understand that Mr. Hampton had implemented a very carefully thought-out plan to teach a bunch of very unique individuals how to think, dress, live, and act as a team.

On another occasion, I spent an entire weekend of off-duty time going over my clothes locker with clear varnish and wax. I was really proud of it when the Monday morning inspection came around. Mr. Hampton walked into my room, took one look, and said, "Very nice, Candidate! Report to my office after inspection." I wasn't sure if I should be happy or not; the little elf wore his familiar grin on his face, and I'd seen it before.

After the inspection, I reported to Mr. Hampton's office, "Sir, Candidate Boyle reporting as ordered, sir."

"Have a seat, Candidate. First, I'd like to tell you how great your clothes locker looked. How long did it take you?"

"Sir, Candidate Boyle. Two days, sir."

"Well, Candidate, how do you think the rest of the flight is going to like it when I inform them that they are going to have to spend Saturday and Sunday varnishing and waxing their clothes lockers until they look as good as yours!"

I spent the next two nights sanding and, the following weekend repainting, my clothes locker so that it would resemble all the other clothes lockers in our flight. I had been taught that we did everything as a team. A lesson that would later prove useful in Vietnam.

The day we graduated was bright and sunny, and, as could be expected, full of joy and happiness and a lot of relief. We had made it, as a team, through the toughest part of flight school, but we still had one mission to accomplish before moving on to Fort Rucker. We arranged for Mr. Hampton to be standing in a company formation outside the barracks, as I and the two other candidates who would be remaining for two weeks, alternately rolled and carried the hated artillery shell down the third floor hallway to the fire escape. With everyone's attention focused on the fire escape and the long shrill wail of Mr. Hampton's *"Noooooooo!"* we let fall the hated shell. There was a huge cheer as, nose first, it impacted the wet lawn and buried itself up to the brass rings at its base. Two weeks later, when I left for Fort Rucker, the shell was still there, a monument to teamwork.

After graduation, I stayed on for two weeks to help Mr. Hampton with his next flight. The rest of my class went on leave, but since my wife had moved into a trailer off post, I decided to stay and save my leave time for later. The morning after my graduation, the new class pulled up in buses in front of the barracks. It was my job as a "super senior" to get on the bus and brief the new candidates as to what they were to do once they got off the bus. Harassment was the name of the game, and everyone had to go through it. Two other super seniors were with me, and we had gone through the same drill eighteen weeks earlier.

We had the candidates get off the bus and line up in four rows, each with his duffel bag in front of him. We knew how long it had taken them to very neatly pack those bags. As was the usual case, Mr. Hampton gave orders that all bags would be turned upside down and dumped on to the ground. Without hesitation, but with a lot of moaning, the candidates dumped the bags. I suspect that the main reason for this was simply harassment, but the given reason was to search for drugs. Not necessarily illegal drugs—any kind of drugs. A flight school student wasn't allowed to take anything, not even aspirin, unless it was prescribed by a flight surgeon. But the bag dumping was really a small harassment compared to some that the candidates would face in future weeks.

Almost immediately, one of the students asked permission to speak to me. Tears were running down his face, and he was visibly shaking.

"Candidate, what's your problem?" I said.

"Sir, I want to quit!"

I couldn't believe what I was hearing. I knew all the crap I had gone through to get to where he was, and he had gone through a lot more than me—the guy had had to go through basic and then sit on his ass for at least a month just waiting for a class. I couldn't understand why, after all that, he would want to quit so quickly. I took him back on the bus and sat him down. Mr. Hampton stepped up into the bus and asked, "What's going on, Candidate Boyle?"

"Sir, Candidate Boyle, may I have a few minutes alone with this candidate, please, sir?"

Mr. Hampton stepped off the bus, and I tried talking to the new candidate. I told him that all he had to do was fall back into formation and the incident would be forgotten. He refused every suggestion and left with the bus. I felt so sorry for that young soldier. It had taken a lot on his part just to reach that first step up the ladder to becoming a warrant officer and pilot. The army didn't make it easy to climb that ladder, and the cadre tested you every step of the way. A wave of sorrow swept over me as I watched the bus drive away with its lone occupant.

"Come on, Candidate, you can't save them all," Mr. Hampton said as he walked over to me.

"Sir, Candidate Boyle. Isn't there something we can do? What the hell is going to happen to him now?"

"He'll end up in a grunt company somewhere. You just may end up having to save his ass in Nam. Don't let it bother you, Boyle. Just take pride in knowing that you made it this far and that the other pilots who make it aren't quitters."

The training for the rest of us continued.

Although we had completed all the classes at Fort Wolters, we still had another twenty weeks of training at the army's advanced flight school at Fort Rucker in Dothan, Alabama. We had been told that if we made it through Forth Wolters, that it was a shoo-in that we would make it through Rucker. My previous army experience had taught me one good lesson about the army—don't believe rumors. So being disinclined to believe either the scuttlebutt or the rumors. I studied and attempted to get the highest grades I could possibly get.

Although there were students who got better grades in flying and in the academic classes, I was able to stay in the upper third of my class. I had to work harder because I had been out of school a lot longer than most of the other students, and nobody cut me any slack because of my age. To most of them, I was a dinosaur who got lost on the way to the tar pit!

CHAPTER THREE

With my wife's Corvair and my Sunbeam Tiger both packed to the roof, we set out for Fort Rucker for the second half of flight school. It turned out to be an interesting drive as neither one of us had ever been through the Deep South before. It's funny the images that people form in their minds about places that they've never seen. Mile after mile, I kept expecting to come upon alligator-infested swamps. Instead, I found a beautiful countryside that was greener than anything I'd ever seen. In one small town in Mississippi, we observed an old black man sitting on the front porch of a very run-down house. Things haven't changed much since *Gone With The Wind*, I thought. We stopped somewhere along the way and got a motel room, and it was there that it finally dawned on me that I was suffering from the same delusion that some of my buddies back at Fort Wolters were suffering. Those who had never been to southern California thought that most movie stars spent all their free time standing at the corner of Hollywood and Vine signing autographs.

The trip was uneventful, except for the occasional overheating of my wife's air-cooled Corvair. The problem was solved when I finally figured out that the stuff I had in the roof rack was blocking the air flow through the vents above the engine. I had arranged to rent a large house trailer by phone before leaving Fort Wolters. When we arrived, I was pleasantly surprised to find a well-furnished, clean trailer located in a beautiful stand of pine trees. It didn't take but a few days to find out that it had one big drawback—our trailer park was located right in the middle of the traffic pattern for one of the many practice fields. So, for the next eighteen weeks, we lived with the sound of helicopters from dawn until well into the night, six days a week.

Providing that they showed up for class and formations on time, married candidates were permitted to live off post, and this, later on, caused some friction between the married candidates and the single candidates who had to get up earlier, clean their barracks, and police up the area around their quarters, and other such duties that we married folk didn't have. Once in a great while, I'd have to go in early and help the single guys, but I think that was a ploy by the tac officer to keep the single guys off his ass.

The term FNG (fucking new guy), which hadn't been used at Wolters, was used a lot at Rucker. It was almost as if Fort Wolters didn't exist, and we were starting from the beginning. We had all looked forward to finally getting out of those little two-place helicopters into something big that could carry thirteen or so troops and was befitting our place in life as officers and gentlemen.

It was just damn rude of the army; when we all went out to the flight line the first day, there they were, Bell 47s, the same make and type I'd flown at Wolters. The Bell 47 was the workhorse of the Korean War. It was an easy helicopter to fly and had great visibility. It was very reliable, and many lives were saved during Korea because of it. During the very early part of the war in Vietnam, it saw a lot of action and was one of the first helicopters used as a scout. When put in the hands of a renowned combat pilot such as CW2 Barrie Turner, it became a lethal weapon. Barrie tried mounting every light weapon known to man on this very slow and vulnerable helicopter. He was known to manufacture his own bombs, feeling that hand grenades were too small, and drop them on enemy locations. The Bell 47 was a piston-engine-powered helicopter, and to new pilots, it held the same stature as a Model A Ford. It was to be respected for what it had accomplished in the past, but it wasn't going to win the race or, in this case, the war. Helicopters had entered the jet- or turbine-powered era, and that is what we all wanted to fly. As wrong as we all were, we thought we knew everything there was to know about how to control a helicopter. Everyone wanted to climb into what appeared to be a huge helicopter compared to the 47, and go on with the task of learning how to fight with it.

There was a little relief when I found out that it would only be for about two weeks or until we flunked out of instrument training. Of all my training, that was the hardest part of flight school. I still don't know how I managed to get through it. If the army had been inclined to start a kamikaze flight school, my name would have appeared at the top of the first class list. My first instructor tried everything, but he just couldn't get the message across to me. So he just plain quit! I tried, but it seemed that the harder I tried, the tougher it became. My second instructor was a different breed of cat and knew how to get a student to learn. He would just remind me that thousands of other dumb FNGs had done it before me, and if I didn't want to end up a grunt, I'd better get with the program. After that two-week adventure, life at Fort Rucker really started getting better.

Fort Wolters' course of instruction had been designed to teach the new candidates what was expected of warrant officers and how to fly a helicopter. At Fort Rucker, the army attempted to teach us what a helicopter could do and what might be expected of us and the aircraft in combat. It became painfully clear that just knowing how to control a helicopter wasn't going to get the job done. There were so many subjects that needed to be learned and committed to memory that I was again faced with the problem of trying to figure out when I was going to find time to sleep. The army really pushed when it came to the map-reading classes, and there was a big difference between the classes at Rucker and those at Wolters. At Fort Rucker, actual maps of Vietnam were used, and in some special cases, they made up maps and Vietnamese names. For most of us, it was our first exposure to the Vietnamese language. It became clear that we weren't going to have the power lines, lakes, roads, and other obvious landmarks to navigate by in Vietnam as we had at Fort Wolters. They taught us how to pick out the slightest rise or fall in the terrain and how to relate it to our flat maps. I spent many long nights in my trailer, with maps spread all over the floor of my living room, in an attempt to learn how to look at something on the ground and then find that same exact spot on a flat piece of paper. Once I had convinced myself that the position was correct, I then had to learn how to convert the position into numbers and letters so it could be recorded. It was difficult, and I couldn't help thinking back some ten years earlier when I had been out in the Pacific on a sailboat with my friend Joe Canutt when he was trying to teach himself how to navigate by the stars. When he transferred the numbers to the chart, they indicated we were in the middle of a mountain range, one hundred miles north of our actual location. When I finally began flying in Vietnam, it became extremely clear why so much emphasis was put on this one class.

Once we had developed a working knowledge of these maps, we moved on to another class, closely related to what we had just learned. One morning we entered a classroom that had bleacher style seating and looked down upon a huge table. The table was, in fact, a large map, depicting rivers, valleys, and hills. The map actually had rises where there were hills and depressions where there were valleys. Each student was given a map that corresponded to the map on the table. This class was intended to teach us how to call up artillery and to direct its fire onto an enemy location. Different scenarios were presented, but it all boiled down to the same thing. They would give us the position of the artillery guns and show us on the map where the enemy was located. It was then up to us, using the maps we were given, to work out the location of the enemy, convert it to numbers and letters, and then call in the artillery. Each time a student gave what he had figured out was the enemy location, the instructor would type the information into a machine next to the large table, and a puff of smoke would rise from the map if, in fact, the student even hit the map. It was really great to watch, a lot of fun mixed with embarrassment and one of the best teaching aids the army had. A year later, I was glad I had paid attention during this course. I was put in a position where I was out of range of normal artillery; there were no jet bombers available, and I requested assistance from the navy. The target, a large bunker complex, was destroyed, and over thirty NVA troops were killed by a ship in the South China Sea, over twenty miles away. I was later told that the ship was the battleship *New Jersey.*

One morning, our flying lives changed forever. We walked into a classroom, and there before us was a very large picture of a Huey instrument panel. We had all just graduated into the jet age! Then we discovered we would be learning how to fly the Huey in the oldest models the army had to offer. But still, we were very happy to finally be getting out of the Bell 47. The difference between the two helicopters was like day and night. The Huey was much larger, could carry many more people, lift much more weight, and carried a crew of four. The turbine engine complicated some things and simplified others. Maintaining the Huey was much more complicated because of the increase in electrical and hydraulic systems and the huge rotor blades. Most of us felt that we were beginning flight school all over.

It was at Rucker that it became apparent why our earlier instruction had stressed teamwork; everything revolved around the group and group actions. Everyone was given a chance to play the leader, whether he wanted to be or not, and then he was critiqued by officer observers. The routine was study half the night, go to class half the day, and fly the other half. There just never seemed to be enough time to get everything done.

Each week that went by, we were being treated more like officers and less like candidate FNGs. I had been at Rucker about six weeks when I was assigned as candidate officer of the guard, a glorified title for guard duty. When I showed up for duty, everyone seemed to be in a panic about something. I found the sergeant of the guard and asked him what was going on.

He said, "Hell, man, everything that can fly is being moved to Fort Benning because of the hurricane."

I said, "If you're talking about Camille, it's clear down around the Texas coast somewhere."

"Not anymore," he said. He made a passing remark about my not letting anything blow away while I was on duty, then disappeared. I had heard a lot about hurricanes, but as a Californian I was unprepared for what I was to see and hear. Within the hour, the sky turned a grayish black, and the clouds were going by like low-flying jet planes. Then it started to rain, but not the way it does in California. Accompanied by a roar, this rain came down horizontally. I had no idea what to do, and I had no orders, so I just watched with my mouth hanging open. When I went into the office to dry off, everyone was clustered around a radio that was giving damage reports from the Gulf Coast. The area around Panama City, Florida, had really been hit hard. Most of the senior candidates, a rank I had not yet attained, had been assigned to fly training helicopters to Fort Benning, Georgia, so that they wouldn't be damaged. The better part of a week was spent rounding up lost pilots and helicopters after the storm had passed. We heard a hundred different farmer's daughter stories and saw a lot of embarrassed red faces in the weeks to follow.

During our last month at Rucker, we were given a mixed bag of assignments, some of which were fun. One such assignment was for a flight of Huey helicopters to fly down to Eglin Air Force Base and pick up a company of Rangers who had been out in the swamps for a week. Each helicopter would have one instructor pilot and two candidates who would trade off flying. The candidate not flying would act as crew chief. My instructor suggested that I get together with the other candidate and fix up a box of goodies for the troops we would be picking up, noting that they had only eaten one meal a day for over a week, and they would be real hungry. So, when the first group of troops was picked up out of the swamp, we welcomed them with cold Cokes, donuts, candy bars, and an assortment of other junk food. Those troops were *happy*, and they really made the three of us feel great. Six months later, I came to understand how those guys felt, when Paul Foti pulled my very scared ass out of the jungle in Cambodia after I'd crashed there with my platoon leader.

During the last two weeks at Rucker and just prior to graduation and receiving our warrants, three very important things were to take place. Only two affected everyone, but we were only told about one, the maintenance exam. Maintenance was one of the toughest courses in flight school, and in order to graduate, it was required that the exam be passed. In the struggle to earn my warrant, I had stayed up late every night, sitting on the living room floor of my trailer, trying to commit to memory all the information I thought might be needed to pass the test. The day prior to the test, I went on sick call with a reason good enough to get me off duty for the entire day. Then I headed directly to the offices of our civilian instructors to take advantage of their offer to help. I was hoping for a miracle.

Four instructors, separately and together and taking turns, went over everything that I should be expected to know for nearly four hours until they were satisfied that I would be able to pass.

The following day, everyone, including me, was sweating the test. I picked a seat next to the smartest candidate in the class, just in case I needed some extra help. As it turned out, I flew through the test, but there was one answer I wasn't sure about. I looked to my left and saw what the class brain had marked for that answer and changed my answer to his. As it turned out, that was the only answer I got wrong, but I still scored the highest in the class.

For the last half of my time at Rucker, I was not the only one in my family going through training. My wife and all the other wives were also being trained on how to be "good army wives." They had to attend mandatory teas and were instructed on what to wear, how to walk, what to say and what not to say, and what they could do in the presence of a general officer. I was pleased to find out that it was not the place of an officer to carry groceries or to walk under an umbrella. One prior-service candidate, who was even older than I, was asked why his wife had not attended some required function. From where he had been sitting next to me, he rose to his feet. The veins were standing out on the side of his neck as he came to attention and almost yelled, "Sir, Candidate Rodgers. I joined the army, my wife didn't. She decided that she had better things to do, sir."

We all went into shock. This candidate had not come from the reserves, but had been a sergeant with over ten years service behind him. His wife attended the rest of the training functions. Unfortunately, he was killed six months later when his helicopter struck a wire, just north of Saigon.

I had been instructed to report to the company area one morning, rather than going straight to class. We had only been told that we were going out on a field situation and would probably not be getting back until late that night. I smelled a rat, but really didn't know what it was. When I showed up at the company area, my field jacket was stuffed with candy bars and oranges. I was reminded of a situation some eight years earlier in basic training when the army got real secretive about a field trip that lasted well into the night.

"Hey, Boyle, what's with the field jacket?" Roger Riepe asked. Roger lived in the same trailer park as I did.

"You afraid that those old bones might get a little cold? It's only been in the nineties the last few days!"

"Eat my shorts, Rog," I said as we climbed onto the bus that was to take us to an undisclosed location. Within minutes of leaving the company area, we were driving through a pine forest where the trees were so close together that it would be close to impossible to walk between them.

After fifteen minutes or so, the bus pulled off the paved road onto a narrow dirt road, then continued on for about another five minutes before stopping near three other parked buses. Other troops were standing around. We were within a week or so of getting our wings, commission, and graduation, and most of the formal bullying had disappeared. So, it came as somewhat of a shock when a very big, extremely ugly soldier, wearing a uniform right out of a Mexican B war movie, yelled,

"Attention! Everyone down the trail on the left. Double time, *now*!"

Nobody had the balls to ask the guy who he was; we just did it. The trail ended at a set of three bleachers that had been arranged in a semicircle. Another oddly dressed soldier was pointing at them and yelling for everyone to "Get your skinny asses into the bleachers and sit down. No talking!"

Riepe was three rows in front of me and turned as he sat down. I saw the expression of bewilderment on his face and read his lips as he mouthed, "What the fuck. Over?"

A man who identified himself as a captain (he had to; you sure couldn't tell from his Mickey Mouse uniform) informed us that we could relax; the yelling was just to get our attention. We were there to learn about how to avoid being captured and what we could expect if we were ever captured. All the different aspects of E & E (escape and evasion) were covered. The oddly dressed people were very well informed and knew how to teach a class. We were told that they were wearing distinctive uniforms to clearly represent an enemy. Every hour or so we got a ten-minute break to use the portable latrine or just to look at booby-trap displays they had set up. That went on until about 2:30 in the afternoon.

At one point, Rog said, "You think they are ever going to feed us?"

"Hell, I don't know," I replied as I munched a Snickers bar. "You want one of these?" I opened the large pocket on my field jacket and carefully let him look in so as to not disclose my stash to the rest of the class.

"Hell, yes," he said as he palmed a Mars bar.

"I've got oranges in the other pocket if you're interested." He looked at me questioningly.

"Why, how come you brought all this stuff?"

I wanted to say, once a cop always a cop, but I just told him that I had a funny feeling about the day's activities.

It was 4:00 P.M. before they loaded us back on the buses for another short trip. This time, we were being taken to be fed. That feeling of mistrust in my gut didn't get any better when the buses stopped at a fenced compound and everyone was ordered off the bus. Rog looked at me and said, "Boy, the army can sure pick some shitty places to serve lunch!"

As we walked through the front gate of the compound, I began to take mental notes. The place was shaped like a football field but only about half as long. Left of the entrance gate appeared to be just flat ground; to the right were four small, bamboo-roofed shacks, two on each side of the compound, leaving a large walkway between them. The compound was fenced with barbed wire, a strand about every foot, to a height of eight feet. Next to the entrance was a guard shack. My mental survey was interrupted by Dick Henke, "Jerry, you got any idea what the hell is going on?"

"Just keep your eyes open and don't believe a word they say," I said.

That brought a look of distaste to Dick's face. Even more than the average candidate, Dick wanted to graduate in the worst way. He loved flying and was a natural pilot. We had become close friends at Fort Wolters, and we tried to cover each other whenever the situation called for it. He trusted the army and didn't like anyone putting it down. I didn't feel it was necessary to explain that I trusted the army, also; it was just a few people in the army who worried me.

We were given a tour of the four shacks, each of which was designed as an interrogation/torture room. One had a hand-cranked generator that could be attached to the person being questioned. Another had a deep hole that was full of snakes, over which the person being questioned could be suspended by the heels then lowered. After the tour, we were led back to the open area of the compound and shown a wooden trapdoor, beneath which was a box about the size of a coffin where a person would be put to "sweat it out."

About that time, somebody in the group had the balls to yell, "When do we eat?"

"Thought you'd never ask," was the reply of the self-proclaimed captain. "Have a seat on the ground, and we will serve you just as soon as it gets hot." Within minutes, two enemy soldiers came through the gate carrying a large steaming pot and placed it on a circle of rocks in front of us. The captain, chest puffed out, walked over to the pot and lifted out a ladle full of whatever was in it.

"I can tell you that this is a lot better food than you can expect if you should become a POW," he said.

Rog gave a big sigh of relief, but before Dick could say "I told you so," someone noticed that the pot also contained what appeared to be a dead frog. The captain quickly removed it, then everyone was issued a small tin bowl and a large spoon and told to get in line. Nobody was allowed to decline the invitation, not even the ten or so army doctors, mostly captains, who were also required to complete the course.

"Okay, listen up, troops," one of the enemy-type soldiers yelled. "After you have filled your bowl, go over to the sweatbox and have a seat on the ground, and the captain here will tell you guys what you all will be doing for the rest of the night."

Rog sat down beside me with his bowl of slop.

"Jerry, you found anything in it yet?"

"Nah, just potatoes and a bunch of unidentifiable stuff. How about you?"

"Negative, but Dick found an eyeball in his; I think he's out in the bushes puking."

About that time, someone held up a set of rattles from a snake.

"You got any candy left, Jerry?" Rog asked.

"No, but how about an orange, it's in my field jacket over there by the sweatbox."

Things began to settle down, and the enemy captain reappeared in front of the group. Two of his helpers carried in a large board and placed it on a stand. On the board was a large detailed map.

"You are here," the captain said, pointing to the far right-hand side of the map. He went on to explain that we would be divided up into groups of five. "Your mission will be to travel from *here*"—pointing to the bottom of the map—"to here." He pointed to the top of the map. He went on to explain that the distance, in a straight line, was about three miles, and that the traveling would be easy except for a couple of things. He explained further that the sticker bushes were pretty thick in some places and that enemy soldiers would be waiting to intercept us along the way.

"If you are captured, you will be brought back to this compound and subjected to some of the fun and games my men have arranged for you candidates and officers," the captain continued.

"Believe me, gentlemen—you don't want to end up here before the official end of the problem. There will be no physical disputes between you and the enemy. That means you cannot overpower your captors and escape. Once back here, you're more than welcome to attempt to escape, but I feel obliged to tell you that it has never been done."

We were then divided into groups of five, and one person

was put in charge of each group. My leader turned out to be a medical-type captain, a wimp.

I knew that rank has its privileges, but that captain couldn't even read a map. The rest of us decided that we would just have to make strong suggestions when it came to command decisions. The enemy captain had advised us that we would be dropped off by buses at half-mile intervals. The operation would start one hour prior to sunset and end when everyone had reached the objective, a large bonfire shown on our maps. The enemy captain added, "You will *all* remain at the fire until everyone is accounted for, for however long it takes. Got it, gentlemen?"

A big moan rose from the group.

As the bus disappeared down the narrow dirt road, leaving five of us standing like little boys lost, I unconsciously reached into the pockets of my field jacket with both hands. Empty. I wondered why I hadn't brought more food.

"Let's get off this road," I said, and we moved into the trees. I suggested to the captain that we cheat a little and start immediately instead of waiting for the appointed time. I wanted to cover as much ground as possible during the daylight. He just said, "No, we'll wait."

We had each been issued a flashlight, but only one compass and one map. At the given hour, we started toward our objective. At first the going was very easy, but it was impossible to travel in a straight line because of the trees. The sticker bushes tore at our clothes, but didn't slow us very much. Less than an hour after beginning our little walk in the woods, the map showed us to be approaching a road. I suggested to the captain that he let me go on alone to check out.

"Boyle, don't cross the road, just check it out and report back."

"Yes, sir, Captain."

"Don't call me sir; we're all equal—right now anyway."

"Okay, boss." I started off. Hell, he's not so bad after all, I thought.

As I approached the road, the trees became thinner, with very little brush to use as cover. I noticed along the route that I had traveled, old commo wire and leaf-filled foxholes. The area had been used before but not recently. I stayed back from the road twenty yards or so. To my right, less than a quarter of a mile, the road made a sharp left turn toward our objective.

The trees on the other side of the road were not as thin as on my side, and it would have been very easy for someone to be watching me from the cover they provided. To my left, the trees closed in on the road, almost forming a tunnel.

I suggested to our captain that we proceed up our side of the road and take cover in a few of the old foxholes until it got dark, then cross the road. The captain wanted to check it out for himself and then decide. We approached the road and stopped where I had stopped earlier. It was decided to wait for five or ten minutes to see if we could detect any movement. Our big problem with the E & E drill was that the enemy knew that we were coming, knew the routes we would be taking, the times, everything. We had also concluded that none of the enemy troops were really officers, just enlisted men (EM) who were out to stick it to the officer candidates and the RLOs (real live officer), a term used to distinguish the difference between warrant officers and commissioned officers.

After we had convinced ourselves that nothing awaited us on the other side of the road, we decided to cross, one at a time. I requested permission to cross first. It had nothing to do with being brave, I just wanted to get the drill over with and find something good to eat.

Using all the cover possible, I made my way to the edge of the road, stopping at the tree closest to the road. As I stood to cross the road, an enemy truck came around the curve to my right. I felt bare-ass naked as I turned around and ran back toward the trees and brush. There was no doubt in my mind that they had seen me. I yelled, "Get back in the heavy brush; a truck's coming." As I yelled, I went ass over teakettle into an old foxhole that I hadn't seen. I lay there, not moving, trying not to breathe. As I went headlong into the foxhole, I heard the screeching of brakes as the truck came to a stop. Then footsteps sounded, and I was grabbed, then loaded into the truck, along with the medical captain, who had not gotten to the heavy brush fast enough. Everyone else had managed to elude our pursuers. With the exception of two enemy guards, the captain and I were the only ones in the back of the truck. I had a sick feeling in my stomach, but kept telling myself that it was from too many candy bars.

The truck came to a stop and then began backing up. When it had come to the second stop, the flap was raised at the rear of the truck by someone on the outside. As our two guards climbed out of the deuce-and-a-half (2 1/2-ton truck), I looked over at the captain and said, "Hang in there, boss, don't let them get to you." He got a puzzled expression on his face but said, "You worry too much, Boyle."

"Damn right, I'm worried, sir. They've got snakes and spiders and no telling what else in this place."

"No talking. Get your asses off the fucking truck you bunch of dumb Yankee pricks," was our welcoming speech to the POW compound. In a vain attempt to make light of the situation, I said "Excuse me, Mr. Mickey Mouse, but is that any way to treat a couple of officers?"

For my effort, I was pulled off the truck and thrown to the ground. "Blindfold the son of a bitch and tie his hands behind him," said one of the half-dozen enemy behind the truck.

"Hey, I thought there wasn't going to be any physical stuff," I said.

"That was then, this is now. Throw the son of a bitch in the sweatbox; we'll have some fun with him later." The captain was also blindfolded, and his hands tied behind his back.

"Do you like to play telephone?" the captain was asked in a singsong voice.

I heard the squeak of the rusty hinges as the door was opened to the sweatbox.

"Down on your knees, asshole." Hands pushed me down into a kneeling position. Then a foot was quickly applied to my back, and I was shoved into the shallow box, landing on my side. They tried to close the door, but it kept hitting my shoulder.

"Lay on your back, asshole," was the next command. I did. The lid was then closed, and I heard the clasp being closed and what sounded like a lock being snapped into place. I was able to get the blindfold off by rubbing my face on the door above me; only three inches or so separated the tip of my nose and the lid of my coffin. Something was sticking me right in the middle of my back, and I couldn't move my hands enough to get at it. My head about went through the lid when I heard the first scream. Either the captain was a damn good actor or their hand-cranked generator was not just a show piece. One thing was for sure, I had no intentions about sticking around for my audition. Either panic or faulty rope tying, prompted by the screams coming from the other end of the compound, allowed me to get free of the rope binding my wrists. I had to squirm around to get my hands out from under me, and that's when I discovered that my flashlight was what had been sticking me in the back.

I pushed against the sweat-box lid with my head. My eyes and face were immediately covered by a fine trickle of dirt filtering through the cracks in the lid. Real smart, Boyle, I thought as the dirt now mixed with the sweat on my face. I spent precious minutes squirming out of my field jacket, then tried to get the dirt out of my eyes. My efforts had revealed that there was about two inches of movement in the lid. I closed my eyes, rolled as far as I could to my right, and braced the lid open with my left shoulder. I lay there, peeking through the crack, looking directly at the front gate of the compound. Two guards stood talking on the outside of the fence, close to the small guard shack. Every few minutes, they would walk off in opposite directions and then return, sometimes going inside the guard shack.

Clearly, if I was to attempt to get out of my coffin, the best time to do that would be when they were inside the guard shack. At least, I would know where they were. The second scream was like a knife being stuck in my back. I felt myself getting panicky. "Calm down and think, Boyle," were words that flight instructors had repeated to me many times while practicing recovery from engine failures. I ran over in my mind what I'd seen when we toured the compound. The main fence posts were poles driven into the ground, and at the corners, they were braced by large tree limbs that still had the bark on them. The sweat box was within a few feet of one of those fence corners. The thought occurred to me that once I got out of the coffin, all I had to do was run toward the fence corner, jump up, using one of the corner supports as sort of a spring board, and vault over the top. Hell, if Steve McQueen could do it in *The Great Escape*, I figured I could do it.

I decided that, if nothing else, I'd give the enemy something to really piss and moan about, but when? I didn't have to wait long for the answer to my question. Another scream sounded, and it had the same effect as lighting the afterburners on a jet engine, only this afterburner was strapped to my ass. I hit the lid of my coffin with all the force I had in me. The lid exploded into chunks and pieces of splintered wood, and I found myself standing in the dim light of sunset. I heard a voice yelling, "Escape, Escape!" It may have been one of the guards, or it could have been mine. Sweat was pouring into my eyes, my legs felt like rubber, and if I didn't get my heart to slow down, I'd die right there. I turned toward the corner of the fence and what I saw almost caused me to throw up my arms and give up. I hadn't remembered one very important detail. The corner post was braced on the outside of the fence not the inside as I had remembered, which meant that I could not use the brace as a step. I had also forgotten the roll of barbed wire around both the top and bottom of the fence. I was really panicked now, but decided to go for it. I didn't like the other alternative. I jumped the roll of barbed wire at the base of the fence and caught the second rung of wire, from the bottom, with my right foot. As I pushed myself upward, the strand of wire I was standing on broke loose from the corner post, but not before I was able to get my arms over the top rung. I found myself staring into a roll of barbed wire that was doing a real number on my face. The wire under my arms had torn through my uniform and was ripping away at the flesh. Mentally I was about to give up, but my feet and legs were still trying to climb the fence and escape. A popping and tearing sound filled my ears as the entire corner of the fence collapsed under my weight.

I looked to my left and saw one of the guards rounding the other fence corner with his rifle raised. He was yelling for the other guards to help him. I felt desperate as I tore at my uniform, trying to get untangled from the barbed-wire roll on the top of the fence.

The guard yelled, and I glanced toward him just as he tripped on a root, fired his rifle, and landed in a pile. I didn't wait to help him up, but ran for the tree line as if a pack of dogs were after me. I ran until my lungs were about to burst, then I found a large pile of leaves alongside a log, and proceeded to bury myself. The slightest movement made the leaves rustle, but in my state of mind, the sounds were more like exploding firecrackers. I held my hand over my mouth thinking, it'll take a real deaf son of a bitch not to hear my breathing. Only once did I hear footsteps close enough to worry about, but they passed and never came back. After about thirty minutes, a voice I recognized as that of the enemy captain started yelling to me that I could come back in now. That I really escaped and they wouldn't do anything to me. "Yeah, sure thing, asshole. Stuff it in your butt," I whispered out loud.

Two hours later, and in complete darkness, I decided to get the hell out of there. The only place I could go was a small building located about one hundred yards outside the compound that we had been told was neutral ground. I was sore all over, and my flashlight was still in the bottom of the sweatbox, along with my field jacket. I felt what I thought was blood trickling everywhere on my body, but didn't know if it really was. The POW camp and the small building were lighted, so I had no trouble getting a direction to travel, it was just all the stuff I kept tripping over that pissed me off.

As quietly as I could, I entered the dark back room of the small, two-room building. I couldn't trust anyone and wasn't about to announce my presence to the voices I could hear in the front room. I cupped my hands and lit a cigarette. I noted the glow of a small red light in a corner. I crawled over to it and found a coffeepot and a box of donuts. I was in hog heaven as I stuffed a donut in my mouth and poured a cup of coffee. I found I could only hold the cup with my left hand; the other hurt too much. I tiptoed to the other side of the room and sat down in a stuffed chair. I had just finished my third donut when the lights came on and someone said, "Hey, Sarge, what do you want in your coffee?" I had no place to go, so I just froze.

"Well, what do we have here; no don't tell me; let me guess. You are the escapee."

I stood up and tried to salute, because this guy was a real live major, wearing a real uniform. I couldn't raise my arm high enough to salute, and the major yelled, "Sarge, go get the medics and make it fast." Only then did I do a personal survey. I looked as if someone had taken a very sharp rake and gone over my body from head to toe. Both hands and both arms were torn open from the barbed wire, and my uniform was in shreds. My face was caked with a mixture of dried blood and dirt, and I had lost my hat sometime during the escape.

"Major, is it over now, or am I in trouble?" I asked.

"It's over for you, son, and you did great. But you sure pissed off Sergeant Brown. He tells me that you destroyed half of his compound during your escape."

"That makes it all worthwhile, sir, knowing that I pissed off that lying son of a bitch."

The major walked me to the front office of the small building and then went back and got me a fresh cup of coffee. Within a few minutes, the sarge returned and advised the major that the medics would arrive in a few minutes, as soon as they got through treating one of the prisoners.

I wonder if it's the captain from my team, I thought to myself.

As promised, the medics showed up. They treated all my injuries, then gave me a shot of something.

"Excuse me, sir," I said as the major walked back into the

room. "Do you think someone could pick up my equipment for me, it's still in the sweatbox?"

"Don't you mean what's left of the sweatbox, Candidate!"

I just smiled and shrugged my shoulders but didn't reply.

"You'll be able to pick the stuff up yourself before we go back to the company area," the major continued. "Besides, the camp commander wants to have a word with you about all the damage you did to his equipment."

"I'm sorry, sir, but I'm not going back into that place for anyone or anything, not even you, sir."

The major just laughed, "You don't have to go back inside, Candidate, they will bring the stuff out to you at the front gate, and that's it. I'll be right there with you and nothing funny is going to happen."

The major and I walked from the small building over to the front gate of the compound, where the camp commander was waiting for us. As I had suspected, Capt. Mickey Mouse was a sergeant. He was holding my flashlight and field jacket and had a big smile on his face, which really pissed me off.

"You really tore up my little enclosure here, Candidate."

"Not as much as I'd like to tear up your face you rotten, lying son of a bitch."

"At ease, Candidate," the major said in a soft but commanding voice.

"Did you learn anything, Candidate?" the Sarge asked.

"Yeah, Sarge, never trust EM!" I said.

"Wrong, Candidate, never trust the enemy," he said.

I got the message and felt just a wee bit foolish.

The following morning I was called up in front of a company formation and congratulated by the battalion commander for being the first candidate ever to escape from the POW camp.

The last month of flight school was devoted to subjects that would only have use in Vietnam. We knew, beyond a reasonable doubt, that most of us would be in Nam within a month, regardless of what we had requested on our "dream sheets" (a request for assignment, on which we were given three choices of locations in the world). The previous month, I had put in a request to be allowed to attend Cobra transition school after graduation. My request had been approved, and I had orders to report to Hunter Army Airfield at Savannah, Georgia, the week following graduation.

In 1969, the Cobra was the newest flying weapon the army

had. To me, it was a beautiful woman, just thirty-six inches wide, then one of the fastest helicopters in the world, and it carried more firepower than any other single weapon the army had in its inventory. The Cobra carried only two people, both pilots, sitting one behind the other. The AC, or aircraft commander, sat in the backseat. With a few minor exceptions, both pilots could fire all the weapon systems from either seat, and both positions were equally important to the mission.

In those last few weeks at Rucker, each time I saw a Cobra, memories flooded back to my first look at one as a very new candidate at Fort Wolters. My civilian helicopter instructor at Wolters, Mr. Comi, had sent me to the PX (post exchange) to "Buy a watch or get the hell out of flight school." Mr. Comi had the dubious and unfortunate task of attempting to teach me how to fly a helicopter. Early on, we had discovered that we both had flown out of the same small airport in southern California. The same FAA check pilot, Mike Dewey, had signed us off when we became private airplane pilots. I thought, this will be a shoo-in; this guy is my buddy, and he'll go easy on me. Unfortunately Mr. Comi didn't get my mental message, nor did he appreciate my sense of humor.

Mr. Comi had instructed me to get a wristwatch. He had noticed that I wasn't wearing one and suggested that all pilots should have one. The suggestion had been made a week prior, but on this day, he made it an order—"Get a watch by tomorrow, Boyle." It didn't matter to him that I was broke after having to buy extra uniforms, boots, and gold-plated brass. He just said, "Do it, or else."

At the end of the day, I felt like hammered dogshit as I walked into Mr. Hampton's office and requested permission to go down to my car in the parking lot.

"Why do you need to get into your car, Candidate? You know it's off-limits to you."

"Sir, Candidate Boyle. I've been ordered to have a watch by tomorrow, and I don't have one; furthermore, I can't afford to buy one. So I thought if you would be so kind as to lend me some garden hose, I'd just go down to my car and end it all, sir."

"Get serious, Boyle."

"Sir, Candidate Boyle, I have a small aircraft clock in my car that I thought I could use until I get my next paycheck, sir."

"Okay, Boyle, but make it quick. You've got to wax the halls tonight."

I had lied. The part about the aircraft clock was true, but this thing was far from being small. It weighed about three pounds, was three inches thick and five inches in diameter, with one through twenty-four on the dial.

The following morning Henke was laughing his ass off as I tried to hide the clock inside my flight suit. I finally decided to suspend it from my dog-tag chain and zip it up inside my flight suit. I couldn't wait for Mr. Comi to ask me what time it was, but it wasn't until we were about through flying for the day that I noticed him giving me the once-over, apparently looking for my watch.

"What time is it, Candidate?" he asked.

"Would you please take the controls, Sir?" I asked.

"I've got the controls; now what the hell time is it?"

As if in slow motion, I unzipped the front of my flight suit and slowly pulled the huge clock up out of my flight suit where it had been resting on my stomach.

"It's 3:30, Mr. Comi, sir."

He waited until we were on the ground, and the blades had quit turning to vent his anger and possibly some hidden laughter.

"I told you to get a *watch*, Candidate, specifically a wristwatch, not some fucking grandfather clock. Come to my office as soon as you're through with postflight inspection and have tied the blades down."

I had almost completed my inspection when I heard the door slam open against the side of the office. As I looked up, the very short form of Mr. Comi was storming across the flight line like a rhino in heat. Behind him, four other instructors wedged themselves into the small open doorway to watch the drama unfold. My first and only thought was, "O shit, what do I do now! He came to a stop about two inches from my face and puffed up like a horse that doesn't like wearing a saddle.

"Here is your pink slip, Candidate, for not following orders, and here is twenty bucks from those dickheads over there in the doorway to buy a fucking watch. Now get your stupid ass on the bus and don't even think about showing up tomorrow without a wristwatch, and I'd like to emphasize *wrist*watch."

"Yes, sir, Mr. Comi."

As I ran to the bus, the clock hanging outside my flight suit swinging from side to side, a small cheer went up from the other instructors who were walking out to Mr. Comi. He was standing on the tarmac, hands on hips, laughing.

On my way to buy a watch, I noticed a beautiful helicopter

parked on the helipad across the road from the PX. A few other candidates were walking around it in circles. I've always loved aircraft, especially the beautiful North American P-51 of World War II fame. There before me sat something like a P-51 with rotor blades. It was sleek, with no sharp corners. Everything was curved and smooth, and the sun danced on the Plexiglas cockpit canopy. The closer I got to it, the bigger it became, until standing next to it, I found it impossible to look inside the backseat. The other candidates were making all sorts of wild guesses about how fast it must be. I didn't say a word. I wished I could have just sat down on the lawn, alone, and looked on, alone with only my dreams.

Graduation went off without a hitch, and ranks right at the top of my proudest achievements. Because Cobra school was only a month long, we had decided that my wife and son would visit her grandparents in Nebraska. I drove them to the airport.

Later, finishing up a few last-minute duties, I had gone to the PX.

"Well, Mr. Boyle, how does it feel being an officer?"

I turned around to find one of my last instructors giving me a visual inspection.

"It feels great, sir, but it is a little embarrassing having to salute all the time."

"When do you leave for Nam?" he asked.

"I've got orders for Cobra school, sir." I felt my chest swell.

"Cobra school, huh, have you bought your little headband yet?"

"I'm sorry, sir, but you lost me somewhere."

"Well, Mr. Boyle, it's a known fact that anyone who flies Cobras has to have some kamikaze blood in his veins. Get into an ARA (aerial rocket artillery) outfit, and you'll be okay," he said and started to walk away.

"Wait," I said, "We need to talk."

"Meet me in the O-club tonight, and I'll fill you in. See you later."

That was to be my last night in Alabama. The trailer was clean, the car packed, and all my buddies had already left for home before going to Nam. I felt a strange sensation that I really couldn't put my finger on. Roger Riepe and his wife had left for Oregon, and Dick Henke, his girlfriend, and parents were on their way to Clare, Illinois. Hell, I was lonely. It was the first time in over twenty weeks that my time hadn't been planned by some unknown major at headquarters. Never one to consume copious amounts of alcohol, I had pretty much stayed out of the NCO club and officers club. That night I had absolutely nothing to do, so I headed for the O-club in search of answers to all the questions I had about Nam.

The most important piece of information pounded into every candidate was don't wear your hat inside the club. If you forgot, the bartender would be quick to point it out by ringing a large brass bell that hung easily within reach above the bar. If you were already in the bar when you heard the bell, it was instant joy, for it meant you got a free drink. If you heard the bell, and you were unfortunate enough to be wearing your hat, it meant instant bankruptcy!

As I walked through the front door, I remembered to remove my hat. After being an officer for only one day, I was feeling conspicuous and self-conscious, but nobody was paying any attention. As I made my way toward the bar, I heard, "Hey, Boyle—over here!" I scanned the room and finally spotted the tactics flight instructor. He was sitting with two other instructors who looked vaguely familiar.

"What's this shit about you going to Cobra school—are you nuts or something?" said one IP (instructor pilot) who obviously had been drinking long before I arrived.

"Na, he's a lifer," said the IP who had invited me to the club. "Gonna make the army a career."

"Well, it won't be a very long career if he's going to be a hotshot gun pilot," said another.

I was beginning to feel like a mouse in the corner, listening to people talk about me.

"So why do you want to be a Cobra pilot, Boyle?" my IP asked.

Feeling I had taken enough crap, I just said, "Well, I was told early on that slicks were for kids, so I decided to fly something designed for real mature individuals."

"I'm happy for you, Boyle, not because you're going to Cobra school, but because you waited to say that until after graduation or you would still be doing push-ups."

"So, what's so bad about flying Cobras?" I asked.

"Order us some drinks, new guy, and maybe we'll tell you," said the drunkest of the three IPs.

I ordered a round of drinks. "Think about this, Boyle," my IP said. "The Cobra is only thirty-six inches wide. It's got everything packed into those thirty-six inches that the Huey you've been flying has, plus more. What do you think's gonna happen when a .51 caliber comes flying through your Cobra? Something's gonna quit. At least in a Huey, there are lots of open places a bullet can pass through without taking out something you really need, like an engine or hydraulics. I would suggest that you become accustomed to yelling banzai, because you've just signed up for the army's kamikaze pilot school."

About all I could come up with was, "Yeah, but . . ." Just more Vietnam bullshit stories, I thought.

"You look as if you don't believe me, Boyle. I didn't get these two Purple Hearts falling out of a whorehouse window on Tu Do Street!"

"Did you fly Cobras?" I asked.

"No, I flew medevac, and most of the pilots I hauled out were in body bags or didn't make it more than a few days. I never hauled a live Cobra pilot, does that get your attention?"

"Look, you guys were there. If you *had* flown Cobras, who's got the best outfit? Where would you have chosen to fly?"

"Ash and trash are the softest," my IP said, referring to flying supplies.

"But Cobras don't fly ash and trash. ARA is the best, wouldn't you say?" and the other two IPs nodded approval. ARA is short for aerial rocket artillery. If a unit under attack was out of normal artillery range, they could call in ARA, which usually consisted of two or three Cobras.

"Stay away from the 1st Cav though, those guys are always in trouble. They have a lot of Cobras, so when you get to Bien Hoa, or wherever you end up, try and stay clear of the Cav. The Cav is a big outfit, though, so if you do find yourself assigned to the Cav, whatever you do, don't get stuck in the 1st of the 9th!"

I couldn't resist. "How come?"

"Well, you know all those guys you just graduated with; well, they'll probably all end up as replacements for pilots killed in the 1st of the 9th!"

"That's just plain bullshit," I said. The drinks were taking effect.

"Well, maybe not all of them, but a big percentage."

Other people in the club started looking our way.

On the next round of drinks, the waiter leaned over and whispered something in my IP's ear. "He says the club manager says to keep it down."

One of the other IPs said, "Boyle, let me try to explain it in terms even an FNG can understand. Have you ever played chicken?"

"You mean with a car?"

"No, with a rooster, you dumb shit—hell yes, with a car. It's the same game between a Cobra and the NVA. The Cobra is diving at the NVA and firing its rockets and minigun, and the NVA is standing his ground throwing a stream of .51-caliber bullets back at the Cobra. All is equal up to that point; the eventual winner has to come up with a psychological advantage. With cars, the way to gain the psychological advantage is to lean out the window and throw the steering wheel away. I just thought you should be aware that the 1st of the 9th has already thrown *all* the steering wheels away."

I left the club wondering if I had made a mistake requesting Cobra school. I was also wondering if I could find my way home. I did.

The following afternoon, after driving all day with a hangover, I arrived in Savannah. It was a beautiful city, with streets running through tunnels of overhanging trees. Hunter Army Airfield was on the southern edge of town, and it didn't take long to check in.

"Candidate Boyle reporting as ordered, First Sergeant. I mean, *Mr.* Boyle." My face turned bright red.

"That's okay, Mr. Boyle. Just about all the new warrants do it."

"Where do I find the BOQ, First Sergeant?"

"Well, Mr. Boyle, as Joseph and Mary were told, there's no room at the inn. Here's what I want you to do. First go out and find a furnished apartment. When you do, call me and give me the address. Next, call the phone company and get a phone. That will take about two weeks. When you get your phone, call and give me the number. After that, I want you to call me once a week and assure me that you are still alive!"

"But, First Sergeant, what about Cobra school?"

"Oh yes, let's see here . . ." The first sergeant fumbled through some paperwork. Okay, Mr. Boyle, you're scheduled to start Cobra classes on the fifteenth of January. Until then, just call me once a week."

"But, First Sergeant, that's almost two months away."

"Just go down to finance and get some advance pay so you can get your apartment and phone. If you have any problems, just give me a call."

I was back to being a snowbird again, only this time I didn't have to pull KP!

I found an apartment on Savannah Beach, got a phone, and became a tourist. I entered my Sunbeam in a road race at Savannah International Race Way and won second behind a Shelby Cobra. I spent Thanksgiving with Dick Kohler, my old training officer from Ventura Police Department. He'd left the PD in 1961 and joined the FBI where he was a training officer at the FBI Academy. Dick gave me a great tour of Washington, DC, and I missed meeting J. Edgar Hoover by only one day.

At Christmas, I drove to Nebraska in a new Coupe De Ville that I'd bought in Atlanta, and picked up my wife and son. We stopped in Roswell, New Mexico, on the way to California, and visited Sonny and Dusty Jones, who were like parents to me. My son got his first horseback ride there. Then on to California, each week making sure I called the first sergeant to tell him I was still alive.

The first week of January, 1970, I flew back to Savannah. Even then, I had to wait a week before the start of the transition course into the Cobra. For a week after my arrival back in Savannah, I would drive out to Hunter Army Airfield just to look at the parked Cobras. Occasionally, I would get out of my car and spend a lot of time just walking around one of them, much as I had done ten months earlier at Fort Wolters, when the thought of actually flying a Cobra was just a dream. Now that dream was about to come true, and I couldn't wait for my first flight.

Every good pilot should know his own limitations and that of the aircraft he was flying. The first few days of the transition course were spent learning the different systems on the Cobra and any major differences between the Cobra and a Huey. The obvious big differences were its speed and weapons systems. The speed of the Cobra could ruin a crew's whole day if they didn't adhere to some very strict guidelines. Up until this time, we had been taught that if an engine failure occurred, for any reason, the pilot should lower the collective immediately in order to maintain sufficient rotor RPM to accomplish a good autorotation. With the Cobra, it was necessary to slow down before lowering the collective. Failure to slow down could result in an overspeed and possible failure of the main rotor system. In simple terms, this meant that you then took on all the aerodynamics of a bathtub! We studied how the minigun was operated, loaded, cleaned, and maintained, and the same went for all the weapons systems. I kept thinking to my-self, Get this preliminary crap over with, I want to go fly.

Finally, after three days of intense study, the day came for the first flight, and it was more than I'd ever expected. Climbing into the front seat of this beautifully sleek Cobra, so named by retired general Hamilton H. Howze, then employed by Bell, because its bite meant sure death, I thought my heart was going to break out of my flight suit. It was faster than anything I'd ever flown. Being in the front seat was like being strapped into the clear plastic nose cone of a low-flying jet plane.

It became clear why my IP at Rucker was so set against flying the Cobra, even though I don't believe he had ever flown one. I had the feeling I was sitting in a glass bubble with only the seat for protection. He was also correct that everything in a Huey had been packed into a thirty-six-inch-wide helicopter, but he had not considered the speed of the Cobra. When the Cobra's width was combined with its speed, it made for a difficult target to hit. But it still took a lot of getting used to not having a lot of metal around you, as in the Huey.

The first week was spent getting to know the Cobra from the front seat. The second week was spent in the backseat, learning emergency procedures and the location of all the circuit breakers that controlled the flow of current to all the ship's systems. The third week was spent learning the weapons systems, and finally, the last week was spent firing the weapons and practicing autorotations (controlling the helicopter during engine failures) and other emergency procedures.

The day of graduation, I left for home in the little Sunbeam Tiger. On the seat next to me was a beautiful piece of parchment given to me at graduation. At the top of the paper was a drawing of a diving Cobra helicopter, superimposed over a coiled snake. It read "This certificate is awarded to WO-1 Jerome Maitland Boyle, in recognition of his qualifications as a pilot of the world's first attack helicopter, the Bell AH-1G Huey Cobra" and was dated 13 February 1970. It also just happened to be Friday the thirteenth, but I was much too happy to care, even though I felt physically ill.

I made it as far as Atlanta, then spent two days in a motel, so sick I couldn't get out of bed. Once back on the road, I drove all the way to North Hollywood without stopping for anything but gas and food.

CHAPTER FOUR

I had said my good-byes to my wife, family, and friends and was on my way to San Francisco. The flight was only about an hour, but it seemed to drag on forever. I had, it seemed, forever to go over in my mind all that had happened the last few days. I had made it a point to go back to Ventura and to the police department, to show the guys the brand-new, shiny uniform that I had worked so hard to attain. The welcome I received from everyone was more than I had ever expected.

"You still don't outrank me, Boyle," Lieutenant Dynge said as he walked out of the detective bureau. Behind him, holding the door open was Tom Burke, who motioned me in. I walked over to my old desk and sat down, feeling at home the way you do after being gone on a long trip.

"You're lucky the chief isn't here," Dynge said.

Burke started laughing and said, "Yeah, we really pissed him off big time."

"Okay, what the hell did you guys do now?" I asked.

"Well, you know all those graduation announcements you sent us in November?"

"Yeah, what about them?"

"Well, the good lieutenant here and I decided that the chief should be made aware of your graduation, also, so we slipped one under his door."

"I sort of find it difficult to believe that that would piss him off that bad!" I said.

"Well, we weren't sure he found the first one, so we've been putting one under his door every week. He's not real happy with you right now, Boyle, and we're too old to join the army if he ever finds out who's doing it."

We all had a big laugh and then walked back to the squad

45

room to get some coffee. Lois, the chief's secretary, was leaving the room as we entered and stopped to say hello. She was a good secretary and was very loyal to a man whom everyone else in law enforcement hated. After she had left, Dynge said, "Look, Boyle, I want you to keep your head down over there and don't get hurt or anything."

"And don't forget to stay away from the women; they've got stuff over there that makes your dick fall off!" Burke added.

"I'll try," I said, "but did you guys really put that stuff under the chief's door?"

"Hell yes," Dynge responded. "We didn't tell anyone else though, so keep it to yourself. He's got spies all over the place."

As we walked out the side door headed toward the parking lot, Burke said, "You know, Boyle, you're really lucky."

"How's that?" I asked.

"Well, when you do end up killing a bunch of those NVA gooks, you won't have to file a million pages of reports and have everyone in the States trying to figure out if you fucked up or not."

"Yeah, Tom, I know, but if I screw up over there, the gook who kills me won't have to file any reports either."

"Look, Jerry," Dynge said, "if you should happen to win any medals or stuff like that, let us know, and we'll get it in the local paper for you."

"And under the chief's door, too," Burke added.

"You guys promise to write if I send you my address?"

"Hell, yes," they said. Burke added, "We'll send you all the *Footprinter* newsletters and anything else you need."

As I walked into the airport at San Francisco, I was still reviewing the past in my head when I heard "Hey, Jer-reee," and at once came out of my dream world to find Mike Moysard throwing his arms around me. I started to turn a little red-faced, but then thought, Hell, anything goes in the big city by the bay! Mike and I had been friendly competitors in police pistol matches. I had called him a few days in advance, and he had agreed to drive me up to Travis Air Force Base, where I was to catch my flight to Vietnam.

I may have been taller than Mike, but he was a hell of a lot stronger than I.

"Okay, Mike, you big savage policeman, put me down before I have to call the MPs."

Mike's arm looked like hams sticking out of a short-sleeve shirt. Mike headed up the special-weapons team for SFPD and felt it really necessary to stay in shape. He was also an ex-Marine, having served in the French and Indian War or something about as far back as that. I pointed out to him, every chance I got, that the Marines might be the first in, but it was the army who had to rescue their asses when they got in over their heads. That sort of conversation always prompted ethnic slurs about Mike's being an Italian cop from New Jersey and me being a no-good Scotch-Irishman from Hollywood. I had also learned never to attempt to outdrink Mike, so when he suggested that we make a quick stop at the local cop bar, I declined.

We had a good dinner at Mike's house, along with his wife, Jan, two daughters and a son, two dogs, and a couple bottles of wine. My flight from Travis AFB was not until well after midnight. Mike had to work the next morning, so we decided that he would drive me up early and just drop me off. The initial effect of the food and wine had been to relax me, but now, driving across the Bay Bridge, the mood had turned from relaxed to somber to depressed. As I watched the rosy glow of the lights on the bridge flash by, I started to wonder whether the idea of going to Vietnam had been a good one. It's a little late to back out now, Boyle, I thought to myself.

Mike, sensing that I was somewhere else in time, said, "I sure hope you're a better shot with that Cobra than you were with a pistol!"

He knew immediately that type of statement would not go unheard.

"You big asshole, I could outshoot you with a slingshot," I yelled. Mike flipped his badge at the woman in the booth, to get out of paying the toll.

"You big, dumb mick, I could outshoot you falling down drunk—or don't you remember," he said. Mike knew that anytime he wanted to change the course of a conversation, all he had to do was bring up one incident that will live forever in my mind.

In 1967, Ventura had sponsored a police pistol match, which was attended by over fifty different police departments from California and Arizona. Mike, who was captain of the SFPD pistol team, had arrived in Ventura, with the rest of his five-man team, two days early. According to Mike, the early arrival was to "acclimate the team to the surrounding conditions." "Acclimation," as defined by SFPD, was to sit around the motel pool while getting drunk.

Within hours of their arrival in Ventura, the police department received a call from a motel manager advising that he had a bunch of drunk cops sitting around the pool waving guns around, and his guests were becoming very nervous. I was sent to calm down the situation, and explained to the five-member team that cleaning and dry-firing their weapons while sitting around the pool wasn't in the best interest of police-community relations.

I was captain of Ventura's team, and my team and Mike's were among the top ten in California. Mike and I were also in the top ten as individual shooters, and by the time of the Ventura match, I was ahead of Mike in points. In order to gain an advantage over Mike and his team, I attempted a little subterfuge. I invited all the members of Mike's team up to my house, in Ojai, for dinner and a party the night before the match. Then I scheduled Mike's team to shoot at 8:00 A.M. the following morning. Everyone from my team attended, and we provided transportation to and from the party. Of course we made sure that Mike's team received copious amounts of booze, but we stayed sober ourselves.

Late that night, after he'd dropped off two very drunk shooters at their motel, Larry Lotton, a member of my team, said, "Hell, we don't have anything to worry about. Those guys are so drunk that I'll be surprised if they are able to find their guns in the morning, let alone find their way to the pistol range."

I had arrived at the range around 7:00 A.M., and with the help of the range master, Sam Hall, and the rest of my team, set up the targets and anxiously awaited the arrival of Mike and the rest of the team from San Francisco. At one point, Larry Lotton came into Sam Hall's office laughing. "You've got to come out here, Jerry, and take a look at this."

A black SFPD station wagon was parked in the driveway with all its doors open. All was silent except for the sound of regurgitation. Mike was sitting on the floorboards of the station wagon, feet on the ground, with his head between his legs. Another member of the team had just exited the men's room so green he looked like a leprechaun.

"Okay, you guys, time to shoot—let's get out to the firing line," I said in the loudest voice I could muster.

"Boyle, you are a rotten son of a bitch," Mike said as he stood up, holding onto the open door.

"Would you like me to help Mikey on with his pistol belt?" I asked.

"Stuff it in your butt, you rotten Irishman; we don't need any more of your help."

Sam Hall walked up and said, "Jerry, I don't think I should allow them out on the course in the condition they are in."

"Don't worry about it, Sam. They seem to be just fine."

Sam just shook his head and walked out to the course. Because we were also competing, we could only stand back, at a distance, and watch the pitiful scene unfold before us. Mike and his team had trouble just loading their pistols, let alone walking.

I couldn't bear to watch Mike and his team, so I walked back to the range office.

As I walked through the door, Ed Graves looked up from cleaning his pistol and said, "How much do you think this will cost you, Jerry?"

"I figure about a hundred bucks in steak and booze, but it'll be worth it to beat those guys." Just then Lotton ran into the office, all out of breath, mumbling something.

"What did you say?" I asked.

"I said they cleaned the targets, all of them. All four of those hung-over assholes shot perfect scores."

"I don't believe it. How could they do this to me!" I cried.

"Well, Sam's bringing the targets around now. You can see for yourself," Lotton said.

All that money, down the tubes, I thought.

Mike and I said our good-byes at the curb in front of the terminal at Travis AFB. Mike had suggested coffee, but I had a long wait, and he had to go to work in the morning, so we hugged, shook hands, and he was gone, headed back to family and friends; I was headed toward a place that I was already having serious doubts about. I'm the type of person who says the glass is half empty rather than half full!

The flight was long, with two stops, one in Alaska and one in Japan. To me, it was like being on a bus full of prisoners on their way to court. There was little conversation, and I couldn't find anyone who looked even vaguely familiar. Bloodshot eyes peered out the windows as the 707 touched down at Tan Son Nhut Air Base, just outside Saigon. As we taxied toward the terminal, I was amazed at the different types of combat aircraft taking off and landing, and parked in concrete revetments. Everyone seemed to be rushing around. Jeeps pulling carts loaded with bombs and rockets, fuel trucks, and aircraft taxiing with their canopies open. I was impressed, but I was also very tired and sleepy.

CHAPTER FIVE

A blast of hot air hit me in the face as I walked down the stairs to the concrete flight line, a big contrast to the blast of thirty-below air that had greeted me at Anchorage, Alaska, while we waited for the plane to be refueled.

Almost instantly, I felt my uniform beginning to soak with sweat. The real attention getter was not the heat, though; it was the odor. It smelled like an anchovy pizza that someone had left out in the sun for a couple of weeks.

All my life I had been leery about going places I had never been before. Anxious, excited, but suspicious best describes my feelings that day in March 1970, as I walked to where the buses were waiting to transport me and the rest of the people on my flight from Tan Son Nhut Air Base to the reception station at Bien Hoa for in-processing. For those returning for a second tour, the processing would take only a day; for those of us on our first tour, which was just about everyone, we could expect to be at the reception station from three to five days.

We had a short briefing, which amounted to telling us where the mess hall was located and where and how we would be informed as to what to do next. We were also made to understand that possession of U. S. currency was against the law, and any such money must be exchanged for money, commonly referred to as "funny money," the military had printed. I was assigned a place to sleep, as were the other officers in my group. Still, I had not found anyone who looked familiar. My attendance at Cobra school had separated me from the rest of my Fort Rucker class by almost four months. I had grown used to having close buddies around, and now felt very much alone, and I must admit, a little frightened. My escape has always been sleep, and that's just what I did. I awoke the following

51

morning, early, feeling like I had been chewing on an old
sweat sock all night. Let's see, what do I do first? I thought.
Being a creature of habit, I started looking for a coffee pot.

I sat in the mess hall, sipping the hot coffee and trying to
down a piece of toast that hours before had turned into roofing
material. I had slept well through the normal breakfast hours.
Thank God, the army always has coffee going, no matter what
time it is.

We had been told to check the bulletin board in front of the
processing building. My name appeared on a list of new arriv-
als to have their teeth treated with a new stuff called fluoride,
but not trusting the army, I decided to pass the fluoride treatment. I was next scheduled to show up at a building for issue
of necessary combat equipment, but that wasn't until 1:30 in
the afternoon, so I headed back to the mess hall for a few more
dozen cups of coffee. Things were moving too slow, and I
wanted to get assigned to a unit. Being a former mess sergeant,
I walked back to where the mess sergeant was sitting at a
small desk, and complimented him on how great his mess hall
looked. Without getting up, he stuck out his hand and shook
mine, and said, "Have a seat, Mr. Boyle."

As briefly as I could, I explained my background as a mess
sergeant in the Reserves, which really broke the ice. "How do
you know how many people you're going to have to feed every day with the amount of folks they must run through this
place?" I asked.

"It's not all that hard. We can usually plan on getting two
planeloads a day in and the same amount out."

"Well, I'm impressed, Sergeant. Most people don't realize
how much goes into running a mess hall and all the work involved." Then we got down to the nuts and bolts of his operation.

For the rest of my time at the reception center, I had free run
of the mess hall and could eat at any hour I decided.

At 1:30 P.M., I entered the building to receive my equipment.
A pilot's issue was somewhat different from that of a combat
grunt. I received a .38-caliber revolver, which was ancient
compared to what I was used to firing, and a holster. Although
clean, the blueing on the metal was very worn. It did not have
adjustable sights, and it took superior strength just to pull the
trigger. I wished then that I had brought my beautiful Smith &
Wesson, with its six-inch barrel and its less than two-pound

trigger pull. I knew I could hit what I shot at with the Smith & Wesson. The one issued to me would better serve as a fishing weight. Although I had brought the helmet that I had worn since starting flight school, I was issued another one, which I never could get to fit right. I left the building carrying two duffel bags full of crap that, seventeen months later, I would turn in, covered with mold, having never been used, much less removed from the bags.

I hauled, drug, and carried the bags back to my sleeping area and tried to repack some of it.

"Hey, Boyle, the sergeant over at reception said to give you this," a blond lieutenant said as he dragged his duffel bag over to his bunk. "He said to fill it out and return it ASAP."

The paper he had handed me was a request for assignment, what we call a dream sheet. It was not a secret that no matter what anyone put down on that paper, the army was going to send you wherever it thought you were needed the most. I shoved my unpacked equipment under the bunk and, with dream sheet in hand, headed for the mess hall. As I entered, I saw that the mess sergeant was again sitting at his desk, so I walked back and said, "How you doing, Sarge? Mind if I pull up a chair?"

"No problem, Mr. Boyle. What's that you got there in your hand?"

"Ah, just a dream sheet," I said. "I don't have the names of any of the units I want to get assigned to, only the one I don't want to get assigned to."

"And who might that be?" the sergeant asked with a smile on his face.

"Well, Sarge, I was told to stay the hell away from the 1st Cav, and that anything would be better than getting assigned to them."

"No problem, Mr. Boyle, just put down 'Anything but the 1st Cav,' but I don't think it will help a hell of a lot. You know that they are going to send you anywhere they want, and that little piece of paper isn't going to change a thing."

"Hey, Bill," the sergeant yelled at one of the cooks back in the kitchen, "What would be a good outfit for this new-guy pilot to get assigned to?"

"Anyplace around here is great. There's all kinds of flying jobs, like flying generals around and stuff like that, and the generals never go anyplace until after all the shooting has stopped anyway."

"Thanks," I said, and wrote, "Anything but the 1st Cav Div" on my dream sheet.

"Honestly, Mr. Boyle, the 1st Cav has been taking a lot of losses in the Tay Ninh area lately, so don't be surprised if you end up in the Cav. By the way, what do you fly?"

"Cobras," I said.

His face fell as if his mess hall had just flunked a big inspection. "I hope you'll remember me in your will, Mr. Boyle."

"That's a pretty shitty thing to say to a friend, Sarge."

"You don't understand, Mr. Boyle, it's sort of a joke. We all do it. Everyone makes up a little will and leaves stuff to their buddies. You know, just in case. You better get that back to reception, Mr. Boyle. I'll talk to you at supper."

The sergeant's remark brought a quote to mind, "Many a true word is spoken in jest."

The sergeant who took my dream sheet looked at my simple request and smiled. "We'll see what we can do, Mr. Boyle, but I can't promise a lot. Most of the country around here is controlled by the VC and the Cav. Check the board in the morning and again after lunch. Your orders should be up sometime tomorrow. Oh, and good luck."

I went back to my bunk and tried to cram all my equipment into one bag, but it was impossible. I had something else to worry about now instead of just where I was going. I lay on my bunk, looking at the steel ceiling, wondering how the hell I was going to carry all the crap they had issued me.

I fell asleep while thinking over that heavy problem. I was awakened by a loud, unbroken roar. It took a minute to shake the fuzz out of my head, and only then did I realize that it was raining, and raining harder than anything I'd ever heard before. Two lieutenants were sitting not ten feet away from me; I could see their lips move but couldn't hear a word they were saying. I got up and headed for the mess hall. The rain felt good, but I was soaked to the skin in the short distance between my building and the mess hall.

"Hey, Mr. Boyle, how did it go?" the mess sergeant asked from behind the serving line.

I waited until I got to the other end of the building and then said, "Okay, I guess. I won't know anything for sure until tomorrow sometime."

"You want some coffee, sir?" one of the cooks asked.

"Sure would. Home come the place is so empty?"

"Hell, sir, we quit serving at 7:00, and it's almost 10:00 now."

"Boy! I must have jet lag or something. I had no idea it was that late."

"You hungry, Mr. Boyle?" the sergeant asked.

"Yeah, but you've got everything put away already."

"I could fix him one of our special sandwiches, Sarge," the cook said.

"And what kind of sandwich might that be, Sarge?"

"We get a filet mignon every once in a while that's supposed to go to the officers, but we always keep it and make sandwiches at night with it. Would you like one?" he asked.

The three of us sat around shooting the breeze and eating steak sandwiches until I thought I would burst.

Finally I had to get some more sleep. "Thanks for all the good food, and I sure hope you saved some of that meat for the officers," I said. We all had a big laugh. "I'll see you guys in the morning for coffee."

"But it is morning, sir," the cook said with a smile.

"Well, I'll see you when I get up then."

The morning orders didn't have my name, but the ones posted in the afternoon did. I was to proceed to the air base at Bien Hoa and board a flight for Phuoc Vinh, wherever that was. Upon arrival, I was to report to the 1st Cav headquarters for further assignment. Oh shit was the only thing that came to mind, but at least I was assigned. But what was I getting into?

"I'm sorry about your orders, Mr. Boyle, but when someone noticed that you were a Cobra pilot, it didn't leave them any choice. The Cav is at the top of the list for all incoming Cobra pilots. Seems they are really short right now for some reason," the personnel sergeant noted from behind the counter.

"You sure you don't have a nice soft Stateside assignment lying around somewhere in that pile of paperwork?" I asked.

"If I did, Mr. Boyle, I'd be buying those wings you are wearing and taking the job myself. You'll be okay, sir. They're a crazy bunch up there, but some pretty good people, and they look after each other."

A spec four walked with me to the door and pointed out where I should get the bus to Bien Hoa Air Base.

A couple of hours later, as the Huey helicopter departed Bien Hoa and headed north—at least I assumed we were headed north—I sat looking at the flat country passing beneath me. There had been little conversation between me and the four other new guys who had boarded the helicopter with me. We shared one bond in that none of us had a clue as to what the hell we were doing. I have always hated not knowing what to expect, but there I was on my way to somewhere, to do something, with somebody.

The helicopter crew was talking and laughing over the intercom, but we didn't have any idea what they were saying to one another because we weren't wearing helmets. Once in a while, the door gunner on my side would lean over and point and yell, "That's the Saigon River," or that's the road to someplace I'd never heard of before.

Within minutes, we were flying over jungle so thick that it was impossible to see the ground. Only once in a while did I see the sun reflect off what must have been a stream or swamp, and then it was gone.

The flight lasted for about thirty minutes, and then we were circling a large military base. I saw one runway that was surrounded by one-story buildings, parked helicopters, airplanes, and vehicles. As soon as we landed, the EM who had accompanied me on the flight were met by a sergeant, and their gear was loaded into a truck, and off they went. I was left standing on the flight line, bags in hand, wondering what now? as the helicopter departed. Then a jeep pulling an APU (auxiliary power unit, used for starting aircraft) pulled up and the driver said, "Can I give you a lift, sir?"

The thought of having to carry those two bags plus two helmets wasn't all that thrilling, and I said, "Yeah, that would be great."

"Where are you going, sir?"

"Well, I'm supposed to report to Cav headquarters for assignment."

"Great, I know just where you want to go. Throw your stuff in the back, and we'll be out of here."

Within minutes, we had pulled up in front of a walkway that was lined on both sides with white rocks. The first thought that came to mind upon viewing the rocks was that some poor son-of-a-bitch enlisted man had to paint those damn things, and I'm sure glad it wasn't me. My driver pointed to a building along the walkway and said, "That's where you want to report in, sir."

I thanked him for the ride and then asked, "You don't happen to know if they've got any good ARA units here, do you?"

"I don't think so, sir. Our troop Cobras pretty much handle

whatever comes up, but you could check over at Quan Loi. I think Blue Max is over there somewhere."

It took three trips, but I finally got my bags to the office that the driver had pointed out.

"Warrant Officer Boyle reporting as ordered, First Sergeant," I said to the first sergeant seated at the desk.

"Well, Mr. Boyle, I see here that you're indefinite, does that mean you plan on staying in this man's army?"

"Yes, First Sergeant, it does, but it was the only way I could get Cobra school."

"Well, that's good, Mr. Boyle. I'm glad to have an honest soldier around. The spec four over there will show you where to put your equipment and where you'll be sleeping until we can get you assigned. We can always use another Snake pilot," he said without looking up. "Jones, show Mr. Boyle where the mess hall is and the O-club after you get him settled in at the barracks, that way he won't get lost." The first sergeant finally looked up from his pile of paperwork, smiling.

Jones helped me drag my bags into the barracks and put them on an empty bunk.

"You got a poncho liner, sir?" Jones asked.

"Yeah, why?"

"Well, you can just use it for a pillow, and it will save you having to draw bedding and then have to turn it back in."

"Sounds good to me. Thanks for the helpful advice. Now, let's find the mess hall and the O-club."

Spec Four Jones headed down one of the red-clay streets, with me alongside. "Over there on the left is the O-club. If you decide to go in there, you might want to sit by a door or a window just in case."

"In case of what?"

"We take incoming—you know, rockets and mortars. But more often than not, some drunk grunt takes it upon himself to toss a CS grenade into the place, just for fun, sir."

"Getting tear gassed is not all that much fun. Take it from someone who knows," I replied. "What time do they open up, do you know?"

"Well, sir, it's usually just after dark. Not much flies around here after dark except incoming mortars and rockets. Which reminds me, there is a bunker right around the corner from your barracks, just in case you hear the siren go off. You'll probably only be here a few days though, so don't worry about it."

"You mean I'll have to move again!"

"Probably so, sir, unless you are assigned to Charlie Troop. All the other troops are out in the field at different locations. Don't worry, sir, you'll get the hang of everything real quick," he said with a shit-eating grin.

I spent the next two hours between my bunk and the mess hall, drinking coffee. The mess sergeant wasn't nearly as friendly as the one at the reception station. As far as he was concerned, I was just another FNG there to get in his way. So it was with great pleasure that I observed the sun go down, and hoping to find some new friends, headed for the O-club.

I remembered to remove my hat as I walked through the door and headed for the far end of the bar, where nobody was seated. There were about twenty people at the bar and seated at the few tables.

"What'll it be, matey?" the bartender asked as I sat down at the bar.

"Have you got a bourbon?" I asked.

"Oh God, another FNG pilot," he said.

"Sure, they've got just about anything you want to drink," said a big, tall first lieutenant.

"Where you bound for?" the bartender asked as he slid a glass of brown liquid across the bar in front of me.

"I'm really not sure yet. Do you have a Coke to go with this, and maybe some ice?"

"What do you fly?" the tall lieutenant asked.

"I fly Snakes," I said, using the slang term for the Cobra and attempting to try and act not so much like a new guy.

"Hey, Mr. Williams, said the lieutenant, motioning to a warrant officer sitting at the other end of the bar. "We've found ourselves an unassigned Cobra pilot."

A couple of other officers followed Mr. Williams down to where I was sitting. All of a sudden I felt surrounded, much the same as a piece of raw meat in the middle of a pack of wild dogs.

"How'd you like to be a part of Apache Troop?" asked one of the warrant officers.

"I was sort of hoping to get into an ARA outfit; is that what you guys do?"

"Well sort of," Williams replied. A loud groan came from the lieutenant whose flight-suit name tag read Coons.

"Look, Boyle, you don't want to get into some eight-ball ARA outfit. What you want is Apache Troop. If you like flying Cobras, we have a place for you," the lieutenant said.

"Hey, Hugele, you're a new guy—tell this young pilot about Apache," Williams yelled at another officer standing at the bar.

"Hi, I'm John Hugele, and I'm a little drunk, but I'm here to tell you that if Gen. George A. Custer could have called upon Apache Troop, the Little Bighorn would have been known for nothing but good trout fishing!"

"Mr. Williams, is there a chance that you could find an empty seat on your bird for Mr. Boyle here?" Lieutenant Coons asked.

"No problem," Williams replied.

"Look, you guys get his gear squared away, and I'll take care of the headquarters' routine. What size hat do you wear, Boyle? I'll put in an order for you while I square away your paper work," Lieutenant Coons said.

"Seven and three-eighths, but is that all it takes to get assigned? Are you sure this is all on the up and up?" I asked.

"Okay, it's settled then," Williams said. "Let's go get this young pilot's gear and be on our way. Welcome to Apache Troop, Mr. Boyle."

Shit, I'm being kidnapped, I thought as I climbed into the back of the Huey. "Hey, I thought nobody flew at night around here," I said to Lieutenant Hugele as he got into the helicopter with as much grace as he could muster.

"We, uh, don't, uh, fly combat missions at night; this flight was sort of an emergency flight. We needed some stuff, uh, beer from the PX. Our O-club ran out last night, and there was damn near a riot," he said.

As the Huey lifted off the ground into a very black sky and headed west, Mr. Williams, who was doing the flying, turned around and said, "Welcome to Apache Troop, Boyle."

Lieutenant Hugele said, "You'll really like our outfit, we're the best troop in the 1st of the 9th."

"The what!", I said.

"The 1st of the 9th—why? Have you heard of us?"

"Yes, sir, I've heard of you guys. Is it too late to turn around and go back to Phuoc Vinh?"

"I think so. Why, did you forget something?"

"Yeah, my balls!" I said as I put my head between my legs, and got ready to kiss my ass good-bye.

CHAPTER SIX

I'd been staring out the open door on the right side of the Huey, when something broke my plane of vision, and I jumped back.

"What's the matter, Boyle, something bite you, or were you just having a bad dream?" Lieutenant Hugele asked.

"No, sir," I answered. "Nothing bit me, and you guys are living proof that a guy doesn't have to be asleep to have a bad dream."

"There are a whole bunch of dead little rice eaters that shared the same opinion," the lieutenant responded in a more formal tone.

I figured that I was pushing my luck just a little too far, and decided to shut up before I really got myself in over my head.

"That's Nui Ba Den you're looking at, Boyle. We own the top and the bottom, and Charlie owns everything in between. The place has thousands of hiding places and lots of caves. Charlie just sits up there and directs in his mortars and rockets when they have a few to spare. He must be having a surplus because we've been getting rained on pretty heavy lately."

I couldn't resist sticking my foot in my mouth, "Why don't you just go up there and clean them out?"

"It's already been tried. The VC have held that part of the hill since the Japs were here and probably long before that. They lost a lot of people; the French lost a lot of people, and so have we. So, it was decided to just let them have it if they want it that bad. You'll get a better look at it in the morning, and I think you'll see just how tough it would be to try and re-take the place. It can't be all that easy on Charlie either, having to try and live up there."

The helicopter banked sharply to the left and started to descend. Within minutes, we were hovering into a black revetment, with other helicopters outlined nearby by the glow from the running lights.

As the Huey settled down inside the revetment, up drove a small, four-wheeled vehicle called a mule. I got off the Huey and started to drag one of my bags with me.

"Hey, Boyle, give me a hand here with the beer," Lieutenant Coons said.

"But what about my gear, Lieutenant?"

"Look, Boyle, quit calling me lieutenant, just call me Red. Everyone else does. As soon as we get the beer over to the O-club and the EM-club, you and Thornton here can come back and get your gear. Besides, I still have to find you a place to spend the night."

Eager arms were waiting at the entrances to the clubs, and the beer was off-loaded in seconds. Red told me to go get my gear and meet him over by the mess hall. I got up in the front of the mule with Thornton, and we headed back toward the flight line.

"Hi, my name's Jerry," I said to the driver.

"How you doing, sir. My name's Evan Thornton, but nobody uses first names around here. They just use their last name or their aircraft commander number, or if they're a platoon leader, they're either Red, White, or Blue. You just flew in here with Lieutenant Coons, who is Red Platoon leader, and Lieutenant Hugele, who is Blue Platoon leader. Didn't they tell you?"

"Have you ever heard of the little Lindberg law?" I asked.

"The *what*, sir?"

"Forget it, it doesn't matter anymore." It'll be okay I thought to myself. The first sergeant back at Phuoc Vinh will miss me in the morning, and they will eventually find me, and I'll get out of this house of cards.

"What ya fly, Mr. Boyle?" Thornton asked.

"Snakes."

"You must be Mr. Webster's replacement."

"I'll bet he was sure as hell glad to get out of this place." I said.

"I don't think so, sir. See, he was killed three days ago."

I met Red—Lieutenant Coons—at the rear of a long wooden building that Thornton had pointed out to me as being the mess hall. Red told me that the commanding officer wanted to speak to me in the morning.

"The one thing I forgot to bring, sir, was an alarm clock."

"Don't worry, Mr. Boyle, things will move a little slow for you the first day or so until you get settled in. Besides, the room I've found for you is right next to the flight line, and I can assure you that you won't have any trouble waking up when the first bird fires up. We call it first light." I later chose to call it "Apache sunrise" because it was usually pitch black and scary.

"How come so early, Red? Doesn't it make seeing the VC a little tough?" I asked.

"We usually only fly when the low bird can see down through the trees. Before that time, he's a sitting duck. He can't see into the trees, but the VC have a clear picture of him. But we've had the firebases along the border getting hit almost every night now. The VC come across the border as soon as it gets dark, hit a firebase about 3:00 A.M., and then get back across the river into Cambodia just as the sun comes up. If we're lucky, we sometimes catch them trying to cross just as the sun comes up. Grab one of your bags and follow me. I'll show you where you'll be sleeping. You'll have a little cleaning up to do, but you'll have pretty much the whole building to yourself. What's left of it anyway." There was a smile in his voice.

Red left me on the small porch of a long wooden building. The bottom half had overlapping boards, and the top half was screened in. At some point, someone had taken it upon himself to nail up boards on the inside of the screen so that the building was completely enclosed, at least that's what it looked like in the dark. There were light fixtures inside but no bulbs, and I spent a good thirty minutes digging through my bags before I found the flashlight that had been issued to me at Bien Hoa. After looking around the inside of the building, I chose the first room on the left, the southwest corner. It had the least amount of junk stacked inside. I spent the next few hours just cleaning the place up. Everything in the room was covered with a thick coating of dirt and fine sand. The room itself was six feet wide and ten feet long. The bunk was made of wood boards and was about three feet above the floor. Above the bunk was a wood frame with a piece of steel runway grating, and on top of that was a layer of sandbags, stacked two high. Sweat pouring off my face, I rolled up my poncho liner, and lay down. There was absolutely no air circulating in the room, but I was too tired to worry about it.

I awoke the following morning to the familiar sound of a helicopter. Red had been right, there was no sleeping in when you were right next to the flight line! Another problem manifested itself when the helicopter outside my room decided to take off. Sand and dirt were blown between the cracks in the wooden wall. Everything that I had swept out the night before had now been redeposited inside my room. Oh well, I thought to myself, I'll take care of that problem in a hurry. But right now I want to find the closest coffee pot.

Compared to the previous night, the morning air was cool, and really felt good as I covered the fifty yards or so to the mess hall. When I walked through the door, I noticed the kitchen area to my right, a large area, in which I was standing, that was designated for the enlisted, and at the far end, to my left, a smaller area designated for officers. Still feeling more at home with the EM than with officers, I started to sit down with my coffee in the EM section.

"Hey, Boyle, come on back here and sit," said someone sitting in the officer area. It turned out to be Mr. Williams, one of my kidnappers. He started to introduce me to the half-dozen officers who were just finishing breakfast.

"Sir, this is Mr. Boyle. We picked him up along with the beer last night," Williams said to a captain who stood up and offered his hand.

"Good morning, Mr. Boyle. I'm Captain Funk. I'm the commanding officer of Apache Troop."

I was really caught off guard. I didn't know if I should salute, sit down, or what.

"Have a seat, Mr. Boyle, we can get all the formal stuff taken care of after you've had your breakfast."

"Well, how did you sleep?" Williams asked after the CO had excused himself and left the mess hall.

"Not too bad for the first night in a strange bed, if you can call that thing a bed. Do I have the whole place to myself?" I asked.

"Yeah, right now anyway. Everyone moved out last month after it got hit by a mortar. The guy who was living where it hit dug his own bunker and now lives underground. When you get a chance, you should go check it out. It's really neat," Williams said.

"Do you know where I can get something to cover up the cracks in the walls to keep the dirt from blowing in?"

One of the officers told me to try supply. He thought that they might have some plastic or tar paper.

After I had drunk a half-dozen cups of very strong coffee, I left the mess hall and walked to the building that Mr. Williams had pointed out as the troop headquarters building.

Upon entering I was greeted by first Sergeant Sparacino, who had me fill out and sign a stack of paperwork.

"Welcome to Apache Troop, Mr. Boyle," the first sergeant said as I handed him back the papers. "The CO is expecting you. He's right through that door."

I knocked on the wall outside the open door, and said, "Sir, Warrant Officer Boyle reporting for duty, sir."

"Have a seat, Boyle. I'm going to assign you to the lift section, Mr. Boyle; we're short a pilot over there right now."

"But sir, I'm a Cobra pilot and went indefinite just to get the school, sir," I said, almost coming out of my chair.

"You are whatever in God's little green acres I want you to be, Mr. Boyle, do you understand!"

"Yes, sir." I said. My voice sounded like that of a seven-year-old being chewed out by his first-grade nun.

"You're dismissed, Mr. Boyle," he hissed.

I did a beautifully executed about-face—for having both my head and my tail between my legs—and headed straight out the door without stopping. I almost knocked over Lieutenant Coons as the screen door closed behind me.

"Well, how'd it go with the CO?" he asked.

"Not very well."

"Why, what happened?"

"Hell, Red, I don't know. He says he's going to put me in lift, and I just told him I was a Snake pilot."

"Don't worry about it, Boyle." He laughed. "I think I know what the problem is. You go back to your room and get that squared away, and I'll see what I can do with the Old Man."

An hour later, Red showed up at my opening (my room didn't have a door) and said I was in his platoon.

"Thanks, Red, how can I ever thank you?"

"You'll probably want to kill me in a week, Boyle. I don't cut anybody any slack, especially FNGs (fucking new guys). After lunch go out and preflight 074, and just you and I will go for a little flight this afternoon," he said with a funny look on his face.

"What else can go wrong? I'm only here twelve hours, and I've already pissed off the CO." I said.

"You didn't piss off the CO, it was just his way of testing you. What you really have to worry about is learning how to become a good Xray (the pilot in the front seat of a Cobra).

Learn your job, and learn it well. A lot of people's lives may depend on how well you can read a map and how well you keep your cool when everything around you is turning to shit. I stuck my neck way out to get you into Apache Troop, and with the Old Man to get you assigned to the Red Platoon. I'm not asking you not to let me down; I'm ordering you."

"I'll try not to, Red." I wanted very much to ask him if he'd ever been a nun in another life, but kept my thoughts to myself.

"Go over to supply and draw a set of maps of the AO (area of operations). Somebody over at the TOC will show you how to fold them and mark off our area. Oh, and, Boyle, you better go over emergency procedures," he said.

The TOC (pronounced tock) was the tactical operations center for Apache Troop. All information from the units operating out in the AO or from division or brigade headquarters was funneled through the TOC. Maps and charts were pinned up on the wall in front of soldiers who were monitoring the numerous radios in front of them. It was usually a very busy place to be and was manned twenty-four hours a day.

I found a sergeant named Delorme, who was willing to take the time to help me out with my maps. The first thing I noticed was that Apache Troop had a huge area of operations. Tay Ninh was approximately fifteen miles east of the Cambodian border. The border generally followed a small river, but in some places it did not, and that meant that the Xray had to know exactly where he was at all times. Where there were trails and roads to compare against the maps, the chore was not that difficult, but where there was nothing but jungle and just about everything looked the same, most pilots wanted to pull their hair out, Sergeant Delorme explained to me.

"Well, sir, I think you've got just about all the maps you'll need right now. Have you met the first sergeant yet?"

"Yeah, I met him when I had to see the Old Man this morning. He seems like an all right guy, but the Old Man, wow, I think he must be on the rag or something."

"Naw, not really. You know how an animal goes around pissing on trees to stake out his territory? Well, sir, you've just been pissed on by the Old Man. He was just letting you know that this is his territory, and things get done his way, or else. You ought to feel lucky. When a new Scout pilot comes in, they hand him a calendar that only has five months on it. He's told that if he makes it longer than that, he can come back and pick up the other seven months!"

I left the TOC, shaking my head, not knowing for sure if I was being put on or just what, but I was soon to find out.

At the end of the day, I was ready to go AWOL. The first part of the flight had been interesting, with Red explaining how a "Pink" Team worked and how it got its name. The Snake or Cobra Platoon was referred to as the Red Platoon, and the Scout Platoon was referred to as the White Platoon. When a Red and a White flew as a team, they became a Pink Team. For some missions, a quick reaction force of troops from Blue Platoon was along. Then the team was called a Purple Team.

Red showed me how important it was to always keep the low bird in sight, no matter what. If for some reason I had to look at the map or, for any reason, take my eyes off the low bird, I was to let the AC know so that he could watch them. One of us had to have him in sight at all times. I was very impressed by Red. The first thing that struck me was that he really had his act together. The second thing that struck me was the volume of his voice. This guy doesn't have to write letters home; hell, he can just walk outside and talk to them, I thought to myself.

Everything went along great until we got to my working knowledge of the Cobra. When Red had told me, earlier in the day, to go over emergency procedures, he wasn't kidding. He chewed on my ass so hard and long, I'm sure I could have put in for a Purple Heart.

"Boyle, you've got to be the dumbest Xray I've ever flown with. Didn't they teach you anything about emergencies in Cobra school?" he yelled.

"Most of the time was spent learning the weapon systems, sir."

"Don't try and bullshit me, Boyle, I went through the same school. I want you to memorize all of the emergency procedures and the location of every circuit breaker in this damn helicopter. If something happens, and I can guarantee that it will, you won't have time to think, you have to react immediately. You won't have time to look at the circuit breakers or try and think about what to do. It has to be an unconscious reaction. Do I make myself clear, mister!"

It was difficult to tell if he was yelling at the top of his voice or just speaking regularly; they both sounded the same, but he had made his point.

"Yes, sir, Red" I said, knowing very well that everything he said was true. A few questions later, Red said, "Boyle, I hope you never get interested in genealogy."

"Why's that, Red?"

"Because, mister, you're liable to find out that your father was really a goat. You take the controls and see if you can find your way back to base; I've had about all I can take for one afternoon."

With the grace of God and a lot of luck, I was able to find my way back to Tay Ninh, and Red only yelled at me ten or so times. Flying the Cobra from the front seems strange at first and takes a lot of getting used to. I couldn't get over the feeling that I was sitting on a diving board that was covered with grease, over a pool filled with alligators. Because of the shape of the Cobra, I felt as if I was always pointed down hill. I kept pulling back on the controls to bring the nose up and that would actually put the Cobra in a climbing attitude. Every time I did it, Red would yell at me. I found it difficult to believe that someone who had yelled as much as he had that afternoon, was still able to speak, let alone yell.

As we landed, there was a conversation between Red and the TOC, but I was too preoccupied trying to get my maps refolded to understand what they were talking about.

"Boyle, when you get through tying down the blade, go over to the mess hall and just wait for me; we may have a mission."

I'd only been in the mess hall long enough for one cup of coffee when Red stuck his head through the door and said, "Boyle, let's go. We've got people in contact."

As the Cobra was already fully armed, we only made one brief stop to refuel, and then were off, headed due north. Red briefed me on what was going on; "We've got an ARVN Ranger unit with two American Special Forces advisers that just broke off contact with the VC, and they've got one wounded. One of the ARVN Rangers got shot in the head and he's in pretty bad shape. They've called for a medevac bird and want us to cover them when they pick up this guy."

Red handed me his map over the center console that divided the front and back seats, and told me that he had circled the location.

"Copy it off onto your map, Boyle, and hand mine back."

The location was very close to the Cambodian border, in an area of swampy clearings surrounded by thick jungle.

"You do remember how to fire the turret, don't you, Boyle?"

"Yes, sir, but I'm not worth a shit with the chunker," I said. (The chunker was the 40mm grenade launcher located in the nose and next to the minigun.)

"Don't worry about the chunker; just use the minigun, but only if and when I tell you."

Red was in radio contact with one of the American Special Forces advisers, who advised that the medevac hadn't showed up yet. I was still having trouble understanding everything that was being said over the radio, but the adviser doing the talking was out of breath, and that made it even harder to understand. I did, however, understand that they were still on the move, trying to find a big enough opening in the jungle canopy so that the medevac chopper could lower a stretcher down to them. He was asked by Red if they were still in contact, and answered no but thought that the VC weren't very far behind them.

I kept thinking, God, I'm glad I'm not down there in that swamp with a bunch of VC trying to kill me.

"Okay, Boyle, make sure the turret works, and I don't mean fire it," Red said.

The sight was located between my legs and moved up and down, left and right. Wherever I pointed the crosshairs of the sight, the turret turned and pointed the guns. "Everything seems to be working okay, Red."

I heard more radio conversation between Red and somebody other than the guy on the ground.

"That was the medevac. He says he'll be here in about five minutes. We'll just lay off here to the west so as not to draw too much attention to those guys on the ground. I'm not real happy with the idea of the medevac ship having to hover to pick up that guy, and I don't think the other pilot is either," Red said with concern.

I still didn't know for sure exactly where this group of ARVNs was and neither did Red. Under normal circumstances, they would have popped a smoke grenade, but they were afraid it would give away their position. It had been decided that the people on the ground would pop a smoke only when the medevac ship got close to their position.

On one of our passes over the jungle, the American on the ground told Red that we had passed right over them, so we now had a pretty good idea where the team was located. Red advised the pilot of the medevac that he would talk him into the general location and then the Ranger on the ground could direct him from there. The team was about twenty yards inside the tree line on the south side of an open area that ran east and west, about three times the size of a football field. Red kept the Cobra about one-quarter mile west of the western end of the clearing, flying back and forth, north and south.

From that position, Red talked the medevac chopper into the general area where we thought the team was located, as they had decided not to use smoke to mark their position. I felt like a mouse in the corner, just watching, not really knowing if there was anything I could do to help. Between radio calls, Red tried to explain what we were doing and why, for which I was very grateful. Red had explained that two things were accomplished by staying away from the team on the ground and remaining over the jungle west of the open clearing. First, we were not pinpointing the team on the ground, and second, we were staying in a position that made us a difficult target.

I heard the team leader say to the medevac pilot, "Okay, you're right over us now; back up just a tad. Okay, hold it right there."

I could see the crew chief kneeling in the door of the Huey, guiding a wire stretcher down through the trees while holding onto a steel cable attached to the winch mounted in the doorway.

Everything seemed to be taking much too much time, and the radio conversations were becoming more tense by the minute. The pilot of the Huey was yelling at the team leader to hurry up, and the team leader was telling him that they were having trouble getting the wounded man strapped into the stretcher.

Red turned the Cobra east and headed along the south side of the clearing. I was watching the hovering medevac Huey. A cloud of leaves and small branches was being generated and blown about by the downwash from the rotor blades of the medevac. Something, possibly a tiny flash, caused me to look away from the Huey and to my left. I didn't see anything at first and then a steady stream of tracers erupted from the tree line on the northern edge of the open clearing. I had never seen anything like it before. Greenish white balls of fire, about the size of a softball, were coming across the clearing in front and below us and passing directly under the hovering medevac. Everyone seemed to see it all at the same time, except the team on the ground. Between each of the tracers I could see, I knew there were at least four more bullets that weren't tracers.

Red yelled, "Get on the minigun and hit the tree line."

The minigun came to life with a burring sound. I couldn't tell exactly where along the tree line the tracers were coming from because they weren't lighting up until they were halfway across the clearing. I worked over a large area of the tree line, and then Red said, "Hold it," and he fired four pair of rockets in the same direction.

The Cobra banked sharply to the east and then south as we headed back toward the medevac helicopter.

The medevac was just beginning to accelerate forward in a climbing left turn, away from the direction of fire.

"What the hell was that thing, Red?" I asked, sweat pouring out of my helmet. My flight suit was also soaked, and I really hoped that it was just sweat.

"That was a .51-caliber antiaircraft gun. Don't ever try and duke it out with one; you'll lose every time."

Red was interrupted by an excited, very out-of-breath Huey pilot over the radio. "We're real sorry that we weren't able to get your man, but those gooks damn near blew us out of the sky."

"What are you talking about, we hooked up the stretcher just as you took off. You've got him hanging under you," the team leader said.

There was a long pause, and then the medevac pilot said, "We didn't know you had already hooked him up. I told my crew chief to blow the cable so we wouldn't get it hung up in the trees."

"Oh my God, oh no," said the tear-filled voice of the team leader.

Just listening to the emotional voices brought tears to my eyes. I was either sweating a lot or had wet my pants, but I was too scared to really care.

We flew up alongside the medevac and asked him if they were okay. The pilot said they hadn't taken any hits, but he was obviously very shook up over what had just happened. I asked Red if we were going to go back and try and get the gun, and he just said, "We'll talk about it later."

Red stayed alongside the medevac helicopter until he was sure they were okay. I felt a sick sensation well up inside me as Red turned the Cobra and headed back in the direction of the ARVN recon team. I wanted to curl up in the fetal position in the armor-plated seat. I was scared, but I could tell from the tone of Red's voice that he was very displeased with what had just occurred, and although I had a lot of questions I would have liked to ask, I kept my mouth shut. I was already scared shitless, and I didn't want or feel like giving Red any reason to start yelling at me.

"Tiger Four One, this is Apache Red, how do you copy?" Red called to the recon team leader.

"I've got you loud and clear," the still shaken team leader replied.

"What the hell went on down there?"

"We had to unhook the stretcher to get our man into it, and then, just as we got it all rehooked up, that son of a bitch pulled pitch and drug him up through the branches; then he blows the cable and drops him into the treetops somewhere," the team leader said, crying out the words. "We're down here now trying to find him, but I think it's going to be impossible," he continued.

"Do you want me to try and get a QRF (quick reaction force) for you?" Red asked.

"No, I've already contacted my headshed (headquarters), and they told me to move south to an LZ (landing zone) and secure it. They're going to insert a company-size force. If Charlie has got a .51 down here, we're up against more than just a VC patrol. I'd sure be grateful if you guys would stick around until Blue Max shows up. They're going to prep the LZ for the insertion."

"No problem. You got any idea when they'll be here?" Red asked.

"I called them on the other radio when the shit hit the fan, so it shouldn't be very long now. Are you guys okay? Those tracers looked mighty close to you."

"Yeah, we're fine, but I think my front seat just got his cherry broke. I can't even see the top of his head, he's sitting so low in the seat."

"I don't blame him one bit. At least I've got a few trees to get behind," was the reply.

We flew cover for the ARVN recon patrol until Blue Max showed. I had remembered to mark the approximate position of the North Vietnamese .51-caliber antiaircraft gun, and relayed it to the flight leader of the three-Cobra, Blue Max team. By this time, the recon patrol had moved far enough away from the area of contact so the team leader on the ground popped a smoke to mark his location for the Blue Max team. At that point, Red told the Special Forces team leader on the ground that we were breaking station and returning to Tay Ninh.

The flight back was conducted in almost total silence, broken only by short radio calls between Red and the TOC and the control tower at Tay Ninh. We stopped at the refueling point and took on fuel and then parked in one of the revetments.

"Tie the blade down and then meet me in the mess hall, okay?" Red said.

"Okay, Lieutenant, uh, I mean Red."

The crew chief walked up to the Cobra and opened the ammo-bay door on my side, stood on it, and opened the cockpit canopy.

"Well, how'd it go today, sir? Looks like you got to do a little shooting."

"Okay, I guess," I said, a little embarrassed by the huge pile of cigarette butts on the floor around my feet. I climbed out of the cockpit and sat down on the open ammo-bay door. The crew chief was taking a count of how many rockets he would need to bring over from the ammo dump to rearm the Cobra.

"You look a little pale, Mr. Boyle. Don't you feel good?"

"I'm okay, I guess. I just had the shit scared out of me. I've never been shot at before, but it didn't seem to affect Red at all."

"Hey, don't let it bother you, Mr. Boyle. Hell, everyone gets scared. I bet if you ask Red, he'll tell you that he was just as scared as you."

"Yeah, well, if he was, he sure didn't show it," I said, looking at the ground.

"Hell, sir, Red's probably the best Snake pilot in the whole damn Cav. He gets scared just like anybody else. The secret is keeping your cool while you are being scared to death."

"Does he yell at everybody, or is it just me that pisses him off?"

"Hell, Red yells at everybody if they screw up. Mr. Bartlett came in the other day looking like Snow White. I didn't know if he was scared or just pissed to the max. So don't feel bad; Red doesn't play favorites.

Changing the subject, I asked the crew chief if he knew where I could get some plastic to patch up the cracks in the walls of my room.

"The unit across that road just moved out, sir. You might want to have a look around there, but be careful. The MPs don't like us taking stuff out of other units' buildings. I would suggest that if you try, you do it after dark."

I started to tie down the blade, and the crew chief said, "I'll take care of that, sir, after I've finished my inspection."

I thanked him and headed for the mess hall to meet Red.

As I walked toward the mess, I couldn't get rid of the thought of that poor ARVN, strapped into the stretcher, hanging up in some treetop back there in the jungle. Just thinking about that and the memory of the antiaircraft rounds flying by us made me get weak in the knees all over again. I began to wonder if I had made one hell of a mistake by thinking that I had something to offer the army and Apache Troop.

As I walked into the mess hall, Red was sitting back in the officers' section speaking with another lieutenant. As I walked up to where they were sitting, Red introduced me, and added that he was also the mess officer. The lieutenant, as if by some prearranged signal, excused himself and walked toward the kitchen. I had the distinct feeling that I was in for an ass chewing, but much to my surprise, Red just said, "Have a seat, Boyle. Well, what did you think about what went on today? Have you got any questions?"

"Yes, sir, I do, but I'm not exactly sure how to go about asking them. Do you think I could get a cup of coffee before we really get into it?"

"No problem, how about bringing me one, too, black."

I set two cups of coffee down on the table, really not knowing where to begin. This man scared the shit out of me, and the last thing I wanted to do was give him an excuse to start yelling at me.

Red broke the ice by saying, "That armor seat doesn't really cover very much when you are as tall as we are, does it?"

The ice was broken. I said, "I see you noticed how low I was trying to get in that damn seat."

"Yeah, I noticed, but don't feel bad, everyone does it at first, and some never get over doing it. So don't worry about it."

I felt as if a big weight had been lifted off me. I wasn't as chicken as I thought ran through my mind.

"Red, why didn't we really go after that antiaircraft position, we had plenty of ammo left?"

"Look, Boyle, I want to impress something upon you right now, and I don't want you to ever forget it. I've told the rest of the platoon, but this is really the first time we've been able to talk. Don't, and I mean *don't ever*, engage a .51 antiaircraft position. Getting hit by a .51 is like being hit by an eighteen-wheeler truck. There isn't one piece of armor plate on that Snake out there that will stop a .51, and if one hits you, something is going to quit working—usually a lot of things quit working. The odds are stacked in favor of the .51. Besides, if there is one .51 down there, chances are there are a couple more. You get suckered into going after the one you see, and then two more open up on you, one from each side. You don't have a snowball's chance in hell of getting out of a situation like that without getting hit. Take my word for it. If we do find something like that, we report it and hope that the artillery or air force can take care of them. Do you get the picture, Mr. Boyle?"

"Yes, sir, Red, and thanks for taking the time to explain. What do you think will happen to the ARVN in the tree?"

"Well, from what I heard over at the TOC, he was about dead when the medevac showed up. They inserted a company and are looking for him and the .51 right now, but I doubt that they'll find either one. Look, Boyle, I'm going to schedule you to be the Old Man's Xray tomorrow. It's more or less just being on standby 'cuz you won't have a low bird."

"Is the Old Man going to be checking me out also, is that the idea?"

"Quit worrying about the Old Man. Every Xray takes his turn being on standby with the Old Man."

"I feel a little funny calling him the Old Man. I think I'm older than he is, and after today, I feel like I could be his father."

"You'll get the hang of things soon enough, and then it will all just be routine. We better get the hell out of this mess hall so they can set up for evening chow. Don't forget to go over those circuit breakers and emergency procedures tonight. I think you now know why they are so important. I'll see you first thing at the briefing in the morning, or maybe in the club tonight," Red said as he got up and walked out.

I felt relieved, not only because he hadn't found a reason to yell at me, but because what I had felt and was feeling wasn't that much different from anyone else. More than anything, I had wanted to ask Red if he had also been scared. But I resisted the temptation, feeling that I might put him in an awkward position.

As I started to leave the mess hall, I stopped by the exit door to fill my paper coffee cup.

"How's the coffee, sir?" said one of the cooks.

"It's great, but I guess I should be filling up on ice water to take back to that sweatbox I'm living in."

"What you need is a fan, sir."

"What I need first is a couple of light bulbs, and then maybe a fan."

He turned to another cook in the kitchen. "Hey, Sarge, okay

if I take off for a couple of minutes? I'm going to help out Mr. Boyle here. Come on, sir, I've got an extra fan you can use and maybe a light bulb, too." He opened the door.

As I followed this happy-go-lucky young cook toward a row of buildings, I found out his name was Mike Cutts. He was from Azle, Texas, and seemed really happy doing what he was doing.

He went into a building while I waited outside. A few minutes later, he emerged with a white desk fan under his arm and a light bulb sticking out of his shirt pocket.

"You can have the light bulb, sir, but try and get your own fan as soon as you can. You can pick one up in town or have someone pick you up one at the PX in Phuoc Vinh. Be careful of this one though; it has a tendency to walk all over whatever you set it on."

"This is really great, Mike. Now all I've got to do is find something to seal up all the cracks in my room, and I'll be all set."

"Set that stuff down a minute; I want to show you something; maybe you could do the same."

I followed him back inside the building, and about halfway down the hall, he opened a door. The inside of the room looked as though it had been paneled with wood.

"That looks great. How did you do it?" I asked.

"No sweat, sir, just go down to rearm and get a bunch of empty rocket boxes and nail them up on the wall. You got to break them up first, and then just use the boards to cover up the cracks. After you get that part done, I'll show you where to get the tar paper to make the wood stain with."

"Okay, Mike, if you say so. Thanks for the light and fan. I'm sure I'll sleep a little better tonight with some air moving around the room."

I unloaded my newfound fortune in my room and set out to walk across the road to the area that an engineer outfit had just left a few days earlier. I first located a door the same size as the opening to my room, then an old runway light that someone had put up in what the departed unit had used as a bar, along with a small stainless-steel sink. I couldn't get the sink loose from the cabinet it sat in, so I just pried the whole thing away from the wall. I stacked my newfound loot next to a door and went back to my room to await darkness.

I lay on my bunk, feeling the rush of air from my newfound fan. The only problem was that every few minutes I had to get up and reel the damn thing in as it wanted to run around the room like a puppy on a leash. In the middle of one of my recovery missions, I found out that I was not the only person who lived in the building. Another warrant officer was standing in the opening to my room watching me reel in my fan.

"How's it going? You must be the new guy. I'm Mills, Jimmy Mills. I'm in the room next to you," he said.

"Glad to meet you; I'm Jerry Boyle. I thought I had this rattrap all to myself."

"Well, you've got to look pretty hard to see my bunk. It's under all that metal and sandbags next door. I see you've already found a fan and a light bulb. Damn light bulbs are worth their weight in gold around here. I think the price is up around two bucks apiece now."

"How come so much?" I asked.

"Seems they go directly from the ship to the black market, and that's where we have to buy them if we want them. By the time a guy gets one going through the normal channels, he's usually already on his way home, one way or the other. So guard that light with your life. What's with your fan, anyway?"

"I can't get it to sit still. It keeps wanting to go AWOL on me!"

"I think I can solve that problem," Mills said, reaching into a pocket of his flight suit. "We'll try the ole grease-pencil-in-the-fan trick."

I watched as he grabbed hold of the fan and then slowly inserted the grease pencil through the metal screen on the front of the fan until a loud twang was heard. Then he shut the fan off and looked at the blades. Only one blade had a mark from the grease pencil on it.

"Yep, blades are out of track. Now all we have to do is bend this here blade back and try it again. What we're trying to do is get the grease pencil to mark all three blades at the same time."

It took about three more attempts, and the twang sound changed to a burr, and when the fan was turned off, all three blades showed a mark from the grease pencil. Mills set the fan down on an orange crate that I was using as a table and turned it back on. The first think I noticed was the different sound the fan made. It now hummed, and didn't rattle as before. It also remained on the crate without moving a fraction of an inch.

"Where in the hell did you learn to do that?" I asked in amazement.

"I had the same problem with my fan some time back, and

I remembered watching the maintenance officer tracking the blades on a helicopter. I just thought, if it works on a helicopter, why the hell wouldn't it work on fan blades, and it did."

"That's great, Jimmy. Thanks a lot. I was really getting tired of chasing that damn thing all over the floor."

"I'm Apache Two Seven, by the way. I see you're scheduled to be the Old Man's Xray tomorrow."

"How'd you find out?"

"It's posted in the TOC. If Red knows for sure what's going on for the next day, he posts it on the board in the TOC. Otherwise, we just find out at the morning briefing. You'll find out that things really change during the night, depending on what the gooks do. You'll like flying with the Old Man, if you fly. He only goes out when the shit hits the fan, so you get to go right to where the action is."

Just what I need, I thought. "So, what do I do, just wait in the TOC, or what?"

"No, just stay in the troop area. If you hear the siren go off, run like hell for the Old Man's Cobra and be ready to take off."

After eating dinner, and meeting most of the other pilots in the troop, I secured my newly stolen equipment from across the road. It took three trips, but I got all the stuff I had stashed, and never saw an MP. My fan was working perfectly, and the steady stream of air really felt great as I attempted to align the door and install the hinges. Finally, the door was on, and I gave up on all my other home improvements, at least for the night.

Jimmy Mills, my newfound building mate, was down at the other end of the building, putting together a model airplane. I decided to just lie down and enjoy the rush of air from my most prized possession, the fan!

I couldn't help but think of all the events that had taken place that day in such a short period of time. I could not get out of my mind the thought of that South Vietnamese soldier, still strapped into the stretcher, either lying on the ground or hung up in a tree somewhere. From the bits and pieces of information I overheard at dinner, the soldier spoke English well and had become good friends with the American advisers. Besides being scared out of my shorts, I remembered how frustrated I had become at not being able to actually see the location of the antiaircraft gun. It appeared to me that the tracers were not lighting up until they were halfway across the clearing. At least their firing had stopped momentarily when I raked the tree line with the minigun.

I thought to myself, I've got to ask Red about those tracers and also why they didn't hit the medevac Huey. They were sitting ducks and should have been shot down.

The ticking of the old windup alarm clock that I had borrowed from the TOC and the hum of the fan were making my eyelids very heavy. I turned out the light and closed the door, and was asleep within minutes.

"Mr. Boyle, Mr. Boyle, wake up."

Someone was in my room, shaking one of my feet.

"Time to get up, Mr. Boyle," the voice said as I opened my eyes to the light of a flashlight. It was the spec four from the TOC, whose duty it was to make sure that every pilot scheduled to fly that day was up or awake.

"Did you wake Mr. Mills?" I asked.

"No, sir, he's off today."

I swung my legs over the edge of the bunk and turned on the light.

Briefings were held in the TOC, and the pilots scheduled to fly were told what had taken place during the night. During my first briefing, we were told that it had been relatively quiet during the night except for a probing action that took place at FSB (fire support base) Hannas. The NVA had dropped mortars on the base, which was within a half mile of the river that acted as the border between Cambodia and Vietnam. They had also probed the defenses of the FSB by sending sappers up to the barbed wire, but made no real attempt to get through it.

Two Pink Teams were scheduled to check out the area along the river in the area of Hannas and the area between the FSB and the river to see if they could find anything of the NVA force from the night before.

Everyone was pretty sure that the NVA were already back across into Cambodia because Hannas was so close to the border.

I checked the board in the TOC and found out which Cobra the Old Man and I had been assigned. As the Xray, I did the preflight. After that, I went to the mess hall.

"Everything okay, Mr. Boyle?" the Old Man asked as I walked toward one of the tables with a plate of breakfast in my hand.

"Everything seems okay, sir," I said as I sat down.

"Has anyone explained what you are to do in the event of a scramble?" Captain Funk asked.

"I think so, sir. If the siren goes off, I'm supposed to run like hell for our Snake and be ready to take off."

"You've got the idea, Mr. Boyle. If I need you for any reason, where are you going to be?"

"I'll either be right here, in the aircraft, or in my room, sir. I'm getting too old to run very far, sir."

The CO just smiled a little, and that scared me more than if he hadn't said or done anything. I wonder if this guy ever let's his hair down, I thought to myself.

Most of the talk around the table was about things that had happened before I arrived in Apache, so I just sat and listened. The topic on everyone's mind seemed to be the increase in NVA activity along the border. Not being able to cross the border and try to strike where they knew they could hurt the NVA the most was a real source of frustration to everyone, but everyone had been given strict orders not to cross the border. The pilots of the two Pink Teams and one lift ship had already departed, having eaten quickly in order to be in the area of FSB Hannas shortly after first light.

I was still feeling scared from the day before. But these pilots that I was eating with didn't act scared. They were a happy-go-lucky bunch of nut cases and practical jokers. I was almost afraid that someone was going to ask me if I had a case of yellow jaundice or something. Sitting there, looking at their faces and listening to them speak, I found no hint that they, too, were feeling the things that were going on inside me. Shooting and being shot at weren't discussed in life-threatening tones, but more on the scale of a college panty raid. Apache Troop was a fraternity of fighting brothers who supported each other in much the same way the members of a football team do. From water boy to the coach, everyone worked as a team, and everyone wanted to score that first touchdown. I could sense the team spirit, but how did I get ahold of it and stop feeling scared?

I was walking across the flight line, having just borrowed a manual on the Cobra's emergency procedures from Mr. King over at the maintenance section, when the siren on the roof of the TOC went off. Within seconds, the flight line looked like a covey of quail had just exploded out of the brush. There were people running in every direction, but mostly toward the parked aircraft. I had only to run about twenty yards, and I was at my Cobra.

The crew chief, who was just as close as I was, had beaten me to the Cobra and had opened the ammo-bay door, which was used as a step for getting in and out of the aircraft. I was strapped in, with my helmet on, when Captain Funk arrived and climbed in the backseat.

"What's going, sir?" I yelled, not being able to turn around because of the shoulder straps.

"The lift ship took some hits over by Hannas and tried to make it back here, but didn't make it. He had to set it down in a clearing," the CO yelled back at me over the whine of the huge turbine engine coming to life.

Normal, by-the-book start procedures were thrown out the window when it came to a scramble. A great deal of pride went with being the first helicopter off the ground following the siren going off, but this was not going to be a pride-filled day for the CO.

"Are you ready, Mr. Boyle?"

"Yes, sir, ready."

The Cobra started to lift off the ground and then plunked back to the surface of the flight line, after rising only a few inches. Again the CO tried to lift the Cobra off the ground, but he had the same results. The Cobra would lift a few inches off the ground, and then the rotor RPM would bleed off, and we'd settle back to the ground.

"Shit," the CO exclaimed. I thought I knew what the problem was, but remembered the last time I had voiced my opinion to the CO, and the resulting ass chewing, so I kept my opinions to myself.

"What the hell's wrong with this thing?" the CO yelled as Jimmy Mills's Cobra, parked down the line from us, lifted out of its revetment and was gone.

The CO opened his side of the canopy and said, "You cool it down, Mr. Boyle, and then shut it down. I'm going over to see if maintenance will check it out. Anyway, it's too late for us to go; they've already secured the lift ship and its crew. Nice job, Mr. Boyle. I'm glad to see that you got here as quickly as you did."

"No big deal, sir. I was damn near standing next to it when the siren went off," I said, and then thought, Hell, he's not such a bad guy after all.

The CO came around to the left front of the Cobra, where my canopy door was open, "Look, Mr. Boyle, I'm going to go back to the TOC and see what's going on. Why don't you get maintenance to check out the bird."

"No problem, sir," I replied as he walked away.

I shut down the engine, and then walked over to the maintenance section across the flight line. The crew chief walked with me, and we talked about what had happened. I really didn't want to say what I thought had happened, I wanted someone else to discover it. After a short conversation with the maintenance sergeant, the three of us walked back to the parked Cobra.

"Would you climb in and start it up for us?" the maintenance sergeant requested.

I climbed into the backseat, went through the prestart procedures, and pulled the starter trigger, located under the throttle.

"I want you to do everything just the same as the CO," the sarge said.

When the throttle had been opened all the way, I said, "Okay, Sarge, that's all of it, and it wouldn't come off the ground."

"Didn't he beep it up?" the sarge asked.

"I don't think so, Sarge."

"Well, hell, no wonder it wouldn't fly. Beep it up, Mr. Boyle."

The beep button was really a switch located at the end of the collective, which also housed the throttle. After the pilot rolled the twist-grip throttle all the way open, he still had to use the beep button to bring the RPM up into the range necessary for flight. The left thumb was usually used to accomplish this task.

We suspected that, in the excitement of the moment, the CO had just forgotten to beep the engine up to the proper RPM.

"I'm going to put the crew chief in the front seat, for balance, and then I want you to see if it will hover. Okay, Mr. Boyle?"

The Cobra came off the ground with no problem, and I was sure that the problem had been solved.

"Look, Sarge, I can't go back and tell the Old Man that he fucked up; what am I going to tell him?"

"Why don't you just tell him that we had to adjust the linear actuator!"

"Great idea, Sarge, you should have been a diplomat."

There was no lie in telling the CO that we had to adjust the linear actuator. It was the part attached to the fuel control on the engine that was controlled by the beep button.

The CO was not concerned when I told him that we had discovered, and fixed, the problem, and accepted the explanation without question. His only concern was that it would fly when next called upon to do so.

I'm not sure if Captain Funk ever learned the true story as he never mentioned it again. One thing was for sure, I wasn't going to be the one that said anything.

CHAPTER SEVEN

I was already awake when the sergeant from the TOC pushed the door to my room open.

"Good morning, Mr. Boyle, how'd you sleep last night?"

"Sort of off and on." I had been awakened around 1:00 A.M. by what sounded like distant thunder. I also heard the noise of flares being fired along the "green line," the base perimeter, which was made up of barbed-wire fences and bunkers manned by soldiers. I saw the eerie glow from the magnesium flares because their bright light leaked through the cracks in my wall as they swung, back and forth, beneath small white parachutes while drifting slowly toward the ground. I heard popping sounds as flares were fired into the air, and walked to the north end of my building and out onto the open porch to see what was going on.

Nervous would be a conservative way to describe how I felt standing on the porch, in my shorts and T-shirt. I could see the glow of cigarettes through the open backside of the bunkers closest to me, and the outline of a few troopers who had chosen to take up positions on top of the bunkers to escape the heat.

The flares made a strange sizzling sound as they floated toward the ground, and their swinging back and forth made the shadows of stationary objects look like they were actually moving. In the far distance, I could see dull flashes of light on the horizon, followed by a muffled boom. The sequence between flashes and booms soon made it apparent that I wasn't watching lightning but explosions of some sort.

"What the hell was going on last night, Sarge?" I asked as he turned to leave my small room.

"Hannas got hit real hard. They've got quite a few

wounded, but nobody killed. They're going to medevac out the worst ones at first light. You're scheduled to fly with Mr. Mills, and your low-bird pilot is Mr. Reardon. You'll be covering the medevac when they go in to pick up the wounded."

"Okay. Great, Sarge." I said as I put on my flight suit and boots. "I'll see you in the TOC in a few minutes."

The briefing had been short, as usual. I was to be Apache Two Seven Xray this day, and our Pink Team would be covering the medevac ship while it picked up the wounded at FSB Hannas. We were told that a large force of NVA regulars, supported by heavy machine-gun fire, mortars, and rockets, had attempted to get through the barbed wire on the west side of the base. Those that had succeeded in getting through the three separate rows of barbed wire had been killed, along with a lot of others who had been killed or wounded while still trying to get through the wire. After covering the medevac, we were to work the area west of Hannas, toward the river, and see if we could find any of the NVA who had not made it back across into Cambodia yet.

I left the TOC and headed for the flight line with my arms full of equipment. I was carrying my helmet, a flak vest, survival vest, a .38-caliber pistol in a shoulder holster, a thermos, an armful of maps, and a flashlight.

The preflight of 502, the tail number of the Cobra assigned to Jimmy Mills and myself, didn't take very long. The crew chief had already gone over the Cobra once, but had left the engine doors open so I could check it out for myself. I stowed all my gear in the front seat, except my thermos, and walked the short distance back to the mess hall.

The conversation had absolutely nothing to do with war. It centered around things that had taken place in the bar the night before, or the other favorite pastime, rat catching. Everyone, it seemed, was trying to come up with new and different ways to catch rats, and as there was an overabundance of rats at Tay Ninh, everyone had plenty of stories to tell. Little or nothing at all was said about the mission that day, or the dangers involved. It was as if they didn't exist.

I had been in Apache Troop five days and was beginning to learn that, although we fought as a close-knit team, each individual had his own way of coping with the war. It was up to the old guys to teach the new guys how to fight and survive, but it was up to each new guy to model his behavior after whoever he thought coped with the stress the best. I was to learn that everyone was different.

The sun had just risen as we took off from Tay Ninh, followed closely by Mike Reardon in the Hughes 500 light observation helicopter or Loach, more commonly referred to as the low bird when flown as part of a Pink Team. The medevac helicopter would be departing about fifteen minutes behind us. Mills had explained to me that would give us a chance to check out the approach route to Hannas that the medevac would be using. I was really glad to see that Mills had brought his own set of maps with him. This was to be my first-ever flight as part of a real Pink Team, and I wasn't all that sure I'd be able to keep us located on the map. I wasn't too worried though, Mills had been in Apache Troop since September 1969, and Mr. Reardon had survived being shot down numerous times since August 1969, so I was with a couple of old timers who really had their shit together.

Reardon brought his low bird up alongside the Cobra, and then took a position slightly in front and lower, which made it very easy for me to keep him in sight. All four doors of the small helicopter had been removed, and I could easily see both Reardon and the torque—a Loach's doorgunner—seated on the right side of the low bird. The torque sat directly behind the pilot, which enabled him to see and shoot at anything and everything the pilot was seeing. An observer sat in the left-front seat, holding a red-smoke grenade in his left hand, with the pin pulled, and an M-16 rifle in his right hand. If the low bird took fire, all the observer had to do was let go of the grenade, and the red smoke would go off, marking the general location of the enemy position and giving the Cobra a visual target to shoot at.

The torque also carried smoke, fragmentation, and white phosphorus grenades (referred to as Willie Petes), a large box of ammo for the M-60 machine gun, and usually, against regulations, a large quantity of C-4 plastic explosive. All this, combined with the fact that they were sitting right on top of over fifty gallons of jet fuel, made the helicopter a flying bomb. So dangerous was it to fly in low birds that it was Apache Troop's policy to assign any pilot or crew member who wanted out to other less dangerous duties after they had been a Scout for five months, no questions asked. Some chose to remain in Scouts longer than required, and some didn't, and there was never any criticism of those who chose to get out of Scouts.

I had become a serious believer in all the stories I had been told about the 1st of the 9th, and was beginning to feel like "one of the boys," but still had a lot of painful lessons to learn.

"Apache Two Seven, this is Dustoff Three Niner, are you up this push?" the pilot of the medevac helicopter called.

"This is Two Seven. Where you at?" Mills replied.

"We just left home plate and should be over the spot in about fifteen. How copy?"

"Yeah, I got a solid on that. We're going to check out the east side, so plan your approach in from that direction. That way you won't be overflying where all the action was last night. We should be there in about five mikes so the timing will work out just great. Over."

Usually the low bird stayed at altitude with the Cobra until the team had arrived at the area to be reconed, making the low bird less likely to be shot at before that was useful.

"Hey, Jimmy, how about turning on the ECU (environmental control unit, better known as air conditioning)?" I asked.

Mr. Mills turned on the ECU, and the interior of the cockpit was immediately filled with a reddish brown powder.

"What the hell is this stuff?" I groaned into the intercom.

"Sorry Boyle, I forgot that we were in five-o-deuce."

"What the hell difference does that make? What is this crap coming out of the vents?"

"Everyone that's flown this bird in the last two weeks has had the same problem."

"Well, how the fuck did so much dirt get inside the cockpit?"

"It's not dirt, Boyle, it's dried blood."

I reached over and turned the vents so that they were no longer blowing the cool red dust in my face. I felt myself beginning to sink a little lower in the armor-plated seat as I asked Mills, "How'd it happen?"

"See that aluminum patch in your doorframe, under your left armpit?"

I lifted my left arm, and sure enough, there was a three-by-three-inch aluminum patch on the bottom edge of the door.

"When we get back, take a look at the patch in the armor plate on your seat, and you'll also find one that I'm looking at right now on my instrument panel. There is also one just under my right arm where the bullet exited the bird."

"Key-rist, what the hell happened?"

"I think it happened about two or three weeks ago. They were covering their low bird and took one .51 hit. It came in just under your arm, went through the side of your seat, missing the Xray's butt, through the instrument panel, through the aircraft commander's right leg, and kept right on going back out the right side, just under where my right arm is now. The AC bled to death before the Xray could get this thing on the ground and get to the backseat to try and stop the bleeding. Damn near tore his leg off."

It was silent for the next few minutes, and without any conscious input from me, my body moved to the right side of the seat, as far away from the aluminum patch as I could get. I could only imagine the horrible feeling the Xray must have felt as he fought to get into a position to help the wounded AC.

The silence was interrupted by Mr. Reardon's voice from the low bird. "Hey, Two Seven, I'm going to start letting down now."

"Okay, but watch your ass, Bo," Mills said.

I was to find out that Mills called everyone Bo when he got nervous.

Mills had contacted Hannas to let the firebase know we were going to be in the area and to advise them that the medevac was approximately ten minutes away. Mills explained to me that we always made contact with a firebase prior to getting close, in order to find out if they were going to be shooting any artillery in our direction and to get a general briefing as to what the situation was near the base.

The firebase advised us that there had been little action during the night to the east side of the base, and that all their guns were pointed to the west, where all the assaults had come from.

Looking down at Hannas and the area around it from thirteen hundred feet, the firebase reminded me of a giant keyhole running east and west, with thick jungle marking the border of the keyhole. Hannas itself was located in the large circular portion of the keyhole at the east end, with the narrow portion of the keyhole stretching west toward the Cambodian border. The radio operator at Hannas had explained that most of the action had come from the tree lines at the northwest and southwest sides of the narrow part of the keyhole, right at the point where the large circular portion began. He further advised that nothing had occurred since about one hour prior to daylight. Because the low bird normally didn't monitor any radios except that from the Cobra, Mills relayed all this information to Mr. Reardon.

We took up our position over the low bird, flying large counterclockwise circles, while the low bird flew small clockwise circles less than twenty-five feet above the trees. The primary purpose of the low bird was to gather information and relay it to me, and I recorded it all. The scout's mission had not changed since the eighteen hundreds and before. Only the equipment had changed. Apache Troop Scouts, their pilots, torques, and observers could read a trail just as well as the Old West scouts. They could tell me if there had been recent use on the trail, and usually put the use down to within twelve hours, sometimes closer, depending upon the condition of the ground and how close the trees allowed them to get to or see the trail. They were also looking for hidden bunkers and anything else that would provide information concerning the movement or intentions of the Viet Cong or NVA. In order to do this, they had to fly low and slow, which made them a sitting duck for an enemy soldier hiding behind a tree. The weapon that the crew of the low bird had to worry most about was the RPG (rocket-propelled grenade). The Russian version of the bazooka, it was meant to be used against armored vehicles, such as tanks. An RPG round exploded on impact and usually totally destroyed the Scout low bird—if it struck it at all—and the crew. The small, low-flying low bird made a difficult but not an impossible target, as shown by the number destroyed. Just about everyone looked upon the Scouts of Apache Troop as people to be revered; a person had to have balls the size of Godzilla to be a Scout crew member.

"Two Seven, we've had a lot of recent use down here," Reardon called from the low bird.

"Okay, Bo. Watch your ass. The medevac bird should be here anytime now," Mills said.

"Okay, then maybe we can move over to the west side so we can have a little fun. I understand they still have gooks hanging in the barbed wire down there," Reardon said as he peered through the jungle canopy, always seeking any kind of movement.

I called Reardon and asked him if the recent use was heavy or light, as I knew the people in the TOC would want to know.

"Heavy, real heavy, and I'd say since the last rain."

This type of information was referred to as spots. When the

low bird gave me information, I would record it, and pinpoint on the map the exact location he was referring to. Then I would record the map coordinates and combine all the info into one spot report.

"Jimmy, do you want me to call this in to the TOC?" I asked.

"Nah, wait until we get a few more so I don't have to keep changing frequencies."

We were in touch with the firebase on the same radio we used to call the TOC, and Mills wanted to be able to talk to the firebase in case something came up.

"Apache Two Seven, this is Dustoff Three Niner, how's it going?"

"No problem yet. My low bird has found a lot of recent use on the east side, but no people yet. You about ready to go in?" Mills asked the medevac pilot.

"Yeah, we're right out your right side, about a mile."

"Okay, let me get my low bird up first."

It was policy, and good common sense to get the low bird up to altitude and out of harm's way when the Cobra was going to be doing something that wouldn't allow it to keep the low bird in sight at all times. This way we could cover the medevac ship and not have to worry about the low bird.

Mills called Reardon and told him that the medevac was on station and to come on up to altitude, which he did. The medevac ship proceeded in toward the firebase from the east without incident and landed. From where I sat in the front seat of the Cobra, I could see a scurry of activity as the wounded were loaded aboard the helicopter.

Watching the medevac was a real break from watching the low bird. Besides, I had almost a full page of spots by that time, and for a few minutes anyway, I could take my eyes off the low bird and the map, and not have to write anything.

I reached down by my right leg and picked up my thermos, which I'd filled at the mess hall with strawberry Kool-Aid. I filled the plastic cup and took a drink, and then set the half-filled cup on the wide armrest next to the armor-plated seat, and then put the thermos back on the floor. As I looked out the canopy on the left side, I saw a cloud of dust and dirt rising from around the medevac ship.

"We're comin' out, Two Seven," the pilot of the medevac ship radioed.

"We got you covered," Mills responded and turned the Cobra so as to put us in a position above and behind the medevac. This way, if the medevac took fire from either side, we would be able to just turn in that direction and shoot.

I watched the medevac bird clear the tree line on the east side of the keyhole and then begin a rapid climb, using the heavy jungle for cover. When possible, all helicopters avoided flying over open areas at low altitudes; that was just inviting someone to shoot. While staying over the jungle, the helicopter could be heard, but was virtually invisible from the jungle floor.

"Okay, we're out of here, Two Seven. Thanks for the cover. We'll probably be back within the hour to pick up a few less seriously wounded."

"Okay, just give us a shout when you're back inbound," Mills said.

Mills called the firebase and told them we were going to start working the southwest tree line where the narrow part of the keyhole began and work west toward the border.

"I'll be off your freq (frequency) for a few minutes while I contact my headshed," Mills told the radio operator at the firebase.

I heard the radio go through a series of different tones as Mills changed frequencies.

"Timber Four Two, Apache Two Seven, how copy?" Mills called over the radio.

"Apache Two Seven, this is Timber Four Two, go ahead," responded the voice from the TOC.

"Yeah, Timber Four Two, the Dustoff has departed for home plate. Will you let the hospital know they're coming, and my Xray has some spots for you. Let me know when you're ready to copy?"

Mills told me to give the TOC what we had so far and that he would keep an eye on the low bird. He then told Reardon where to start working. It didn't take Reardon long to get the low bird into position; he must have been bored to tears having to follow us around the sky, waiting for the medevac to finally leave the area.

The low bird started the search along the southern edge of the narrow part of the keyhole, keeping orbits over the trees so as to not expose himself by flying out over the open area. The northern edge of the keyhole was over a half mile away, so the danger of small-arms fire from that direction was minimal. Our orbit, thirteen hundred feet above the low bird and a half mile away from him, caused us to cover a lot greater area than the low bird. At first, our orbit took us directly over the firebase, then just south of the northern edge of the keyhole, and then back over the trees south of the low bird. As the low bird moved west along the tree line, so did our orbit move west, with the low bird remaining the center of our orbit.

I was just about finished giving the TOC the spot reports, when Reardon said, "Two Seven, we've got something down here. Clear to recon by fire?"

"Go ahead, Bo, but watch your ass."

"We've got a gook lying on the trail. My torque put a burst into him, but he didn't move. I've got an idea that he only got this far after the firefight last night, but it's not like them to leave somebody unless they were being chased, and they weren't."

"Two Seven Xray, are you through with the spots?" the TOC asked.

"Stand by one, Timber Four Two," I said into the mike. I wanted to hear everything Reardon had to say without interruption.

We had just crossed the edge of the northern tree line in a banking left turn when something slammed the bottom on the Cobra so hard that my thermos was lifted off the floor and landed in my lap. The cup on the armrest to my right, half-filled with strawberry Kool-Aid, erupted like a volcano all over the canopy. Before I could even think about asking what the hell was that, a second something slammed into the bottom of the helicopter.

"Shit, oh dear!" Mills yelled into the intercom, "We're hit."

The helicopter immediately began to roll left and right, and at the same time, the nose was pitching up and down. Judging by the frantic movements of the controls, Mills was having one hell of a time controlling the Cobra.

Mills yelled at Reardon, "We're hit, Bo! We're hit real bad. Get the hell out of there and cover us. We're going down. Are you okay, Jerry?" Mills yelled over the intercom.

"Yeah, I'm okay, just scared."

"Well, what in the living hell is all that red shit all over the windshield?"

"Kool-Aid, Jimmy, those assholes just killed my thermos."

"Eat my shorts," Mills replied. "Call the TOC and let them know we're going down ASAP," was the next thing out of his mouth.

"Timber Four Two, Timber Four Two, Apache Two Seven. *Scramble, scramble!* We're going down just west of Hannas. *Scramble, scramble, scramble!* Two Seven's going down West of Hannas," I yelled into the mike.

"We copy, Two Seven. The Blues are scrambled," was the reply from the TOC.

Mills had his hands full with the controls, but at the same time he was talking with the low bird, telling Reardon that he was going to try for Hannas. I couldn't change frequencies from the front seat, so I called the TOC.

"Timber Four Two, Timber Four Two, contact Hannas and let them know what's going on. We're going to try and make it back to Hannas," I said into the mike.

"I got you covered all the way," was Reardon's reply.

I was impressed. Mills was really keeping his cool, but I could hear fear in his voice, which didn't make me feel any better. I was already scared enough for both of us—you couldn't have driven a nail up my butt with a sledgehammer.

I could see Hannas almost directly in front of us, about two miles away.

Mills said to me, "Boyle, make sure your seat belts are tight; we're going to hit hard. I can't control this thing."

Two miles doesn't seem like all that far to go, especially when you start from thirteen hundred feet, but our Cobra had the aerodynamics of a bathtub.

"Hold on!" Mills yelled, as we cleared the first two rows of barbed wire surrounding Hannas, and slammed into the ground. The ground was very uneven, with holes and mounds of dirt. The Cobra bounced and rocked forward far enough that the rotor-blade tips slapped the ground in front of me.

We're going to flip over, I thought, and closed my eyes. I felt the Cobra rock back and slam back to the ground, flat on its skids. My eyes opened, only to see the rotor blades flex down so low I thought that they were going to take the front of the Cobra off. In hopes the rotor blade would miss my head, I tried to lean forward. But I had tightened the seat and shoulder belts to the point that I couldn't budge an inch. I heard a tremendous bang as one of the huge main rotor blades impacted the tail boom and almost took it off.

"Are you okay, Boyle?" Mills asked.

"I think so, Jimmy. Nice job getting us down."

We sat without moving as the dust and dirt settled around us for what seemed like forever. In actuality, it took less than a minute. My part of the narrow cockpit was a real mess. Maps were scattered everywhere. When the second antiaircraft round had impacted the Cobra, my thermos had been thrown out of my lap, hit the turret gunsight and then broke open on contact with the floor. I was bathed in strawberry Kool-Aid as were the maps, seat, gunsight, and canopy.

"God, what a hell of a mess," I thought to myself, "the crew chief is going to kill me."

"Let's get the hell out of this son of a bitch," Mills yelled over the center console that divided us. He had already removed his helmet and was removing his seat belts. I tried to get the chin strap of my helmet undone, finally said screw it, and unlatched my seat belts. As I reached for the handle that would allow me to open my side of the cockpit canopy, the handle turned without me touching it. I didn't realize it at the time, but the Cobra was leaning a great deal to the right, which put the outside canopy door handle almost out of reach. I heard the ammo-bay door being opened as I pushed open the cockpit door and was then greeted by the most distinguished face I had ever seen. This face looked to have been chiseled out of solid rock, with silver-gray hair and blue eyes that looked at me like a couple of laser beams. The face belonged to a colonel, who I assumed was the commander of FSB Hannas. Apparently I had taken too long trying to get my shit together in the front seat, as Mills was already out and away from the aircraft.

"Where are you hit, son?" the major asked.

"I don't think I am, sir. Just a little shook up."

"Then what the hell is all that?" He pointed at a pool of Kool-Aid that had formed next to my right boot, and some still dripping off the rearview mirror.

"It's Kool-Aid, sir. My thermos broke." As I looked away, I was feeling like a real jerk.

"Thank God for that, son. You gave me one hell of a scare. Now let's get your little butt out of this thing before Charlie starts dropping mortars around us again," the colonel said with a huge grin on his face.

"I'm sorry about the Kool-Aid, sir, I hope—"

"Don't worry about it, son. I saw enough blood last night. I'm just real happy that this turned out not to be blood."

Even an untrained ear could hear the unmistakable thump and low roar of approaching helicopters.

God, that was fast, I thought.

The first lift ship approached, twenty yards from the nose of our crippled Cobra.

"Thank God, the Blues are here," I said as Sgt. Kregg Jorgenson leaped from the still-hovering Huey, followed by Lieutenant Hugele—Blue himself—and other Blues.

As soon as the Huey had disgorged its load of Blues, it departed in a cloud of blowing dirt and debris. As he grew smaller in the distance, the Huey's door gunner, Art Docktor, gave me the thumbs-up. He had a huge smile on his face.

Is everyone in this troop nuts? These guys actually enjoy this shit, I thought. Hell, I hadn't done anything. Maybe the thumbs-up sign meant that I'd just passed my probation. I was just grateful that Jimmy Mills had kept his cool and had the necessary experience to react automatically under tremendous pressure. I remembered what Red had told me, "You don't have time to think about what to do, it has to be an unconscious reaction." He was right. I made a promise to myself right there and then, that when I got back to my room at Tay Ninh, I was going to hit the books again on emergency procedures.

I started to walk toward the tail of the Cobra when something caught my eye, and I froze in my tracks. We had landed between two rows of barbed wire that surrounded FSB Hannas. The entire area was littered with debris of every description, including the human hand that I had almost stepped on. An unconscious reaction made me look to see if both of mine were still attached. I felt very stupid, standing there looking at my upturned hands as if offering up a prayer to God.

Where did the hand come from was my first thought. Then I realized that what I first thought to be debris hanging in the barbed wire, was the remains of an NVA soldier, so torn apart that he looked like a brown gunnysack.

In my fledgling army career, I had never seen anything like that before. I stepped over the hand and continued toward the tail of the Cobra, where Mills and Hugele were looking at the huge hole in the tail boom of the helicopter.

"Want some coffee?" a voice said as my arm was grabbed from behind.

I turned and was looking into the face of the base commander.

"You look as if you could use a cup, soldier," he said with a smile that could melt butter.

"That would be great, sir, but I've got to check with my AC."

I asked Mills and he said, "No problem. No telling how long it'll take to get a Chinook out here to pick this thing up." The Chinook was a heavy-lift helicopter with two sets of main rotor blades that was capable of lifting almost anything.

I walked over to where the colonel was standing. "It's okay with my AC, sir."

"Great, let's go. I'll show you the way through the wire, but watch your step."

As I followed behind the colonel, we wound our way through the maze of barbed wire, past bunkers dug into mounds of dirt. Empty shell casings lay everywhere. The base reminded me of the vacant lot I had played in as a child, where I would dig forts and play war with the rest of the kids on the block. Only, this was for real. It didn't end with the cry of "Dinner!" from some parent standing on a front lawn.

"This is all pretty new to you, isn't it, son?" the major asked as he handed me a cup of lukewarm coffee.

"Yes, sir," I said, wishing I could look at the back of my flight suit to see if someone had hung a sign on me reading SCARED SHITLESS. I couldn't resist asking, "Does it show that much, sir?"

"You mean, that you are new to Vietnam? Oh, it's not all that difficult. Look at you. You've got a fresh haircut, almost new flight suit, your boots still have the flight-school shine to them, you don't have a tan, and you're covered with Kool-Aid. See what I mean?"

"Yes, sir, I do. But you could have left the part about the Kool-Aid out of your description." Trying to change the subject, I asked, "How'd this place get the name Hannas anyway, sir?"

"How long have you been around, son?" the major said with a questioning expression.

"This is my fifth day in Apache Troop and about my tenth in country, sir."

"Well, you sure got off to one hell of a start, didn't you? That explains why you don't know about Hannas. Not too long ago, a firebase like this one was almost overrun one night. The commanding officer, named Hannas, had both his legs blown off. When we built this firebase, we decided to name it after him," the major explained.

"Was he killed?"

"No, he survived. He's about as tough as they come."

In the distance, I could hear the unmistakable sound of a Chinook helicopter approaching.

"Thanks for the coffee, sir, but I think I'd better be getting back now."

"Nice doing business with you, young man. Come back anytime, but how about using the helipad next time!" he said, laughing.

The Blues had rigged the crippled Cobra to be slung out by the Chinook, and the other two Hueys, full of Blues, had returned to Tay Ninh when it had become obvious that they would not be needed. Everyone not needed ran for cover as the massive helicopter took up a position over the Cobra. Only Sergeant Jorgenson was left standing, but barely, as he stood on top of the Cobra, holding onto the rotor mast with one hand and attempting to hook the sling onto the hook protruding from the bottom of the Chinook. The rotor wash from the Chinook set up gale-force winds in excess of one hundred miles per hour. Everything that wasn't firmly attached to something was being blown away.

The hook-up process only took a minute. As I watched from inside a bunker, Jorgenson climbed down from the Cobra only to be blown down to his knees. The Chinook lifted the Cobra with ease, and departed to the southeast with the Cobra spinning beneath it.

As the other lift ship landed where the Cobra had been, Lt. Jack Hugele, the Blue Platoon leader, yelled in a Texas accent, "Come on, Boyle, we're leaving." He didn't have to ask twice, and I ran to the Huey and climbed aboard.

I jumped into a small canvas seat next to Art Docktor, whom everyone called Doc.

"Does this sort of shit happen very much?" I yelled at Doc, trying to be heard over the noise of the helicopter.

"You better get used to it, Mr. Boyle," he said, with a smile.

I thanked Jorgenson, who was sitting on the floor, for hooking up the Cobra.

"Piece of cake, sir," said this kid who could have passed for a fourteen-year-old.

CHAPTER EIGHT

I lay on my bunk, listening to the rain hitting the tin roof. It had started just after midnight as a soft, light rain, the kind that lulls one to sleep. Now, 3:00 A.M., it had become an ear-shattering roar, making sleep impossible. Dumb thoughts came to mind, like why in the hell would anybody with half a brain have tin roofs in a country that gets over three hundred inches of rain a year? The answer was simple, the American troops had introduced tin roofs into Vietnam. Someone, in their infinite wisdom, must have figured that if we have to be kept awake all night by the rain, then so should the Vietnamese. So whenever we left a base and turned it over to the Vietnamese, the next day the closest village had all-new tin roofs.

Thoughts were racing through my mind like flashbulbs going off, or the flashes from the lightning outside. The lightning flashes and the wind-driven rain, were invading my room through the still-open cracks between the old boards that formed the walls of my room.

Closing my eyes didn't accomplish anything, nor did rolling from side to side; the flashbulbs kept going off, and I kept feeling the hard boards of my bunk through the thin sleeping bag.

Screw this crap, I thought; I've got to go out and steal me a good mattress. I turned on my flashlight and directed the light into the far corner of my room. I looked at the pile of lumber that I had collected from the ammo dump and thought about nailing up some of the boards. I shitcanned that idea because it would wake up Mills in the net room.

Mills could sleep through anything, including a mortar attack, but if I did happen to wake him by pounding on the walls, he'd be pissed to the max.

I decided instead to get up, get dressed, and write a letter to Sonny and Dusty Jones, a couple who treated me as an adopted son, and who lived in a town called Muleshoe, Texas.

I wanted to tell them about an incident that had taken place a couple of weeks before my arrival in Apache Troop that, when I first heard about it, I just assumed was one of those bullshit war stories that we always heard about in flight school. But after talking to a few people, I found out that John Wayne wasn't the only guy on the block with huge balls, Apache troop had a whole bunch of them.

The day had started as normal as any other day. Captain Funk wanted to know why other Pink Teams were reporting a lot of use in an area west of Tay Ninh and not far from the Cambodian border. Rick Pierce was to be the low-bird pilot, and with him as the observer was Jim Thomas. Both were warrant officers, and they had an enlisted man in the back, manning the M-60 machine gun. Thomas was along as the observer to learn as much as he could about becoming a low-bird pilot, and Rick Pierce was one of the best at teaching the deadly and dangerous trade. Their high bird was to be Lieutenant Coons and John Bartlett in the Cobra.

Pierce and Bartlett had arrived in Vietnam on the same day, which meant that if they survived, they would be going home the same day, also.

Except for Bartlett, who seemed always to be giving someone something to laugh about, very little was said by anyone as the crews ate breakfast and drank coffee.

Then the crews headed for the flight line to do the ritual morning preflight of the aircraft. After that was accomplished, Red (Lieutenant Coons) called the control tower and requested a takeoff clearance for both Pink Team aircraft, with a west turnout.

"Apache Red, cleared for takeoff; west turnout approved," was the response from the tower.

With the sun just coming up at their backs, the Pink Team headed west to the assigned area. Red didn't have to tell Pierce how to do his job, but he still advised him to be careful because the area, although covered with trees, still had a lot of small open clearings scattered around. All low-bird pilots tried to avoid clearings and exposing their aircraft to the dangers that open areas and their associated tree lines presented.

Pierce was almost halfway through his fuel load when he came upon a trail that showed a lot of heavy use. The trail led in the direction of an abandoned village which had already been checked and rechecked, but no one had ever been found in the area. Pierce reported to Red that there appeared to be cart ruts in the trail, and they looked deep. Whatever had been hauled in the carts was heavy, but he couldn't tell for sure which way they were moving.

Jim Thomas, sitting to the left of Pierce, had no trouble seeing over Pierce's helmet as Thomas was almost six feet three. All Thomas could do was sit and listen and learn to read the trails, a job that didn't come easy because he had to see down through the trees, fly the aircraft, and relay what was being seen to Bartlett, the Xray in the Cobra, so that he could write it all down for the spot reports and locate the positions on the map.

Bartlett already had two pages of spots written down when he saw the red-smoke grenade go off and trail away from the low bird. Bart's heart stopped as did Red's. The red smoke was only used if the low bird was taking fire.

Thomas didn't have to be told to let go of the red smoke grenade that he had been holding in his left hand. The pin had already been pulled when they started the let-down into the recon area.

"Taking fire, taking fire," Pierce yelled into the mike as AK-47 bullets ripped the bottom of the low bird; the large red master-caution light on the dash began flashing, and the smaller red light that read ENGINE OUT went on.

"Red, we're going down," Pierce yelled into the mike.

"There's a small opening to your right, try and make that," Red called back to Pierce.

Bartlett was already following along behind Pierce with the minigun, putting out short bursts to get whoever was doing the shooting to quit. The minigun was an awesome weapon, when it worked. Bart could see the dirt being kicked up by his bullets and the tree branches disappearing as if being run through a lawn mower. He knew he was taking a chance by firing short bursts because the minigun was easily jammed for many reasons, short bursts being just one of them.

Pierce fought to keep the aircraft out of the trees, but knew he was using up all the rotor RPM, and would have little left to cushion the landing if he did make the clearing. The gunner in the back was throwing out everything he could to lighten the bird.

"We're still taking fire," Pierce called to Red, "but I think I'm going to make it."

The clearing was a small one, with a huge bomb crater in the middle.

Bartlett watched the low bird and held his breath. It didn't look like the Loach was going to make it. Little flashes of light erupted from the dark underbrush at the edge of the clearing, which prompted Bartlett's minigun to swing into action, this time in front of the crippled low bird.

Pierce held his breath and dragged the tail through trees at the edge of the clearing and slammed into the ground. Everyone took a giant deep breath, just waiting for the aircraft to erupt into a ball of flames, but no fire started. Bartlett and Red couldn't believe their eyes when they saw three people run out of the cloud of dirt and dust and jump headfirst into the bomb crater.

"Get on the minigun, Bart," Red yelled. "Work over that tree line on the south and see if you can get those assholes to quit shooting."

"Timber Four One (Apache base), this is Red, scramble the Blues. Our low bird was just shot down, and they are in contact."

Most of the enemy fire was coming from the south and west sides of the clearing. The downed low bird provided some cover from the fire coming from the south side, but did nothing to protect the crew from the west edge of the tree line. The bomb crater was huge and appeared to have been made by a daisy cutter, an "instant LZ bomb" that had gone off too low. The daisy cutter was a ten thousand-pound bomb that was usually rolled out the rear door of a C-130 then descended beneath a large parachute. It was designed to go off when it contacted trees. If everything went right, the bomb would level the trees at ground level, creating a large landing zone with no crater in the ground. This one obviously had not gone off until it hit the ground, and in so doing had left a lot of tree stumps sticking up everywhere and a very deep crater.

Thomas had managed to salvage his M-16 rifle and was wearing his pistol. Pierce only had his pistol, but the "Torque" (the machine gunner in the backseat of a low bird) had held onto his M-60 machine gun, but only had about 50 rounds of ammo.

The situation was becoming more hopeless by the minute. Bartlett knew the minigun had to be close to empty, and Red was thinking about the Blues getting chewed to pieces as they tried to hover above the tall tree stumps and offload.

Bartlett felt as if Red was reading his mind when he said over the intercom, "Bart, we've got to get them out ourselves. Save the minigun ammo, but get rid of the "chunker" (40mm grenades) on the west tree line."

The chunker ammo was heavy, as was the full load of rockets, and Red knew he had to get rid of all of it if he was to have any chance at all of lifting three people out of the bomb crater.

Red made a sharp left turn and pointed the nose of the Cobra at the western tree line. Through the front center section of the sleek cockpit, Red could just see the top of Bartlett's helmet as the trees rushed up at them at over two hundred mph. Above Bart's helmet, Red was looking at the tree line through the glowing red cross hairs that reflected off the thin piece of glass that made up the rocket sight.

Whoosh, whoosh, whoosh reverberated through the cockpit as three pairs of rockets streaked toward the enemy positions and the source of the tracers, by then directed at the diving Cobra gunship.

"Okay, Bart—hit 'em with the chunker."

The tree line erupted with explosions as the rockets impacted, followed by the 40mm grenades. On his second tour in Nam as a Cobra pilot, Red knew how to shoot. Better yet, he knew how to hit what he was shooting at. Two more rocket runs were made, which expended all the 40mm grenades and rockets. Red had now committed himself and Bartlett to going down into the clearing to pick up Pierce and his crew.

Red hoped he would have enough power to lift the added weight of three men, and Bartlett was hoping that he had saved enough ammo in the minigun to cover them until they were clear.

Pierce had found out quickly that as long as he and his crew stayed on the west side of the crater and below the lip, they were safe from the fire coming from the tree line. What concerned Pierce was that Red had disappeared from view; Thomas was hoping that the local VC didn't have a mortar in their inventory; and they all hoped that there wasn't anyone crawling up to try and toss a grenade into their position.

Red had flown a little over a mile east of the clearing and dropped down to treetop level before turning back to the west with the bright sun at his back. As the Cobra streaked across the treetops, with very little room between the skids and the branches, Bartlett felt as if he were sitting on a bed of hot coals. Those branches could foul the helicopter's skids and pull it down into total destruction. He also knew that as the Xray he would be up front, looking right into the barrels of a lot of AK-47s once they cleared the trees and stopped over the low-bird crew.

The Cobra provided no protection to Bartlett when being shot at directly from the front, and Bart's sweaty palms and the large amount of fluid running out of his helmet attested to the fact that Bart was keenly aware of this flaw in the Cobra. It wasn't the sort of feeling that he enjoyed, but what a hell of a story to tell back at the officers club if they survived.

Red slowed the Cobra to eighty mph as the edge of the clearing approached. Red hoped that Thomas, a Cobra pilot, would know enough to open the ammo-bay doors on each side of the Cobra; that would give two of them a place to sit, and the other could get on one of the rocket pods.

"Bart, let the gooks know we're here."

As if they don't know! Bart thought to himself. He let go with a short burst from their only remaining weapon.

Thomas was the first to see Red clear the eastern tree line, and knew immediately what Red was planning. He told Pierce how to open the ammo-bay door and did the same with the torque. Thomas decided that he would be the one who took the ride on the rocket pod.

As Red approached the bomb crater, the three-man crew of the low bird moved to the deepest part of the crater.

As Bartlett said many silent prayers that the gun would not run out of ammo, hot brass was landing everywhere from the minigun.

Red hovered the Cobra into the crater, which exposed only the cockpit and rotor blades. The crater's walls made the minigun useless at that point, and the Cobra's pilots could only watch as the ammo-bay doors were opened.

Pierce crawled onto the left door, and the torque onto the right. Thomas was last on, taking a rear-facing position on the inboard right rocket pod. As each man got on, Red had to pull up on the collective to keep the Cobra from settling farther into the hole.

Once all three were on, Red began to try to lift the Cobra out of the crater. Bartlett felt useless because he could see the muzzle flashes form the tree line, but the minigun was still below the lip of the bomb crater. He also wondered how long it would be before a red-hot bullet tore through the thin Plexiglas and put an end to his thoughts of returning to Whitefish, Montana, and the bow hunting that he loved so much. Bart noted that the torque gauge was sitting on the redline, and wondered if Red was going to be able to pull off the rescue attempt. The torque gauge rose above redline as the Cobra came up out of the crater.

Bartlett raked the tree line with the minigun as Red turned the Cobra north and tried to climb above the trees. Pierce and the torque were prone on the ammo bay doors in an attempt to provide the smallest target possible. Thomas didn't have a choice, he could only straddle the rocket pod as if riding a horse, and hope that Bartlett could keep the VC from taking real good aim.

Just as Red turned north, the minigun spat out its last bullet. All they could do was hold on and pray.

Red and Bart both felt the sick feeling in their stomachs at the exact same time. The Cobra was getting real mushy. The rotor RPM was starting to bleed off as Red pulled more pitch into the rotor blades in his attempt to get the aircraft above the rapidly approaching tree line. "*Beep* it, Red! *Beep* it!" Bartlett thought, not realizing he was speaking out loud and into the intercom. Red instinctively moved his left thumb onto the beep button and pushed it forward and held it there. (The beep button is used to fine tune the engine RPM to keep it in the normal operating range.) By holding the button in the full-forward position, Red had run the engine to its maximum output. The change was small, but its effect stopped the rotor RPM from bleeding off and effectively stopped the Cobra from sinking farther toward the trees. With a slight rearward pressure on the cyclic, Red raised the Cobra's nose and cleared the trees at the northern edge of the clearing.

"You can open your eyes now, Bartlett," Red said from the rear seat, unaware that Bartlett's eyes had been the size of dinner plates the entire time or that he had said anything about the beep button. The change had been so small and subtle, but enough to keep all five of them out of the trees.

"Hey, Red—why the hell don't you try eating my shorts with that big mouth, you fuckin' RLO." An RLO is a real live officer, as opposed to a warrant officer.

The pressure was off, and Red and Bartlett were once again

just being themselves. Now the question was what to do with
the three extra bodies they had hanging all over their Cobra.

Mike King, a lift pilot and assistant maintenance officer, had
gone over in his mind what he was going to do with the load
of Blues he had sitting behind him in the Huey. He had already
been told that it was going to be a "hot LZ," full of stumps,
and that he would have to hunt for a spot to put the troops out
while being shot at.

What he saw next took his breath away. Five miles east of
the LZ, he saw a single speck in the sky heading toward him,
and at the same time heard Red call over the radio to cancel
the Blues. With both helicopters closing the distance between
them at somewhere around eighty mph, it didn't take long for
Mike's mouth to fall open at what he saw hanging all over
what had been a sleek-looking Cobra.

Lieutenant Hugele, the Blue Platoon leader, was the only
Blue wearing a headset, which enabled him to listen and talk
to the pilots of the Huey.

"Hey, Blue, you ain't gonna believe what I'm looking at in
front of us." Blue moved forward, out of where he had been
seated, and looked over King's shoulder.

"Holy shit, Mike! I've never seen anything like that before
Those guys have got to be nuts."

"Maybe that's the army's new tourist-class seats," the copilot remarked from the right seat.

Later, King would swear that he could see Bartlett smiling
from a mile away.

"Apache lift, this is Red, let's find a secure area so I can
off-load this extra weight."

Art Docktor, manning the machine gun in the open door of
the Huey, had overheard the conversation through his helmet
and grabbed Sergeant Jorgenson's arm, pulling him over to the
door.

"Take a look at that," he yelled into the sergeant's ear while
pointing at the Cobra, which was about to pass below and to
the left of them in the opposite direction. As both a Blue and
leader of long-range recon patrols (LRRPs, pronounced
LURPS), Jorgenson had seen a lot of things during his six
months in Vietnam, but he, like Blue, had never seen anything
like that. Everyone in the Huey had gotten the message and, to
a man, had the same thought in mind, Why the hell didn't I
bring my camera?

Mike King banked the Huey in a tight left turn and descended to the same level as Red, and was followed by the other two lift ships.

Red picked out a very open area, with a well-used road, in which to land and off-load his very grateful passengers, who were then picked up by King and transported back to Tay Ninh.

When I finished, I placed my letter-writing material under my sleeping bag in an attempt to keep it from getting wet, and then I walked to the door leading outside. The rain had let up a little but would still have been considered a downpour back in the States. The distance between where I was standing and the back door of the mess hall was only about seventy-five yards, but they were seventy-five yards of mud, ass-deep to a tall Indian. Trying to run in that muck could only lead to a disaster, so I walked, taking the biggest steps possible.

Mike Cutts was just going through the rear door and saw me coming.

"Hey, Mr. Boyle, what the hell are you doing out in this crap at this hour?" he asked as he held the door open for me.

"Well, you know how it is, Mike, once a cook, always a cook. I just can't seem to stay away from mess halls early in the morning. Don't suppose you've got any coffee made yet?"

"Comstock was going to open up this morning, and that's the first thing he usually makes; lets get out of this rain and find out."

I really felt at home in the mess hall. Being there, I could get rid of that FNG feeling that normally took four or five months to shake. The cooks also liked an officer who took a real interest in what they were doing and how they did it. Usually the only time an officer paid them any attention was to do an inspection or bitch about the food. Bob Comstock was from El Paso, Texas, but didn't have much of a Texan accent. He and Cutts were easygoing, good cooks and a real pleasure to be around.

The heat from the ovens combined with the rain outside made the mess hall feel like a sauna. I filled a cup with hot coffee and watched as the other cooks showed up for work and started to prepare the morning meal. Instead of walking back to the officer area, I just took a seat at one of the tables closest to the serving line so I could talk to the guys without having to yell. Cutts had found out, within a few days of my arrival in Apache Troop, that I loved bacon. He walked up to where I was sitting and took a seat across from me and set down a plate of hot bacon and a couple of freshly baked biscuits.

"Who are you flying with today, sir?"

"Nobody as far as I know. Red told me to take today off because I was getting too many flight hours. I was thinking about going to the PX (post exchange) as soon as the rain let up to pick up some menthol cigarettes and some other stuff."

"The PX doesn't open until noon, sir, and it's only 4:30. You've got a hell of a lot of time to kill."

"I guess I could go back and work on my room after Mills gets up, but I haven't been able to find any nails yet."

I knew that other people would be showing up soon, so I picked up my coffee and what was left of the bacon and moved back to the officer area. The guys who had been up all night in the TOC were the first to show up for breakfast. One of them walked back to where I was sitting and said that Cutts had told him that I was looking for some nails.

"If you'll come over to supply, sir, I've got a coffee can full of nails you can have." I thanked him and said I'd see him later.

The mess hall started to fill with a lot of troops, officer and enlisted, and I no longer felt out of place by going up to the serving line and filling a plate with more bacon and a couple pieces of toast. As I walked back to the rear of the mess hall someone said "Hey, Boyle—got that room fixed up yet?"

I turned to my left and saw Ron Black sitting at one of the tables, clutching a hot cup of coffee with both hands.

"Hi, Ron, what the hell are you doing up so early, I thought you Slick (Huey lift ship) drivers had banking hours!"

"Who the hell ever told you that load of crap? If you asshole Snake drivers would ever take the time to look up, instead of always down, you just might see that Slick that is covering your skinny ass, besides, what the hell are you doing up so early? The duty roster says that you've got the day off."

"Well, the rain was blowing through the cracks in my room and made sleeping somewhat difficult, so I just got up and decided to get an early start on breakfast, and then go to the PX and buy some cigarettes and see what else I can dig up. You don't happen to know where I can dig up a real mattress, do you?"

He started to laugh, and I could see some of the other officers within hearing distance smiling at my question.

"You'll have to ask Bartlett about the mattress shortage, or the Old Man," Ron said with a huge laugh.

"Why the hell don't you just tell me and knock off this passing-the-buck crap," I said.

"Look, Boyle, Bartlett enjoys telling the story so I'll just leave it up to him. Just understand that there is a grave shortage of mattresses in Apache Troop, but it was for a good cause. You know the PX doesn't open until after noon; why don't you ride along with me for the first flight. My door gunner had to go on sick call this morning, and you could take his place and see what real men do."

"Sounds okay to me, but I've never fired an M-60 before."

"No sweat, my crew chief can fill you in—it's not all that difficult. Why don't you plan on being out on the flight line in about an hour, and we'll get you all squared away."

"All right," I said.

As I left the mess hall, I waved at Mike Cutts and told him I'd see him at lunch.

The rain had eased up to just a light drizzle, and it was starting to get light. As I entered my room, it looked like someone had filled it with bird shot—tiny balls of mud formed by the drops of rain and the dirt had been blown into my room through the cracks in the walls. I couldn't understand why the hell I told Mr. Black that I'd go with him—I didn't know anything about shooting an M-60, and I really did have to get my room fixed up.

CHAPTER NINE

I had only been asleep about an hour when someone pounded on my door and yelled that Mr. Black was waiting for me out on the flight line. I wanted very much to tell whomever it was to just go back and tell Black that I had changed my mind, but before I could think up a good excuse, the person was gone.

As I stepped out onto the rickety wooden porch and into the dim morning light, the first thing I noticed was that it had stopped raining. Little clouds of ground fog still hovered just above the wet red clay that would turn into blowing red dust as the sun rose and baked everything in sight. The air at that time of the morning was so thick you felt as if it could be cut with a knife.

I felt a little out of place as I walked toward the dark green Huey helicopter with an M-16 rifle slung over my shoulder. I had never fired the damn rifle since arriving in Vietnam and felt more comfortable with the old Smith & Wesson .38-caliber pistol the army had also issued me. At least I knew I could hit what I aimed at with the pistol.

I sat down in the canvas seat on the right side of the Huey and put on my helmet.

"Hey, Boyle, you about ready to go, or what?" Black said over the intercom with a laugh in his voice.

"Yeah, I guess I'm as ready as I'll ever be, but you got to promise me two things first."

"And what might that be, new guy?"

"Well, you got to have me back in time to go to the PX because I've just got to get some menthol cigarettes before they run out, and somebody better show me how to work this damn

M-60 back here so I don't end up shooting us down and become another Captain America."

"No problem about the PX. We should be back with time to spare. The crew chief will show you where the trigger is on the 60; that's about all even an FNG needs to know," Black said.

My remark about Captain America was in reference to an incident that had happened a few days after my arrival in Apache Troop. Captain America, as he was called because of the stars and stripes he had painted on his helmet, had been assigned the duty of training a new low-bird pilot. Captain America, a warrant officer called Ty, and his new low-bird pilot, Mr. Everest, had flown out due west of Tay Ninh to an area that was relatively flat, with little jungle but a lot of tall brush. A river ran through the area. For reasons still open to speculation, Ty decided to ride in the back seat and act as the door gunner and do his instruction from that location. Everyone knew it took many hours of practice to circle a target and keep it in the center of the circle so as to give the torque a clear and steady target.

A piece of wood was observed floating down the river, and Ty directed Everest to try circling it while keeping it in the center of the circle as the wood floated down the river. It was really just a practical coordination exercise. At some point, Ty decided to start shooting at the floating piece of wood. Everything was going along fine until Everest overshot the floating target and steepened the bank to keep the low bird close to the target. Ty was still shooting at the target when Everest went to hard right cyclic to correct his orbit. All Ty had time to say was, "Oh shit," as his stream of machine-gun bullets ripped through the ends of the rotor blades. What a hell of a surprise—Everest was expecting Ty to quit shooting, and Ty had not expected the sudden appearance of the rotor blades between him and the floating piece of wood.

Everest was able to get off one call to the TOC before the little low bird fell out of the sky onto a small sandbar in the river in what could be described as a cross between a crash and a hard landing. The incident was bad enough as it was, and Ty knew there was going to be all kinds of hell raised by Captain Funk when he had to report what really happened. What Ty hadn't planned on was that a CBS News crew was at Tay Ninh waiting to get a story on the Blue Platoon's recovery of a downed aircraft. Everest's call to the TOC had sounded the scramble siren, and the shit had hit the fan.

Mike Reardon was the first off the ground with his low bird, followed closely by the two Hueys, one full of Blues and the other full of CBS News crew, headed by Richard Threlkeld.

The Blues had deployed around the downed low bird when CBS arrived. The first question asked of Everest was, "Where did the fire come from?"

"From my right rear," Everest answered.

"What caliber was it?"

"I believe it was 7.62," Everest responded.

"How can you be so sure? And isn't 7.62 a NATO caliber?" Threlkeld asked.

"Yep, sure as hell is a NATO caliber, and I'm damned sure of it because the guy who was sitting in the backseat shot me down."

"Cut! Cut!" Threlkeld said to the cameraman. With the exception of Ty and Everest, who were going to have to stand in front of Captain Funk to explain how they happened to shoot themselves down, everyone was laughing.

Everything I knew about an M-60 could be put on the head of a pin. Morris Piper was the crew chief on Black's Huey. He was a great kid from somewhere in Tennessee. He came over to my side of the helicopter and showed me how to lock and load the damn thing.

The first thing I asked him was why the hell there was an empty beer can attached to the side of the gun. He explained that the M-60 had a tendency to jam, but if the belt ammo was routed up and over the can before going into the gun, it wouldn't jam.

The most enjoyable part of the flight was just sitting in the open door, feeling the air blowing across my face. I began to think that I could almost like a job like this. I didn't have to read a map or keep the low bird in sight every minute. No one was asking me questions about emergency procedures or the limitations of the aircraft, and there wasn't a lot going on over the radio. The only conversations I could hear in my helmet were between the people in Mr. Black's aircraft. I couldn't hear what was going on anyplace else. That was okay with me, and I was almost enjoying just looking down at the thick jungle, some three thousand feet below us, with the little specks of patchy white fog still hanging close to the treetops.

I had just leaned back and lit a cigarette when the Huey made an abrupt left turn and began to accelerate. I looked forward toward Ron Black and noticed the copilot grabbing a map and unfolding it.

"Hey, Ron, what's going on?" I asked.

"Hold on, Jerry, I'm getting the info right now; I'll let you know in a minute," Ron answered. Whatever was going on wasn't good because Ron was pulling the guts out of the engine trying to get to wherever we were going in the quickest possible time.

It seemed like forever before Ron said, "Okay, Boyle, you may have to use the 60, so crank off a few rounds and make sure it works, and make damn sure you got it pointed down."

"Okay, Ron, but what the hell's going on?" I asked as I fired a short burst with the M-60.

"Mr. Everest has been shot down. They made it to a very small clearing, and the crew is okay, but the high bird doesn't think there is enough room for us to land or even hover down. We're going to take a look and see what we can do. The crew has taken cover next to the low bird, and the high bird advises that they are the only friendlies in the area, so if you see anything move besides the crew, shoot it. You got all that, new guy?"

"I got it all, Ron. You just make sure you keep the damn rotor blades away from my bullets. You got that, you old fart?" I yelled back at Black.

"Does anyone know where or what size the gun was that shot them down?" I asked.

"The high bird advises that Everest thinks it was a .51, because it blew a very large hole in the bottom of the bird, came through the floor, through the compressor section of the engine and out the top of the aircraft. He also believes that the gun is just inside the tree line close to where they are."

"I got that okay, Ron. Let's just not join them down there, please!"

Why do I do things like this to myself, I thought. I could be back working on my room or just sitting around the mess hall filling myself with coffee and bacon. Red's words kept running through my mind, "Never duke it out with a .51; you'll lose every time."

The first feeling of fear manifested itself in my butt as it acted like a vacuum cleaner and tried to suck up the canvas seat I was sitting on. Then my palms started to sweat. "Shit,"

I said out loud, nothing has even happened yet and I'm turning into the head rooster of Apache Troop.

"We're just about there," Ron said over the intercom. "Keep your eyes open. They should be coming up on our right side real soon."

The clearing was so small that it flashed by before Ron had a chance to say anything, and as the Huey banked away I had to think back on what I had just seen, something akin to instant replay.

"What the hell is burning back there?" Ron yelled over the intercom.

Piper and I looked at each other and held out our hands, palms facing up.

"What in the fuck are you smoking, Boyle?" Ron asked with a tone that made me feel like hammered dogshit.

It then dawned on me that I was puffing on only the filter of my cigarette.

"Sorry, Ron, guess I've got to try and make every one count," I said.

"Did you get a look at the low bird?" Ron asked.

"Yeah, I saw it fine, but it sure went by fast."

"Okay, new guy, here's the plan. We are going to have to land in another clearing, just south of the low bird about a quarter of a mile. One of you guys is going to have to go get them and lead them back to the clearing we land in."

Without any hesitation, Piper told Black he'd go, but then I opened my big mouth and suggested that he stay with the aircraft as he was the only one who really knew how to operate the M-60 in case they needed it.

"Okay, Boyle, you've got the detail. Just keep your ass out of trouble."

I asked Ron if he would make one more pass between where the low bird was and where we were going to land so I could get a good idea of the direction I needed to go and how far. On this pass, we hung out away from both of the clearings, and I got a good look. It didn't look very far at all.

"No problem, Ron. I think I've got it fine. Let's do it."

The clearing Ron had found was large enough for two or three Hueys. We touched down on a slight rise in the center, with the nose pointed south and the tail of the Huey pointed in the direction of the downed low bird.

Ron swiveled around in his seat and said, "Be careful, Boyle, but hurry."

"Okay, Ron, but do me one big favor will you?"

"Yeah, and what's that?"

"Don't leave without me," I said as I unstrapped my helmet and set it on the seat next to me, and picked up my M-16 rifle.

I felt excited and a little scared as I ran out into the knee-high grass a few yards and then turned right and headed toward the tree line and away from the tail of the Huey. As I approached the tree line, it dawned on me that I had never been on the ground before except within an American base. With that thought in mind, my trot turned into a fast walk, followed shortly thereafter by a slow walk.

Upon reaching the tree line, I stopped and turned around to make sure I was still going in a straight line toward the downed low bird, at least that is what I was telling myself. In reality, I was hoping to see Ron leaning out the door waving for me to come back to the Huey, but there was no such signal.

As I entered the tree line, everything became dimmer and dimmer, and it became impossible to move without making noise.

How the hell do the Blues do it? I kept thinking to myself. They have to do this every day, and I know they can't be making this much noise!

There was no trail, and the going was damn near at a snail's pace. Vines were hanging down everywhere, and the undergrowth was so thick it was impossible to see where I was stepping. I knew that if I tried to find an easier way I'd end up losing my sense of direction toward the low bird, and then I'd really be in deep shit. Then the thought came into my mind that there was a very good chance that I wasn't alone in this semidark mass of bugs, vines, and sticker bushes. "Hell, it didn't look this bad from the air, maybe I'm not going in the right direction; it's still not too late to turn around and go back; I can still see a little light coming through the trees from the clearing where the Huey is sitting. Calm down and think," I said to myself as I turned and tried to move through all the growth in front of me.

I never saw the huge spiderweb, and stepped right into it. Panic is the only word to describe my actions, which for all intents and purposes, closely resembled an Indian war dance. This web felt more like a sticky fishing net than a spiderweb, and I went nuts trying to get it off me. I hate spiders and would rather sleep with rattlesnakes than have anything to do with any kind of spider. I wanted to yell when I saw the huge black-and-yellow thing crawling up the right sleeve of my flight suit. I brushed it off with enough force to clear the center-field fence in Yankee Stadium. The sweat was pouring out from under my army-issue baseball cap, and my heart was beating so hard, I put my hand on my chest in an attempt to hold it in. Never again, I kept telling myself. I can only speak for myself, but having been trained as a pilot, I felt very much out of my element on the ground.

At first I thought I was hearing things, but then the unmistakable sound of a Cobra helicopter in the distance would come and go. It must be circling the low bird because it was coming from the direction that I was headed and where I thought the low bird was. My rifle kept getting caught on vines, and I'd have to stop and back up, in fact everything kept getting caught on something, and the bugs were eating me alive. I believe it was at this point that I made up my mind that should Captain Funk ever decide to send me out on some mission with the Blues, that I was going to go AWOL. I really began to think that I had to be the biggest chicken in the army. So far, there wasn't anything that had happened to me in Vietnam that had not scared the shit out of me, and right that minute, I was scared. Not so much of what might happen to me or being shot, but just not knowing for sure what the hell was out there, if anything, and just how it would manifest itself if I was unlucky enough to run into whatever it might be. If Everest was correct, and he had been hit by a .51, that meant that there were more than just a couple of gooks down here. A .51 isn't the easiest gun to move around in the jungle, and it usually goes along with a fairly large enemy force. I was really starting to talk myself into a panic situation, so I just stopped and listened while the bugs ate me for lunch.

Something bit me on the side of my neck, and I slapped the unseen bug with my hand and felt something soft get squashed against my skin. I told myself it wasn't a spider and wiped the mess off on the leg of my flight suit. The only thing I could hear was the Cobra, but that really didn't mean that the VC or NVA wasn't out there somewhere.

"Screw it," I said out loud, this is taking way too long, and I started moving forward as fast as I could. The desire to move fast was there but the ability was not. After listening to Sergeant Jorgenson and some of the other Blues talk about moving through the jungle, I knew I must be doing something wrong. They made it sound as if it were easy, or at least they didn't bitch about it the way I knew I was going to if I ever completed my mission. I seemed to be getting caught up on everything I touched.

Finally, some light was beginning to appear in front of me, and from the sound of the Cobra, I could only assume it was the clearing I was looking for. I now understood how the enemy could move so freely in the jungle without being seen. The Cobra flew directly over me on a few occasions, and I couldn't see it, so I knew he couldn't see me. I moved up close to the edge of the clearing, keeping some brush between me and the open area. I kept thinking that nobody in his right mind could not have heard me trying to move through all that crap. The thought then came to mind that the crew of the low bird was probably not expecting me, and there was a real good possibility that I could get shot by one of my own guys that had taken cover beside the downed helicopter.

I didn't know if the VC knew how to whistle or not, but I started to whistle as loud as I could. Someone lying prone by the nose of the low bird got up on his knees and took a good look in my direction. When he didn't shoot, I stepped out in the open where they could get a good look at me and started waving for them to come toward me. It only took a few waves, and the three crew members were hot-footing it across the clearing in my direction. I held my breath hoping that they wouldn't start taking fire from the far tree line. Then it dawned on me that whoever shot Everest down could be anywhere. They could have been miles away by then, or walking up behind me. All I wanted to do was get the fuck out of there.

Everest was the first one to get to me. "What the hell are you doing here, Boyle?"

Whenever I'm scared or nervous, I attempt to cover the fact by trying to be funny in hopes that nobody will notice.

"I volunteered, I was the only one in troop that thought your chubby little ass was worth saving, and besides, we're short of low-bird pilots, and the only way I can keep the Old Man from transferring me to Scouts is to save your ass. And I must say I really think yours is really cute, you big savage Scout pilot you."

"Knock off the bullshit, Boyle. Where are the rest of the Blues?"

"I haven't a clue; I'm by myself. If it's not too much trouble, how about us getting our asses out of here and back to where Black is waiting for us. He told me to hurry."

The torque and observer were nodding their agreement, and the expressions on their faces told me that I wasn't the only person around who was concerned about who else might be on their way toward Black's aircraft.

"I'm with you, sir," said the torque, who didn't appear to be a new guy.

"Right this way, gentlemen. I think." I just hoped I could find my way back to the Huey. The torque had brought his M-60 with him, and a short belt of ammo, and the thought ran through my mind that there really is safety in numbers. At least, I felt safer.

The Snake pilot must have seen me and the crew join up, and read my mind because he was now circling the Huey from the sounds I was hearing. There was no way of following exactly the way I had come to the clearing. Everything looked the same, and I had not left a trail. At least, not one that I could follow. So I just started busting through the vines and bushes, not really caring how much noise I made. My only thought was to get back to the Huey and never step foot in the jungle again, ever.

The return trip was made without a word being spoken and seemed to take half as much time as it took me going the other direction. When we finally cleared the tree line, Ron Black's Huey looked like the pot of gold at the end of the rainbow, and none of us wasted any time getting on board.

Ron turned around in his seat as I put my helmet back on. "Well how did it go?" he asked, with genuine concern in his voice.

"Hey, no problem," I said as I choked back the feeling that I wanted to throw up. The look on Ron's face told the story though. I knew that he knew how I was feeling, but he didn't say anything, thank God.

As the Huey cleared the tree line and headed back to Tay Ninh, the Cobra flew up alongside, and the crew of the low bird all waved at the crew of the Cobra. They were all smiles now, but I was having serious doubts that I would ever fit into this group of American kamikazes. I was to later learn that it took months and months of strict training to get to a point that you could piss your pants in fear and have no one notice. My neck was beginning to swell up and get stiff, and I had the feeling that whatever had bit me was more than just a mosquito.

When he noticed the golf-ball-size lump on the side of my

neck, Piper suggested that I go over to the hospital and get it checked, and I just nodded. I felt embarrassed, instead of proud. It was almost as if I had chicken written all over my uniform, and I felt very uncomfortable.

When we landed, I didn't say anything to anyone, but headed straight for the mess hall. Mike Cutts met me at the door and said, "What's wrong Mr. Boyle? You look like shit."

"I just need a cup of coffee and a couple of tea bags if you've got any to spare," I said, as I poured myself a cup.

Mike handed me the tea bags, and I turned and headed out the door. "Thanks, Mike, I'll see you later," I said as the screen door slammed behind me.

Once back in my room I soaked the tea bags in the coffee and then placed them on my neck and lay down on my bunk, hoping that the trick my mother had learned from the Indians in Canada would work on whatever had bitten me.

I awoke sometime in the early afternoon and walked over to the PX. I was able to get a few cartons of cigarettes and a small reel-to-reel tape recorder and some extra tapes. Someone had told me that we could also mail small letter-size tapes home free, and I thought I would give it a try. The swelling on my neck had gone down, and there was no more stinging, but a hard spot under the skin remained. It stayed there for months to come, as a constant reminder not to walk in the jungle.

CHAPTER TEN

By mid-April, I had completed paneling my room with lumber from broken-up rocket boxes. The supply Sergeant had come through with enough nails to finish the job and had given me a few rolls of masking tape, which I placed over the cracks between the boards. It looked really great, and in addition to keeping out all the dirt and dust blown up by the helicopters, the masking tape made it look like there was caulking between the boards.

Mid-April also brought an additional pilot to the building, which until that time, Mills and I had had all to ourselves. He was an FNG by the name of Carl Rosapepe, straight out of Cobra school. I immediately nicknamed him Rosey. At first he didn't care for the name, but it slowly took hold. The best way to describe Rosey would be to say that he resembled Jimmy Durante. We quickly became good friends. In fact Rosey said that Jimmy Durante was his hero—Jimmy wasn't at all sensitive about his nose. Another pilot, who I later showed a picture of Rosey's profile, said, "Good thing he's not hooked on cocaine, he'd go through the world's supply in a week!"

Rosey's arrival was a very good thing—finally there was a Snake pilot who was newer than me, and Red would have someone else to yell at.

Our AO (area of operation) was really beginning to warm up, and aircraft were taking hits almost every day. The firebases along the border north and west of Tay Ninh were all getting hit on a regular basis.

Orders came down allowing us to go right up to the border, but under no circumstances were we to cross into Cambodia, and that sort of order didn't sit well with any of us. The Viet Cong attacked at night and crossed back into Cambodia with impunity as it was getting light. I think the frustration was beginning to take it's toll on the Snake pilots who made it a practice, on the last flight of the day, to fly up to the border, pull the nose of the Cobra up, and fire all the rockets that they might have left and watch them sail over the border into Cambodia.

Apparently, all of our bitching had not fallen on deaf ears. Every day I observed more and more traffic headed northwest along the highway toward the border. At first it was just trucks, then tanks started moving toward the border. Then the heavy artillery guns were being moved up. That's when I asked someone in the TOC what was going on. I was told that it was just equipment for a new firebase and to forget about it. I had not yet been tuned into the rumor mill that usually emanated from the officers club, and because of being a new guy and never one to even like beer, I had tried to find other things to do besides spending a lot of time in the bar.

But I did wander into the bar one night, the reason being that I had just painted some wood stain on the walls of my room, and I couldn't stand the fumes. John Bartlett was tending bar and obviously had been tending himself as well as the other patrons. Bartlett was the senior Xray in the Red platoon, and everyone knew that he was about to become an aircraft commander (AC). Bartlett was feeling no pain when some words were exchanged between him and the White Platoon leader, Lieutenant Brewer, who had obviously had a few beers also.

I couldn't hear what Brewer said to Bartlett as he walked toward the door to leave but nobody missed Bartlett's reply of "Why don't you bite my ass."

Nobody paid much attention because Bartlett was always telling people to bite his ass. He probably used the term more often than the word hello. Everything had returned to normal—normal, that is, for the Apache Troop officers club. Within a few minutes, the door to the club flew open, and Lieutenant Brewer stormed back into the bar and placed a rattrap on the bar in front of Bartlett. It contained a freshly caught rat.

"Why don't you take a big bite out of *this*, asshole," Brewer roared at Bartlett.

Everyone was laughing, and the spotlight was now centered on Bartlett. Bartlett didn't appear to be shaken. He almost acted as if the bit had all been rehearsed. Even I, an FNG, could tell from the expression on Bartlett's face that the young warrant officer was no longer kidding around with the lieutenant.

Bartlett picked up the trap, and a loud cheer erupted from the group. He folded back the heavy spring, which held the dead rat by the neck, removed the lifeless form, and let the trap fall to the floor. Holding the rat in his right hand, above his head, and at arm's length, Bartlett showed it to the gathering of officers as one would show off an Olympic medal or some prize possession, holding it high and moving it from left to right and then back. Without warning, Bartlett brought the rat up to his mouth and bit off its head and then spit it out on the floor.

The laughter of the stunned gathering of officers and gentlemen came to a sudden stop, and the silence was broken only by the moaning of grown men running for the door so that they wouldn't puke inside the club.

From that night on, John Bartlett, from Whitefish, Montana, was known as "Bloody Bart," a title he wore with the same pride as if it were the Congressional Medal of Honor.

I retreated back to my room and its fumes, hoping that no one would make biting the head off a rat a condition of becoming an aircraft commander.

In a later conversation, Bartlett pointed out to me that he and Brewer had developed a mutual dislike in flight school, and it was only by accident that they both ended up in Apache Troop. But whenever they were flying, regardless of their personal feelings, there was always a comradeship and mutual respect. This was true of everyone in the troop, not just pilots—personal likes and dislikes were left behind whenever anyone was in trouble. The guy who disliked you the most was usually the one who went out of his way and risked his life to save yours.

Lying on my bunk, I couldn't help thinking that the group of pilots reminded me of something that I had read about before, but I couldn't put my finger on it. I had never been one to drink a lot. In high school I had always been the designated driver when the rest of my friends got drunk. Sobriety did have its advantages, though, when it came to the girls. I learned early on that the advantage went to the person who was sober. I really worried a lot about what I was going to have to do to fit in with this wild group. Then it came to me. I knew who this group reminded me of, it had to be Pappy Boyington's Black Sheep Squadron. I began to think that, just maybe, all these crazy Apache Troop pilots were the result of reincarnation. Maybe they were all reincarnated Black Sheep pilots who had been killed during World War II.

I never finished the thought. The next thing I knew, it was

morning again, and a spec four from the TOC was telling me it was time to get up.

With Tay Ninh being as close to the Cambodian border as it was, it was not uncommon for the flight crews to come back to base to rearm, refuel, and eat lunch. Twelve-hour flight days were not uncommon, and sometimes we even went to sixteen, but eight to ten hours were the norm. Everyone was tired, and an hour or two break back at Tay Ninh was much looked forward to.

I had finished lunch and returned to my room in hopes of getting a little nap before having to leave again. I had just lain down when a Cobra landed outside my room and blew some of the masking tape off my walls, following up with a lot of dirt. As my room had no windows, I got up, walked to the door leading into my building, and looked out to see who the jerks were that had disturbed my nap. It was Bartlett and Lieutenant Coons, our platoon leader. I watched as they got out of the Cobra and walked to the mess hall.

Bartlett appeared to get along well with Coons, better than any other Xray did. Other Xrays took Coons's attitude too personal, the way I did, and it wasn't until much later that some of us, especially me, understood that Coons was just keeping us alive.

I decided that it was time that I got a little involved in the crazy world of screwing with other people's minds. I had observed Bartlett remove his flight gloves and carefully place them on the front dashboard of the Cobra, laid out very nice and neat, and I decided to stimulate the ongoing war of nerves and practical jokes between him and Red.

I left my room and walked over to the back door of the mess hall and got Mike Cutts's attention. "Hey, Mike, I need a cupful of that Jell-O that we had for lunch."

"Did you really like it that much, sir? Wasn't it kind of watery?"

"No problem, Mike. I just need it for a little joke I want to pull on Bartlett."

Mike returned with a paper cup filled with green Jell-O. "What are you going to do with it, sir?"

"Well, Mike, seeing as how Mr. Bartlett was so kind to park his helicopter so close to my room, I just thought he might get a kick out of some Jell-O in his gloves."

"No shit! Are you really going to do it?"

"If you'll keep an eye on the mess hall and give a whistle if you see either Red or Bartlett leave, I'll do it."

"You're covered, sir." Mike said as I headed out the back door toward the flight line.

I stepped up onto the ammo-bay door on the left side of the helicopter and grabbed one of Bartlett's gloves. I peeled the glove back so that just the holes for the fingers were exposed and poured about a teaspoon of Jell-O into each finger. I replaced it just as Bartlett had left it and repeated the process with the other glove. When I had finished, I walked back to the mess hall where Mike was waiting.

"Somebody is really going to be pissed, sir," Mike said with a laugh.

"Yeah, I know, but I'm betting that he'll think it was Red that did it. Is there somewhere we can watch the flight line without being seen?"

"We might be able to see through the window in the storage room."

It was great. We had a clear view of the Cobra in question; now all we had to do was wait for Red and Bartlett to finish their lunch and return to the helicopter.

Mike and I were giggling like a couple of little kids. I became afraid that one of the other cooks would hear all the giggling and discover what we were up to, so I asked Mike to go back out and see what Red and Bartlett were doing. In what seemed like only seconds, he was back, wearing a huge grin on his face.

"They are just walking out, sir," Mike said as he raised his right hand and covered his mouth to muffle the snickers.

It always amazed me how little, stupid things could bring so much enjoyment. The same thing done anywhere but Vietnam would mean nothing.

Red was first to arrive at the ship and climbed in. As soon as he had put on his seat belts, he started the engine; the high-pitched whine could be heard clearly from our observation point.

Bartlett remained outside, watching the engine cowling for signs of fire during the start, then climbed into the front seat. As was usually the case, he first put on his seat belts and then his helmet. The gloves were always last.

Mike and I held our breath as Bartlett picked up the first glove and shoved his hand into it, his forearm and hand being vertical as the glove was pulled on with his bare hand. The sleeves on Bartlett's flight suit were rolled up to his elbows. The raised arm with the Jell-O–filled glove froze in place. Bartlett never lowered his hand, he just turned it from side to side as if giving the glove an inspection. Then he lowered the hand and put on the other glove, raising his arm as he had done with the other one. He was looking closely at something running out of the glove, down his arm, and dripping off his raised elbow.

Mike and I were going nuts, jumping around the storage room with our hands clasped over our mouths. Our last view of Bartlett was as he turned around in the tight seat and obviously said something to Red, who had no obvious reaction. Then Red pulled the Cobra to a hover, turned, and departed to the north.

Mike and I were ecstatic, but I made Mike swear that he would not tell anyone.

That night the word spread about what had happened to Bartlett. There was not a question in anyone's mind that Red had been the culprit. Bartlett put out the word that he was going to get even, and described in detail how he was going to take a big shit under Red's pillow. For weeks Red inspected his room each night, looking for the elusive pile of excrement. I suspect that Red eventually convinced Bartlett that he was not the person who had doctored the gloves, for the matter finally just died on the vine.

Since I had the next day off, I looked up Mike Reardon, the Scout pilot, and asked him if I could ride along with him in the morning as his observer. I really wanted to see what the low bird got to see instead of just writing it down while riding around in the front of the Cobra. Mike agreed, and I went over to the TOC and asked that I be awakened with the other pilots scheduled to fly the next day.

Because of low clouds and ground fog, we didn't get off the ground until 7:30 A.M. We headed north with Lieutenant Coons (Red) as our high bird. I had become used to a lot of leg room in the Cobra, but my six-foot-two body didn't fit very well in the small low bird, and it seemed a lot louder than what I had been used to. I did enjoy flying with the door off, as the constant rush of air, even though warm, had a cooling effect, and it felt good.

Mike had been in Apache Troop since August 1969 and was the senior Scout pilot, which made me feel that I was in pretty good company.

Most of the flight I spent trying to look over Mike's shoulder and helmet so I could see what he was seeing and relaying up to Red in the Cobra. Everything went by so fast, I couldn't understand how he saw what he did, but I quickly learned that he was very good at his job.

When we finished reconing the area that had been assigned to us, we headed back to Tay Ninh.

Having planned on only going on the first flight, I dropped my gear in my room and walked over to the mess hall to get some coffee and maybe some leftover bacon. I had only been there ten minutes when Reardon came in and said, "Hey, Boyle, grab your stuff, we've got a mission."

Visions of returning to my room to put some more stain on the walls disappeared. The urgency in Reardon's voice prompted me to run to retrieve my helmet and M-16 rifle.

Mike had the low bird running when I arrived. I squeezed into the left-front seat of the very small helicopter and was still strapping in as Mike took off. When I finally got my helmet plugged in, I asked, "Where in the hell are we going in such a hurry?"

"A group of tanks that are operating close to the border are taking sniper fire, and they can't seem to find the guy who is popping off at them."

"Shit, I thought something really big was going on," I said.

"The guys in the tanks think that getting shot at is something really big," Mike said, and I felt as if I had just been scolded.

When I thought about being buttoned up inside a tank in this heat, I realized that had to be worse than getting shot.

It took us about ten minutes to arrive over the tanks, and Red informed us that the tank commander had told him that the sniping had stopped. The tanks were formed up in a line, with the intention of moving to the west. The area was relatively flat, with thin lines of trees to the north, east, and west of the tanks. The southern flank was wide open.

Red directed us to recon the tree lines to the north and west of the tanks as that's where the tanks thought the sniper might be.

"Mike, I thought we didn't fly along tree lines!" I said.

"We usually don't, but we have a good idea that this guy is right along the tree line, and you know us Scouts, we got to go where the action is."

"Yeah, sure, Mike, just make sure the tree line is on your side of the aircraft," I said.

"Don't worry, new guy, we'll take good care of you," Mike said, as he let down in a slow, descending circle.

We started at the northwest corner of the tree line and

worked south along the western edge. All I could do was watch and listen and try once again to see what Mike was seeing and relaying up to Red in the Cobra above us. Mike was always talking to his torque in the rear seat to confirm things that they were seeing. I really thought that I was going blind because, so far, I hadn't seen anything.

Bill, the torque, suddenly came over the intercom with, "I've got a gook behind that one big tree."

"I see him," Reardon replied as he steepened the right turn and went around the tree.

"Stitch him," Reardon said to the torque and, at the same time, informed Red what he was looking at.

The sharp sound of the M-60 machine gun made me jump, and I strained to see where the torque was firing. All I could see was chunks of bark flying off the tree and dirt being kicked up on the ground.

Then the torque came on the intercom with, "I've got two of them down there."

"Yeah, I see them," Mike replied.

"Taking fire," Mike yelled into the radio, and I let go of the red-smoke grenade that I had been holding in my left hand, with the pin already pulled.

As luck would have it, it landed within five feet of the two VC who, along with others, were shooting at us. For a minute, I thought I was having a dream because there were tracers passing directly under the low bird, but they were going in both directions, west to east and east to west.

"Get the hell out of there!" Red yelled. "The tanks are firing into the tree line."

Reardon rolled out of his right-hand circle and made a sharp left turn to the south and did a steep cyclic climb.

I'm not really sure when I started to breathe again, but I was very happy to be out of the area. Once we were at altitude, Reardon turned the low bird around, and we watched as Red put down rockets on the red smoke that was still coming out of the tree line.

Steady lines of red tracers streaked from the tanks and chewed apart the brush and trees at the edge of the clearing. Then, as suddenly as it started, the tanks would quit firing. As soon as the tanks had stopped firing, a single line of tracers would erupt from the tree line and start bouncing off of the tanks.

Red suddenly broke off his rocket runs and started to climb.

The author at Loc Ninh with his two little
Vietnamese friends who like to eat C rations.

Chinook slinging back Cobra that Jimmy Mills and
the author were shot down in during March of 1970.

(left to right) John Peele and the author
at Firebase David.

The author and all his cooks at a temporary
mess hall at Phuoc Vinh.

Mike King inspects wreckage of a recovered
low bird that had been shot down.

The cockpit of "Red's" Cobra after he was shot down south of
Song Be. Photo by B. Fuller.

Looking through the gun sight of a Cobra from the rear seat.

Looking forward from the rear seat of a Cobra.

The "Wild Bunch," (left to right) W.O. Bob Smith, Sgt. Jack Bracamonte, author, W.O. Jeff Houser, Lt. Larry Lilly, waiting for a mission into Cambodia.

Dead NVA outside FSB David. Note that none are wearing shoes or boots. Photo by C. Rosapepe.

51 caliber enemy bullet entered front left canopy door and exited top above rear seat of Carl "Rosey" Rosapepe's Cobra, peppering his face with Plexiglas shrapnel.

51 caliber hole made by same bullet in main rotor blade.

Jim Thomas on right just after returning from Instructor Pilot School (Note squeaky-clean uniform). Rosey is at left, inside our sewer pipe.

My only picture of Norm "Red" Coons, loading his weapon, after our crash in Cambodia, 11 June 1970.

(left to right) Jim Thomas, Jeff Cromar, author, Carl "Rosey" Rosapepe at a 1993 reunion of Apache Troop at Fort Knox, KY. Photo by C. Rosapepe.

Lt. General Paul Funk, left, with author at 1993 Apache Troop reunion. In 1970, as a captain, he commanded Apache Troop.

He advised Mike that Rash One One, an air force OV-10 observer airplane, was overhead and was bringing in a flight of bombers to take care of the gooks in the tree line. Red further advised that another low bird had been shot down about five miles south of us and for us to follow him to the location.

Within a minute, he called us back and said that the low bird had made it to a firebase, and the crew was secure.

The pilot of the other Cobra advised that the observer in his low bird had been hit in the hand and that the low bird had taken over thirty hits.

I looked over at Mike and said, "If you don't have any objections, when we get back to base, I think I'll take the rest of the day off and work on my room."

Mike just smiled but didn't say anything to indicate that he probably knew just how scared I really was. The older pilots knew that everyone got scared, but no mention of fear was ever made. It was almost as if it were an unwritten rule that fear was never a topic of conversation and was a necessary part of the learning process that everyone went through, grunt or pilot.

As I sat in my room, enjoying the blast of air from my fan, I started a letter to Sonny and Dusty. I had to be able to tell someone that I had just had the shit scared out of me. I had to tell someone that I felt I was learning how to fight and be scared at the same time, but that I felt as if I was the only one who was feeling scared. Nobody else even mentioned fear, and it was really beginning to wear on my nerves. I wondered if the aircraft commanders had their own little secret meetings where they discussed their fears so as to not lose face in front of the new-guy pilots.

One thing did become obvious, and that was that there weren't a lot of going-home parties for the pilots of Apache Troop. Most were leaving the country after a stop at the hospital or via a body bag. I decided to do as I felt the other pilots had to be doing—don't think about it, and find something to keep me from thinking about what might happen. I decided to put all my spare time into really fixing up my room, and when that was done, I'd find something else to do.

CHAPTER ELEVEN

The only way I was going to find out where all the good mattresses had gone was to ask Bartlett. Every time I asked anyone about them, I always received the same laughing answer, "Ask Bartlett."

I decided that I would make one of my very infrequent trips to the officers club. Bloody Bart had just made aircraft commander and could usually be found at the O-club, acting as bartender or just sitting around with some of the senior pilots. As I entered the bar, a very drunk pilot walked into me, damn near knocking me off my feet. Normally, I would have just let it pass, but this pilot made some remark about me being a fucking new guy, and I should watch where he was walking. I had been told that rank and seniority were always left at the door of the O-club, but in this case that apparently had been forgotten.

I mentioned that, instead of drinking more beer, he should go out into the jungle and shave a few bananas along with the rest of his relatives.

This prompted a lot of pushing back and forth and a lot of name calling before we were broken up by Red (Lieutenant Coons), my platoon leader, and I was ordered out of the bar.

Pissed to the max, I returned to my room to brood and write more letters, still wondering what the secret of the mattresses was. Almost a week later, while flying as Bartlett's Xray, I got the chance to ask about the mattresses.

It had been one of those long boring days, during which I had written down pages of spot reports, but little else had taken place. That type of day provided welcome relief to pilots, crews, and to everyone else involved, but I wondered if it didn't cause us to let down our guard a little.

"Hey, Bart—everyone tells me that you hold the answer to where all the good mattresses disappeared to. Is that true?"

"Shit, that's a crock of bull! My low bird got shot down, and I needed a lift ship, and I needed him quick. The closest one said he had a load on, and I thought he meant that he was carrying a sling load. So I told him to dump his load and get his ass over to my location ASAP. Hell, I didn't know he had the whole inside of the Huey stuffed full of brand-new mattresses that he had just picked up at Bien Hoa. Kind of funny when you think about it, though. Here we are sleeping on whatever we can get our hands on and Charlie is sleeping on our new mattresses."

"Did the Old Man get pissed off about it?" I asked.

"Hell no, he was my aircraft commander at the time, and he wanted to get the low-bird crew out of there, no matter what it took. Anyway, we didn't find out about the mattresses until after it was all over. But I don't think it would have changed anything. I get real tired telling the story every time someone needs a mattress."

As soon as I had finished calling in all my spots to the TOC, I asked Bloody Bart what had happened to the low-bird crew.

"Yeah, we got them out okay, but they were all wounded. As I said, I was flying in the front seat, and Captain Funk was my AC. Ordean Iverson, he's from Montana just like me, he was the low-bird pilot. Anyway, we were just on a regular recon mission, and I was watching the low bird as usual when Iverson yells, "Taking fire!" and all this red smoke starts pouring out of all the doors of the low bird."

"Captain Funk did a hard left turn and started firing rockets into the area that the low bird had just been over. I just kept my eyes on Iverson to see what was going to happen next. Then Iverson comes on the radio and tells us that he can't keep the bird in the air, that the collective has been blown in half, and that everyone on board has been wounded."

"Holy shit, how did he get it down without a collective?" I asked. (Simply put, the collective is a long tube that is moved up and down and controlled with the left arm and hand. It controls the helicopter's altitude.

"Well, the collective being blown in half wasn't the only problem Iverson had," Bart continued. "His arm had damn near been blown in half. When they took fire, the gooks had to have been almost right underneath them because they got the observer, and he dropped the red smoke grenade inside the aircraft, and the windshield and most of the gauges were blown out. One round went through the collective, blew it in half, then went through Iverson's arm, breaking it. Even if he'd had a collective, he wouldn't have been able to use it because he had no use of that arm."

"Well, don't leave me hanging, Bart, how the hell was he able to land?"

"He put the cyclic between his legs and controlled the collective by sticking the middle finger of his right hand into the stub that was left of the collective and was able to control the pitch that way. It sure wasn't a great landing, but he got it down in a large clearing, and the Old Man and I landed next to them. I jumped out of the Cobra and went over to help. Christ, what a mess, there was blood everywhere. I reached in the backseat and dragged the torque out. He appeared to be dead. Then I got Iverson and the observer out. The observer had been hit in the arm and leg, but Iverson was really in bad shape and had lost a lot of blood. The observer asked how the torque was, and I said I thought he was dead. I just about shit my shorts when he said, "I'm not dead and you better not leave me." Then we started taking fire from the tree line, which made Captain Funk, in the Cobra, a sitting duck. Luckily the Huey that had been carrying your mattress showed up, and while the door gunners put down covering fire, we got the wounded loaded. I then ran back to the Cobra and got going with the minigun until the Huey was out of the clearing. Then the Old Man and I got the hell out of there real quick like."

"What ever happened to Iverson?"

"Hell, Boyle, where have you been anyway? You see him every day in the TOC! He's the Old Man's right-hand man. He spent about three weeks in the hospital, and rather than go home, which he could have done, he came back here and extended his tour."

I didn't say anything, but just sat there, thinking. Then the light dawned—hell, the guy everyone calls "Ord" has got to be Iverson. With so many people in Apache Troop, I still had not gotten to know everyone, and as I remembered, Ord was the real quiet type. The thought also came to mind that Bartlett and Iverson were from the same general area of Montana. Bartlett ate rats and Iverson declined to get the hell out of Vietnam after being wounded and damn near losing his arm. And people accuse us Californians of being a little on the strange side.

"Hey Bart, who's going to take your place as the new Xray?" I asked as we neared Tay Ninh.

"I think it's going to be Magnet Ass, at least that's the rumor going around."

Magnet Ass was Jim Thomas, a pilot whom I had gone all through flight school with. He had been shot down with Pierce while learning how to be a low-bird pilot and then last week again.

On that occasion, Thomas was flying as observer in the left-front seat on the low bird with Mike Reardon. Reardon's torque had spotted a VC running into a hootch and opened fire on him. When they made their next pass over the hootch, the VC stepped out the door and filled Reardon's engine and tail rotor full of AK-47 bullets. The low bird then took on all the aerodynamics of a bathtub and fell straight down, spinning, crashing through the roof of the hootch, just as the Viet Cong ran back inside through the door. The VC was killed instantly beneath the low bird, and Thomas and his crew walked away without a scratch.

As we landed at Tay Ninh, I thought I saw a familiar face limping across the company area.

"Hey, Bart, who's that grunt over there? I pointed at a baby-faced kid who appeared to be about sixteen years old but was wearing the stripes of a buck sergeant and was having obvious trouble walking. "He looks like I should know him."

"Don't know for sure, but it looks like one of the Blues maybe."

About that time Tony Cortez, from the Blue Platoon, walked up to the unknown grunt and shook his hand. When the blowing dust from our rotor wash had settled, both grunts turned to look at the Cobra. The grunt I thought I knew was identified by Bartlett.

"Hey, Boyle, that's Jorgenson, the sergeant who always walks point for the Blues."

"I think you're right, Bart, but I thought they sent him back to the States after he got all shot up for CBS?"

"Yeah, I thought so, too. Can you imagine what his folks thought if they saw him being wounded while they were watching the evening news. Blue said they had packed up all his stuff to send back to the States."

"Shit, he's really going to be pissed if they sold off all his souvenirs." If a person was wounded or killed and had accumulated weapons or other items that could not be sent home, we auctioned off those items and the proceeds were sent back to the person or his next of kin.

Jorgenson had been wounded in both legs in a real western-style shoot-out between him and an NVA point man a few weeks earlier. The Blues had been inserted into the same area where Pierce and Thomas had been shot down while following a heavily used trail. With the Blues was a CBS camera crew and Richard Threlkeld. Little did Jorgenson know that he would be featured on the CBS evening news that very night.

"Damn!" I said.

"What's wrong now, Boyle?" Bartlett asked, trying his best to sound like Red.

"Shit! If I'd been thinking, I probably could have snatched his mattress."

Bartlett started laughing. "You're cold, Boyle, really cold. Besides, I hear the Blues sleep on nails, not mattresses, just to keep themselves sharp.

I had to agree with Bartlett, the Blues were always ready to go at a moment's notice. A lot of flight crews owed their lives to that small, yet very proud group of men. Every pilot in Apache knew that there was a very good chance that his life would be entrusted to the Blue Platoon at some time during his tour. They also knew that they wouldn't want it entrusted to anyone else.

I had witnessed an act of trust by the Blues a few days earlier as I walked across the flight line. It was just after lunch, if you could call it that, and I was walking out to where a couple of guys from maintenance were working on the Cobra that I'd be flying the next day. I'd been in Vietnam two months and was still having a difficult time adjusting to the heat and the bugs and the constant feeling of being dirty. As I walked, I heard the distinct sound of an approaching helicopter. While I was standing in the middle of the flight line, I looked up to make sure that I wouldn't be in the way. Holy shit, I thought, as I saw the Huey approaching from the west with two people hanging fifty feet below it. When it got closer I could make out the ropes coming out of each side of the Huey by which the two men were suspended as they clung to each other. The Huey came to a hover just inside the barbed-wire fence at a height of about seventy-five feet, and then slowly lowered the men to the ground. Two other men then ran up to take their places. They secured the ropes to their webbed harness, grabbed each other in a bear hug, and were lifted up and flown off to the west. The Huey continued to climb and gain speed until it reached an altitude of around five hundred feet. As the distance between them and where I was standing increased, the two grunts hanging under the Huey appeared to be just one person. I stood, as if frozen to the spot, watching as the Huey returned and again the process was repeated. What in the hell are those guys doing? I thought.

As I got to the Cobra, I asked one of the maintenance guys, "Hey, Sarge, are those guys being punished for some reason, or is that the newest way of testing new rope?"

"You've never seen that before, Mr. Boyle?"

"No, what kind of drill do you guys call that anyway?"

"Well you better hope that you never have to make use of it. They are practicing a way to get you out of the jungle in case you get shot down and there isn't any clearing close by, or you're injured and can't help yourself."

"If that's the drill, great. But there is one big flaw in the plan—I don't wear one of those rigs to hook the ropes onto."

"That's why they're practicing, Mr. Boyle, so they can learn how to hold onto you while you're being dragged up through all two hundred feet of tree limbs and branches," the sarge said with a big smile.

"You guys better do damn good work on this helicopter because I sure as hell know I don't want any of those guys hanging onto this body."

The sarge appeared to take offense at what I had said. "What do you mean, sir? Those guys are our Blue Platoon. It's their job to try and rescue you when you get in trouble."

There was tremendous pride in the Apache Blues throughout the entire troop, and it looked like I had just stepped all over my dick with my comment.

"I didn't mean anything by it, Sarge. It's just that I almost knocked Cortez and Jorgenson down the other day with my rotor wash. I only meant that they didn't look big enough to hang onto me." I wanted to find someplace to go hide my head.

Everyone had noticed increased activity in the area, and yet, if someone knew why, they were not talking. The airfield at Tay Ninh had many more cargo flights than usual. The road traffic north out of Tay Ninh was beginning to look like the freeway at rush hour. Every type of vehicle a person could think of was headed up the road, churning out black exhaust smoke and clouds of the ever-present red dust. Everyone seemed to be in a hurry, and everyone had an idea about what was going on.

My years in the Army Reserve had taught me not to believe rumors, but to try and put facts together and make up my own rumor. Until then, the number-one rumor on the hit parade of rumors had been that we were getting ready to pull out of Vietnam, or at least back, because of all the heat that Nixon was taking back in the States. My reasoning told me that unless the United States was planning on departing Vietnam by way of Hanoi, it was headed in the wrong direction. I had also noticed that the maintenance platoon was working day and night on all the aircraft, and that the number of flight hours had decreased this last week. More time off was being given to the flight crews, while supply and maintenance were working their butts off.

Those members of the platoon who were getting short, a term used to describe someone who was within a month or so of going home, were hoping that the pullback rumor would turn out to be true. On the other hand, nobody really believed anything but that we were getting ready for a really big action someplace. The first pick of locations for the suspected action was Cambodia. I can really only speak for myself, but I suspect that some, if not all of us, were a little apprehensive—or just plain scared—about the thought of invading Cambodia. Most of our aircraft commanders could look down at the area they were flying over and, without the aid of a map, pretty much know, within a mile or so, where they were. But none of us had been in Cambodia before. In the past, if the new guy in the front seat of the Cobra became confused or lost, the aircraft commander usually knew where they were and could get the situation straightened out in a hurry. The thought that it was going to be left up to me to do the navigation around an area that I had never seen before was just a little mind blowing. I hoped that there was some other reason for the massive buildup.

Apache Troop, which was greatly undermanned, also began receiving additional personnel. Each platoon was receiving new people, and one of these new people was Paul Foti.

I had first met Paul at Fort Polk, which by then seemed like ten years ago although it was just over a year. Foti was from New York and very much an Italian. He referred to me as the Irish Mick, and I called him the Spaghetti Western Wop, be-

cause of his love for Italian-made western movies. I had taught
Foti how to spit polish his boots and make his bunk the "army
way" when we first met at Fort Polk, and although I had only
known him for ten days before leaving, we had formed a good
friendship. When he first showed up at Apache Troop, I was
really happy to see him and to know that he had made it
through basic training and the forty weeks of hell they called
flight school. I can't recall ever seeing Paul Foti without a
smile on his face or a laugh in his voice. Wherever he was,
you could always find someone laughing. Foti was assigned to
fly lift-platoon Hueys and always seemed to be where the action was.

The air around the TOC had become very tense. Although
Captain Funk, our commanding officer, still scared the shit out
of me, he usually was willing to talk and joke around with the
rest of the officers. But recently that had changed. Some of the
other pilots also noticed the change and guessed that it was because he was getting short. Someone had mentioned that he
would be leaving the troop in a few weeks and we would be
getting a new commanding officer. I had not been in the troop
long enough to be able to yet notice the change that came over
a person, officer or enlisted, when they were within a week or
so of getting to go home. It seemed a little strange that the XO
(the executive officer, who acted on second in command)
would also be acting quiet. I guess the old saying about "once
a cop, always a cop" held true in this case; I smelled a rat and
knew that we weren't being told the whole story.

My suspicions were verified on 30 April 1970. The knocking on my newly stolen door jarred me awake.

Shit, it can't be morning already, I thought. I swung my feet
off the bunk and staggered to the door. As I opened the door,
the first thing I saw was this huge nose, which was attached to
the face of Rosapepe. "What the fuck? Over." I said, still half-
asleep.

"They want us at the TOC, so get dressed. And hurry up."

"What's going on, Rosey, and what the hell time is it anyway?"

"It's only eleven P.M.; so quit your bitching and let's go,"
Rosey said with a laugh.

I slipped into my flight suit and shower shoes and followed
Rosey out the door toward the TOC. It soon became apparent
that everyone was up and about and headed toward the TOC.

As we walked through the door we were directed toward

one of the rooms by a spec four. The place was buzzing with activity, more than I had seen since my arrival. As Rosey and I walked into the room, we were both handed a huge roll of maps and told to pick a place to sit on the floor. Lieutenant Coons (Red) was the only officer standing, and one EM was walking around the room, handing out rolls of wide, clear Scotch tape. Some of the other officers were on their hands and knees, staring at maps that had been unrolled on the floor. The first thing that leapt off the map and hit me right between the eyes like a sledge hammer was the word at the top of the map. *Cambodia!*

The rest of the night was a hurricane of activity. As I looked around the roomful of pilots from the Red Platoon, I had the feeling of being alone. It was as if I had backed into a corner and was just watching everything that was going on, but no one else could see me. It then dawned on me that I was suffering from a terminal case of wishful thinking. I stayed close to Rosey, because when it came to maps, whether putting them together or just reading them, there wasn't anyone better.

All of the Xrays had gathered in one corner of the room and were attempting to make sense of the maps we had just been handed. We had been instructed to cut off the borders around all four sides of each map and then tape them together to make one big map.

"Hey, Rosey, I'll help you carry your map back to the room if you'll give me a hand with mine," I said in a vain attempt to get a smile out of someone, anyone. There was a lot of conversation going on, but it lacked the lightheartedness that I had become used to. Everyone seemed very serious, and it showed most clearly on the faces of the Xray Cobra pilots in their corner of the room. I suspected that everyone shared my apprehension of the unknown. Some had guessed that we would catch the NVA with their pants down and the war would come to a quick end; I didn't share their optimism. To me, Cambodia reminded me of a story I had read as a child, where some unsuspecting human, walking across a bridge, is accosted by a big, ugly troll who has been laying in wait. The human is pulled from the bridge and dragged into the dark water, never to return.

We had been told in the briefing that takeoff would be before first light so that we could cross the border at first light. Avoidance of civilians had been strongly stressed, in addition to all the other usual briefing information. It was early morning by the time we had finished cutting, taping, and marking out areas of operation on our now huge maps. To me, unfolding that map inside the tight cockpit of a Cobra would be like unfolding a king-size mattress inside a Volkswagen.

Finally, we were told to go back to our rooms and get some sleep and that someone would be around in a couple of hours to wake us up. Not a lot of conversation took place as Rosey and I walked out into the very dark company area and headed for our rooms. As soon as I got into my room, I wrote three very short half-page letters to my mom, my wife, and Sonny and Dusty. I then lay down on my bunk, removing only my shower shoes. All I could think about was a question that kept running through my mind. After over a year of training on how to be prepared and how you must always preflight your aircraft, how do you preflight your mind for the unknown?

CHAPTER TWELVE

I didn't have to look very hard to see the thin line of dim light, to my right front, that represented the Apache sunrise as we headed northeast toward the Cambodian border. I managed to unfold the huge map so that I could easily follow our flight path. The erie glow of the red lights on the instrument panel did little to illuminate the map, but I had remembered to put the red lens in my flashlight, and it allowed me to see the map clearly. Just then there wasn't any problem keeping track of our location as we were still over our own AO, which I had overflown many times in the past. Ahead was another unit's AO, over which I had never flown, but I was with Mr. Zeroth, whom everyone called Zero, and I knew that he would give me all the help I needed if I had any trouble with locations.

Almost every sentence had started with the same three words, "I wonder if," followed by every possibility that the human mind could conjure up. None of the pilots knew what to expect when we crossed the border; at least nothing definite had been mentioned in the late-night briefing. If our higher-ups knew, they had kept it to themselves, but that wasn't like the CO or Red.

I just assumed that we all would be operating in the dark for the first few days. Just the thought of not knowing scared the shit out of me, which I'm sure was reflected in the three very short letters I had written after the briefing. I didn't write out a will as did so many others. Hell, I didn't have anything to leave anyone. Only the people who had acquired a few weapons or cameras or other items they felt were worth something bothered making a will. I had only done what the Apaches had done before leaving camp for battle. The saying was short and to the point, "Say good-bye to the ones you leave behind."

The mess hall had opened early that morning because of the takeoff time, and I had been one of the first to grab a hot cup of coffee and a piece of plywood toast. Sipping the hot coffee, I tried to prepare myself mentally for the unknown and unexpected. Compared to previous mornings, the mess hall was strangely quiet, and my thoughts drifted back to the hours that followed the briefing. I had lain on my bunk in a vain attempt to sleep, but everything under the sun was running through my mind. I thought I knew why Captain Funk had been so quiet for the last few weeks except when someone screwed up an aircraft by mistake or through carelessness. I just hoped that the NVA were just as blind as I was, and that we wouldn't be flying into hell come sunrise.

I for one, would rather take incoming than suffer the wrath of Captain Funk, yet Apache Troop could not have wished for a better commanding officer. He was what "commanding officer" was really all about. When he took command of a situation, he really took command, and if he was just passing on orders that had been given to him by someone further up the chain of command, nobody ever knew it. He also was open to suggestions and tolerated more crap than most in his position. He could chew someone out by just looking at them; no words had to be spoken; it was all in the expression on his face. That look told a person whether Captain Funk was pleased or pissed. If he did say something, you knew that you had either done really bad or very good.

"That's the highway leading north out of Quan Loi," I advised Zero in the back seat. "I think we follow it north and we'll come to Loc Ninh and then An Loc."

I really liked Mr. Zeroth. He had a quiet way of pointing out mistakes made by the new guys when he was instructing, and that really was what an AC was.

"I think if you'll check the chart again, you FNG, you'll see that An Loc comes first and then Loc Ninh," Zero said with a smile in his voice.

We had been instructed to refuel at Loc Ninh and that we would be working out of an area at the northeast corner of the small dirt airstrip there. Looking up the highway, all I could see was rubber trees. The area was completely different from what I had become used to around Tay Ninh. Huge plantations of green trees that had been laid out in perfect rows, broken only by narrow dirt roads, except for paved highway we were following north. The view from the front seat of a Cobra is like no other helicopter or airplane I had ever flown in before. After a while the divisions in the windshield became invisible, and I would get the sensation that I was sitting in the front of the Cobra with nothing else around me. This sensation could be a real sense of breathtaking beauty or stark terror, depending on whether I was looking at beautiful scenery or green tracers racing up at me.

We passed Loc Ninh on the east side. Already there was a fury of activity around the small airstrip that had been built years ago by a French rubber farmer who still lived there, apparently immune to the war going on around him.

"Zero, we're about five miles south of the Cambodian border," I said over the intercom.

"Okay, thanks." Zero called the low bird, told him of our location, and then advised him to slow down. At the same time, I felt our Cobra slow and noticed the reduction in speed on the gauges. Knowing I could ask Zeroth questions and not be made to feel as low as a snake's belly, I asked "How come the slowdown?"

"I don't want to be crossing the border until the low bird has enough light to see what he's shooting at."

I felt a little stupid for not already knowing the answer to that question. Among the biggest dangers to the low bird were first-light and last-light missions. Looking down into the trees was hard enough at noon, but when there was little light, the only good target was the low bird. Our low-bird pilot, Charlie Cochran, didn't have to ask why we were slowing down.

Our orders were to disable any vehicles we found, and shoot anything wearing a green uniform or black pajamas or anyone who shot at us. The main objective was to find the large caches of food and weapons that, up until this time, had been immune to the prying eyes of our hunter-killer teams.

"We are at the border," I announced over the intercom. Zero called Cochran and told him to stick close, and we would follow the highway a little farther, staying at altitude until the light got better or we found something.

It seemed to be only a few minutes, but was probably more like fifteen, when Cochran called Zero. "My torque just spotted a truck off to your right about half a mile. Do you see it?"

Zero and I looked to our right, and we both caught the same small flash of what looked like the brake lights of some vehicle.

"Charlie, why don't you come right, and we'll go have a look-see," Zero advised Cochran.

"Hey, Boyle. Are you sure we are in Cambodia?" Zero asked as he banked the cobra to the right.

"Yeah, I'm sure. We're about eight miles southeast of Snuol. Are you going to put the low bird down now?"

"Well if you were the aircraft commander, what would you do?" Zero said.

I had not been expecting to be put on the spot, so I said the first thing that came to mind. "I think I would have turned left instead of right."

"Now why the hell would you do that?" came the roar from the backseat.

" 'Cuz it's the shortest way to Bangkok, and they don't shoot at Cobras over there."

"Yeah, right, Boyle. Right about a quarter mile in front of you is where we last saw what looked like brake lights. Do you think you've got enough light to see into those trees?" Zero asked the low bird.

"Yeah, plenty," came the reply.

"Okay, pick up that road and follow it until it gets to the trees, then you can let down and take a look for our mystery vehicle."

Upon leaving Tay Ninh, I had folded the sight for the gun turret down and out of the way, in order to have more room for the huge map.

"Can I put this damn map away and get the turret ready to fire?" I asked Zero.

"No, spot reports are going to be very important today, and I want you on that map and the low bird every minute. You'll have plenty of time if we need the minigun."

Zeroth was right, the most important part of the mission was protecting the low bird and recording what he found.

"I'm letting down," Cochran advised.

"Okay, but if you're having any trouble seeing, just come back up; we're in no hurry," Zero responded.

My eyes were glued to the low bird as it descended in tight right-hand turns and became smaller and smaller. It may have been difficult for Cochran to see into the trees, but it was also difficult for me to keep track of him in the dim, early morning light that was being filtered through a thin gray cloud layer. Looking down on the area, I could not get over the difference between the way this country looked and Vietnam. The vegetation was different and less dense, a lot more rubber trees, but there was something else that I just couldn't put my finger on.

Then the light bulb went on in my head, and the difference came to me in a flood of recognition. There were no bomb craters. Vietnam was covered with shell holes and bomb craters, and in some places, the landscape appeared more like the face of the moon. But Cambodia appeared devoid of any signs of war.

"We've got a truck down here," Cochran's excited voice boomed over the radio.

"Okay, check it out. But cover your ass," Zero replied.

"We've got people down here," was Cochran's next radio call, green uniforms and pith helmets—" He was interrupted by the sound of the M-60 machine gun from the back seat of the low bird. Out of the corner of my eye, a red light appeared on the instrument panel, which told me that Zero had just armed the weapons system, but we held our altitude and continued to circle the low bird. Finally, Cochran came back on the radio, his voice cracking with excitement. "Okay, here's the story. There were two NVA-type gooks who jumped out of the truck, both with AKs (AK-47 assault rifle). The passenger took off up the road, but my torque got the driver. The jerk made the mistake of firing at us as he got out of the truck, and my torque spot-welded him to the door."

"What's in the truck?" Zeroth asked.

"It's loaded with tires, must be about twenty truck-type tires."

"Okay, the truck's not going anywhere. Let's find the gook that took off up the road," Zero advised.

On our next pass to the west of the low bird, I noticed that the road emerged from the trees into a small open area containing about four small buildings of different shapes. I pointed it out to Zero, and he advised Cochran that he would be coming up on an open area.

"Keep an eye on those buildings. I got the low bird," Zero said over the intercom.

As the low bird's orbits got closer to the open area, I saw a lone figure emerge from the northern edge of the tree line and disappear into a small, red-roofed building that had a stone or brick wall about three-feet tall surrounding it.

"Hey, Zero, I just saw a gook run into one of those buildings."

"All right! Which one?" he asked.

As I told him which building, he was already advising Cochran about what I had seen.

The low bird rolled out of his tight right-hand turns and headed straight for the open area.

"Watch your ass down there; you're not going to have any cover at all, and we already know we've got one bad guy down there," Zero advised.

"The backyard of this place is loaded with fifty-five gallon drums," Cochran said over the radio as he made his first pass by the small building.

"Any sign of our friend yet?" Zero asked.

"Nothing yet. The place has a small door at the front and one at the back, and a small window on each side of each door. It's real dark inside there, and I can't see a thing."

"Okay, go ahead and shoot up those drums, and let's see if there is anything in them worth writing home about. But keep your speed up."

From where we were, we could see the tracers hitting the drums and knew the answer to our question even before the low bird called up his report that the drums were empty. The drums were rolling all over the small walled-in yard, but there was no fire. I was writing down as much information as I could while still trying to watch and keep track of the low bird's movements. I was not permitted to assume that Zero had him in sight also. As I glanced up from my notebook to look at where the low bird was circling at the rear of the building, a flash of light caught my eye, and a string of tracers erupted from the small window on the right side of the front door. Before I could step on the intercom button with my right foot, Cochran's yell almost tore my helmet off.

"Zero, you're taking fire."

"No shit, sports fan. Get clear; I'm in hot from the south."

I pushed the map down between my legs and partially under my butt and then elevated the gunsight for the turret, tearing the map in the process. The crosshairs glowed bright red in the gunsight as I put the point where the two lines crossed directly on the small window opening and squeezed the trigger. The minigun responded with a low pitched burring sound as Zero turned and dove toward the building. The sound of the minigun always made me think of what a bullfrog must sound like as it's being run over by a truck.

I could see the stream of tracers impacting all around the window and pieces of plaster and brick flying in all directions. Then a single *whoosh* erupted from beneath the stubby wings of the Cobra as two seventeen-pound rockets screamed away toward the building, one from each wing. One rocket impacted the wall next to the window, from which we were being shot at, but failed to penetrate. The other rocket disappeared through the window to the left of the door. This is really great, I thought to myself. Finally we were getting to shoot at targets we could see, instead of shooting at a colored smoke rising up through the trees.

My elation was interrupted by a huge explosion inside the building, and it looked like the roof came off in one section, rocketing straight up. Beneath the roof was an ominous black-and-red fireball. For a split second it looked like something out of a Saturday morning cartoon. Then reality set in, and I thought that my life had just ended. I didn't see any way that we were going to miss all the flying roof material that was now only seconds away from flying through the Plexiglas windshield in front of my face.

With my view blocked by flying, red roof tile, I felt my whole body being pushed down and back in the seat with unbelievable force as Zeroth pulled the Cobra into a near vertical climbing right turn. "Too late," I whispered to myself and closed my eyes. Then I felt and heard the terrifying sounds of debris impacting the bottom of the Cobra. A lump developed in my throat the size of a tennis ball.

"Holy shithouse mouse, that was close. Are you okay, Boyle?" Zero asked, having cleared the last of the flying roof.

"Yeah, I'm okay," I said. I opened my tightly closed eyes, "But I think my ass just sucked all the rivets out of the seat. And I was just beginning to think I might like this sort of thing."

We both had lost sight of our low bird and were very relieved when Cochran called and asked if we were okay.

"I think we're okay, but we got hit by a lot of crap flying up from that roof. So far I don't see any red lights on the panel, and it seems to be flying pretty normal. How about you guys; everything okay?" Zeroth asked.

"Yeah, we're fine. That building had to have been loaded with gas or some kind of fuel, the way it went up," Cochran said.

"What do you say we go back and check out the truck, then go back to Loc Ninh? I want to check the bottom of the aircraft," Zero said.

"Okay by me," Cochran said as he turned and headed back

down the road. In seconds, we heard Cochran exclaim, "It's gone; the damn truck isn't here!"

"Boyle, check the map and make sure we've come back far enough," Zero said.

"I'm sure that's the spot, boss."

"My torque says this is the spot. He's sure of it, but there's nothing here. Wait a minute, we've got something," Cochran said.

I watched as the low bird made two or three tight turns, and then Cochran's voice came back over the radio. "We've got a pith helmet down here, and tire tracks off the side of the road where it looks like the truck was turned around."

I was writing as fast as I could while keeping an eye on the low bird. "Okay, lets keep going back down the road. If he pulled off, you should be able to see where. If he kept going, I should pick him up when he clears the tree line where we first saw him," Zero advised.

As he moved back down the road, Cochran's low bird looked like a hunting dog trying to find a wounded pheasant. Without any spot reports being called up for me to write down, I had a chance to look at the map and record the map coordinates for the locations that Cochran had reported before, and of the building that no longer existed—and its occupant.

"I've got fresh tracks leading off to the north. I think the trail was here before, but I don't think it had any fresh tire marks on it," Cochran reported.

"Okay, let's give it a try. But be careful," Zero warned.

From my position, I could see that there were only about six hundred meters of trees before the area opened up again, and beyond that, the area had large clumps of trees separated by large open areas. Cochran continued his search until the tracks reached the edge of the tree line.

"The tracks head out toward that other tree line to the northwest," Cochran reported.

"Hold it there. I think we should go back to Loc Ninh, refuel, rearm, and check out the aircraft. Then we'll come back and see if we can run this guy down."

Zero always had a way of making orders sound like suggestions, and they always went over well. Cochran brought the low bird up alongside our Cobra, and we headed back toward Loc Ninh.

We landed at the south end of the runway, on the east side. The area was covered with huge, black fuel bladders and pallets loaded with crates of ammo and rockets. Zeroth had told Cochran to make sure his torque picked up a case of incendiary grenades so we could set the truck and its load of tires on fire when we found it again. I couldn't get over the amount of traffic that was going in and out of the small airstrip. C-130s and C-123s seemed to be taking off and landing every few minutes.

As soon as we had rearmed and refueled, we hovered up to the north end of the field, away from the runway and close to a stand of rubber trees. A temporary TOC manned by some of the TOC staff from Tay Ninh had been set up just inside the tree line. The Blue Platoon was scattered around the same area, some of them cleaning weapons while others tried to catch up on some sleep.

"Boyle, why don't you go over and advise the RTO (radio-telephone operator) what we saw and give him all your spot reports. Tell him we want to go back and see if we can find the truck as soon as I can check out the aircraft and get something to drink," Zeroth said.

"Okay, boss, but if you find something cold, save one for me."

Walking from the Cobra toward where I could see the RTO with a telephone held to his ear, I couldn't get over the near parklike setting of the place. I tried to imagine how it might have looked before all the different countries had made a battlefield and weapons' test-bed out of that part of Vietnam. Back inside the rubber trees to the east, I could see a small group of buildings that I guessed was the village of Loc Ninh. Two young boys who looked like brothers ran up to me, each grabbing a sleeve of my flight suit. They both had big smiles on their faces and were talking so fast that, had they been speaking English, I don't think I would have been able to understand what they were saying. I did get the idea that they wanted to get a closer look at the Cobra. The two stuck to me like glue until I approached the RTO, who made a number of gestures to the little boys that they were not welcome around the radio.

"Here's my spot reports. Mr. Zeroth wanted me to let you know that he wants to go back to the same area and see if we can hunt up that truck," I said.

"What truck was that, Boyle?" the lieutenant asked, still clutching the radio.

"Right there, Lieutenant—the fifth or sixth spot down on the page."

"Hold on," the lieutenant said, as he held the receiver away from his ear in an attempt to reduce the volume. He began to write as someone relayed information to him over the radio. "Okay, see what else you can find up there. Over," he said into the microphone.

I watched as the lieutenant wrote down map coordinates on a piece of paper and then looked at the spot reports that I had given him.

"Hey, Boyle, look at this. One of the lift ships just reported that his two door gunners, Piper and Docktor, just nailed two NVA riding bikes up that same road where you just came from—at least the numbers are very close," the lieutenant said, picking up a large map pinned to a board.

"Looks close to me. I'll tell Zero," I said as I headed back toward the Cobra.

"How's it look?" I asked as Zero came out from under the tail boom.

"All I can find is a couple of dents in the tail boom, and I don't think they'll cause us any trouble," he said.

I told Zero what the lieutenant had told me of his conversation with the lift pilot who was flying high cover in a Huey.

"Okay, lets get the hell out of here and see what's so important about that area anyway," Zero said as he climbed into the back seat of the Cobra.

I closed the ammo-bay door that he had used as a step, and went around to the left front and climbed in. "Where's our low bird?" I asked.

"He went down to the other end of the field to see if he could hunt up some extra incendiary grenades in case we've got to set some tires on fire," Zero responded.

While we were still going through the start process, Cochran hovered up and gave us a thumbs-up. Cochran's torque was removing grenades from their heavy, waterproof-cardboard containers. The flat red paint indicated that they were incendiaries.

The trip back to the area where the road left the trees and crossed the open area didn't take as long as I thought it would. Things were beginning to look familiar now instead of strange and forbidding as they did on the first flight.

"Stay up here with me until we get over that next group of trees up ahead," Zero called to Cochran, who was flying directly to my left, about two hundred feet away.

The tracks of what we guessed to be the truck were visible in the waist-high grass a thousand feet below us. They headed directly toward the next island of trees in a huge plain of tall grass.

"Let's make a high recon and see if we can pick out anything," Zero suggested.

"Did you hear Williams report the two KBHs (killed by helicopter) on bikes?" Cochran asked Zero.

"No, but my front seat told me, so we know we can probably expect to find more people in this area. Keep your speed up and don't hang your ass out," Zero advised.

As we approached the stand of trees, I noticed it was in the shape of a big donut with something dark in the center.

"Are you seeing what I am?" I asked Zero.

"Yeah, but I'm not sure what the hell it is."

Zero called Cochran, who indicated that he had also been looking at the same thing.

"I am going to go down and check this place out if that's okay with you?" Cochran asked.

"Okay, but play it cool. We know we have people around here, and they know we're looking for them," Zero said.

Once again I watched as the little Hughes Loach went into its tight descending right-hand turns and then straightened out only a few feet off the top of the trees. Cochran headed straight for the open area at the center of the stand of trees and passed it at over a hundred miles an hour.

"Holy Shit!" Cochran exclaimed as the low bird went into a tight right-hand turn and headed back toward the open circle in the trees.

"What'ya got down there?" Zero asked.

"There are tires everywhere, stacks and stacks of tires. I'm going back for a closer look. No telling what may be under the trees with all those tires out in the open," Cochran said.

Once again the red light appeared on the instrument panel in front of me, and I knew Zero had armed our massive weapons system.

"Have you got the low bird?" I asked Zero.

"Yeah, I got him."

"Okay, I'm going to be on the map for a minute," I said.

There were no roads indicated on the map, and I was having a hell of a time finding exactly where we were, but I knew it was going to be very important to be able to pinpoint this spot when we reported back to the RTO at Loc Ninh.

"We've found our truck again, and about ten bikes stacked against a tree down here," Cochran reported.

"That's great, just tell your torque that I don't want that truck to ever move again, whatever it takes."

"I think he got the message!" was Cochran's laughing reply.

"Have you found us on the map yet?" Zero asked me.

"Not yet."

"Okay, you take the low bird and the controls and hand me the map, I have a feeling this is going to be an important spot," Zero said.

I had only flown the Cobra from the front seat a few times, and it was a real sensitive procedure until you had become accustomed to the controls. Because of the very limited amount of room in the front seat, and the fact that the gunsight was between your legs where the cyclic control usually was, the two controls, cyclic and collective, had to be made smaller and located in a different position than where they usually are in a helicopter. The cyclic control was a pistol grip and controlled by my right hand, with my forearm resting on a small arm pad. The collective control was much the same as a bicycle-handle grip, and controlled by movement of the left hand and wrist. Because there was little movement available in these two controls, the movement ratio was three to one to that of the controls in the backseat. All I had to do was think about what I wanted the Cobra to do, and it happened. The pitching and rolling of the Cobra immediately told Zeroth that I had the controls. In what seemed like less than a minute, Zero handed the map back to me with the spot circled in black grease pencil, and took control of the pitching-and-rolling Cobra.

"We're going to be doing some burning down here," Cochran advised.

"Any sign of people?" Zero asked.

"Lots of tracks, but nothing moving and no sign of bunkers," was Cochran's reply.

Up through the top of the trees came a column of black smoke. Just a little at first, and then it became more intense.

"We've got the truck burning and the tires that were still in the back of it, and we messed up the bikes pretty good," Cochran reported.

"Check out the inside edge of the tree line around all those tires, and if it's clear, put the torch to the big pile," Zero advised.

I watched as the low bird circled the huge cache of tires,

throwing incendiary grenades, one after the other, with little effect.

"Any chance of calling in an air strike on this place? We're having a hell of a time trying to get these things to light off," Cochran said.

"I don't know, but I'll give it a try," Zero said.

It took over an hour to get a reply to Zeroth's request for an air strike. Whoever was doing the talking was very sorry, but everything was tied up on more important targets, but they would see what they could do for us in a couple of days. Cochran didn't sound real happy after Zero passed on the fact that we were on our own.

"Well, I'm about out of stuff to start fires with. What do you say we break for fuel, get something to eat, and I'll see what my torque can scrounge up to really start a big fire with?" Cochran suggested.

We landed back at Loc Ninh amidst an ever-increasing flurry of activity. We had never had to wait in line to get fuel before, but today we had to wait in line for everything, even to land. By the time we hovered up to our spot next to the rubber plantation and shut down the engine, over an hour had passed. I had called in my spot reports to the RTO while we were waiting for fuel, which eliminated the need for me to hand carry them over to the lieutenant who was still sitting under the same rubber tree as when I had last seen him. Zeroth took off in search of something cold to drink, and I stayed to check the oil levels on our aircraft. The skin of the Cobra was hot to the touch; the area inside the engine compartment was red hot, and I was sweating like a kamikaze pilot at an American Legion convention.

"Hey, GI!" came the voice of a child from behind me. When I turned around, I thought I was dreaming. There staring up at me were my two little Vietnamese friends holding a cardboard box filled with ice and Cokes. The Coke bottles were the old-fashioned kind that I hadn't seen since I was a kid.

"You want to buy?" I'm sure they knew by the large smile on my face that they had already made a sale.

"Let's get out of the sun," I said, and walked toward the shade of the closest rubber tree. I don't know if they really understood or not, but they were quick to follow. I motioned for them to sit down and wait for me, then I walked over to open cases of C rations.

"Hey, Mr. Boyle, who are your new buddies?" one of the Blues asked. His voice indicated a certain disapproval.

"Just selling Cokes, that's all," I said.

"Well, if you don't die from being poisoned by those two little VC, I might just buy one."

"Yeah, right," I said with a laugh. But the look on the faces of some of the other guys sitting around, including officers, indicated that they were serious. I understood their mistrust. Hell, they had to come face to face with the VC and NVA. Hopefully, I would never have to. In this war of few uniforms, where the enemy looked exactly the same as the people we were there to protect, mistrust came first.

I picked up three boxes of C rats and walked back to where my newfound little friends were sitting, and opened one of the boxes. It was lima beans and ham, and although I loved lima beans and ham, you damn near had to be starving to eat the army's version cold. As I was opening the can, Cochran walked by, did a double take, and said "You're not really going to eat that crap are you?"

"Sure am, but it would taste a lot better hot."

"Hold on a second, I'll show the FNG a little trick," Cochran said, as he turned and walked back to his low bird. He returned in a minute and produced a small piece of C-4 plastic explosive.

"Here, take this and roll it into a small ball. Then scoop out a small hole in the ground, put the C-4 in the hole, and light it. It won't explode unless you step on it, but it will really heat up that can of crap you intend to eat. Just leave part of the lid attached, so you have something to hang onto the can with."

"Thanks for the help. I'll give it a try," I said as he walked away shaking his head.

Everything went just as instructed, and I enjoyed watching the boys pass the can back and forth as I drank one of their ice-cold Cokes. I opened a second box and took out the main-meal can, this time beans and franks. There was only one person I knew who went out of his way to eat that stuff, and that was Rosey. Given the chance, he would eat beans and franks morning, noon and night. The two little boys apparently shared Rosey's taste. The second can disappeared in a flash, along with the crackers, fruit salad, and candy.

When Zeroth indicated it was time to hit the road again, with numerous hand signals the boys told me that they would like to take the third, unopened, box home with them. I told them no and tried to indicate that they could only eat the food there with me. I didn't want to take any chances on the stuff's falling into the wrong hands. Some of the stern faces around me weren't very happy with the company I was keeping, and they especially disliked my feeding the two young boys. I hoped that the boys had understood as I gathered up the leftovers and headed back to Zeroth's Cobra. Walking past the low bird, I stopped and asked the torque if he had acquired anything that might set the tires on fire.

"No problem, sir," he said as he lifted a small tarp exposing a five-gallon gas can with a pound of C-4 plastic explosive taped to it.

"I didn't see anything," I said, and continued toward the running Cobra.

Scout torques took great pride in building superweapons even though there were orders against it. Usually those weapons were made from the discarded aluminum canisters that aerial flares were shipped in. They were packed with C-4, glass, nails, rocks, and anything else that might piss off the enemy if he happened to be too close when it went off. The only thing that went off with a bigger boom was Captain Funk if he caught you with one of the secret weapons.

Two hours before sunset, we headed back toward Tay Ninh, after refueling at Loc Ninh. Behind us we could see the huge column of black smoke rising thousands of feet into the air, a tribute to the ingenuity of the Scout torques. We had spent another fuel load looking for targets after the tires had finally been ignited but had found nothing. It had been a very long day, and everyone was tired but happy. Nobody had been killed or injured, and no one had been shot down.

The mood in the troop area that night was as if we had just won a football game. Everyone had different stories to tell; everyone had found something different to shoot at. No two stories were alike, and each one thought his was the best. The mess hall that night had a constant buzz about it, with an almost partylike atmosphere. After mess came the evening briefing about what could be expected the next day. The CO, Captain Funk, seemed pleased with the way things had gone, and indicated that we would continue the same way tomorrow, with the exception that we would not have to cross the border at first light. We weren't going to surprise the NVA and VC the second day, so we went back to the normal first-light takeoffs from Tay Ninh.

John Williams, who flew Hueys for the lift platoon, was standing in the back of the room as the briefing came to an end. A captain, who John did not recognize, walked up and introduced himself. "Hi, I'm Ken Benton, you're John Williams, right?"

"Yeah, that's right, Captain. What can I do for you?"

"Your CO, Captain Funk, said it would be okay if I asked you if I could ride along tomorrow." The expression on William's face must have conveyed the question that was in his thoughts.

"I'm the division public information officer," the captain continued. "I'd really like to ride along with you and get some idea of what's going on."

"If the CO said it was okay, it's okay by me. Be out at the flight line just before first light and climb aboard," Williams said.

John Williams had spent the entire day just getting back to Apache Troop from Long Binh. He had arrived early in the morning at Long Binh after a long-anticipated R & R. Five days of sun and fun and no getting shot at. When he called Tay Ninh requesting a ride back to the troop, he was told that the shit had hit the fan while he was gone and that he would have to find his own way back.

"Hell, it's only a hundred miles through enemy-held jungle, I think I'll just walk," he told the spec four on the other end of the line, and hung up the phone. I should just hitch a ride to Sydney, he thought to himself as he walked toward the flight line in hopes of finding a ride back to Tay Ninh. Two cargo flights and ten hours later, John Williams arrived back at Tay Ninh, just in time to attend the evening briefing and get his assignment for the next day. Everyone he spoke to had red eyes, as most of the pilots and crews had been up for the better part of the last twenty-four hours. Like everyone before him, he had returned from R & R more tired than when he had left, so he headed for his room in hopes of a rocket-free night of sleep.

CHAPTER THIRTEEN

The morning of 2 May, 1970 began for me not much different from any other morning. As usual, I had gone back to sleep after the sergeant from the TOC had waked me up. The responsibility for making sure I was up usually fell upon Carl Rosapepe (Rosey). After damn near breaking down the door of my room with his knocking, Rosey had managed to wake me up. He waited, sitting on a box that I used for a chair, as I laced up my flight boots.

"Who are you flying with today, Rosey?" I managed to ask though still half-asleep.

"I'll be with Peele," he said.

"That's great, he won't eat your ass out like Coons does. What do you say we get out of this sweatbox and go get some of that great army coffee," I said with a laugh as I stood up and followed Rosey out the door.

The humidity outside couldn't have been any higher without it raining. By the time we reached the mess hall, my flight suit was already soaked. People from all over the troop area were headed toward the mess hall, like zombies from a science-fiction movie.

As Rosey and I walked through the door, the bright lights made my eyes hurt, and I wondered how the guys who had gotten drunk the night before must feel. It was impossible to tell who was hung over and who wasn't. When I looked around, I got the impression that everyone was hung over. I can't recall ever seeing so many bloodshot eyes in one place before. My only thought was that at least I'm not the only one who's tired. I got a cup of coffee and some of the worst army bread anyone was ever forced to eat, and went over and sat down across from Lieutenant Brewer, the Scout Platoon leader. John Williams was just getting up from the table.

"Where you headed for so early, Williams?" I asked.

"The Old Man wants me to haul a load of ammo and grenades up to the Blues at Loc Ninh, and I want to check out the load."

"Are you going to take that PIO with you today?" I asked.

"Yeah, I guess so. He seems to have his act together, and he assured me that the damn CAR-15 he insists on carrying has been worked over so it won't jam."

In addition to having a Huey full of ammo, that was to be dropped off at Loc Ninh, Williams had been made a part of a Purple Team for at least the first part of the day. A Purple Team consisted of a low bird, a Cobra, and a Huey flying above them. The Pink Team that was going to be flying under Williams today included Lieutenant Brewer in the low bird and Lieutenant Coons in the Cobra, both platoon leaders of their respective platoons. Normally, Purple Teams were only used when there was reason to suspect that the danger to the Pink Team was greater than normal. Because the NVA now knew what we were up to, it was decided to put everything we had in the air, just in case they were waiting for us today. There wasn't much doubt in anyone's mind that we were not going to catch them by sitting around as we had the day before.

Williams, although he wished that his R & R could have lasted another week, was excited about today's flight. It was going to be his first trip into Cambodia. In the short period of time he had between returning from R & R the night before and getting some much-needed sleep, he had been filled to the brim with war stories. Now it was going to be his turn to see, firsthand, what all the shouting was about. Also, in the back of his mind, he knew that he had only ninety days left in this sweatbox of a country. Eighty-nine days and a wake-up, he thought to himself.

"Come on, Mr. Williams, let's get this thing into the air so I can cool off!" Morris Piper yelled from the rear of the Huey.

Piper and Art Docktor were the two door gunners, and Lt. Karle Mahler was assigned as Williams's copilot.

"Eat my shorts, Piper!" Williams yelled, "We've got to wait for Captain Benton."

"Are we going to have to get out and come to attention and salute and all that real army crap?" Art Docktor asked.

"Hey, you guys, cool it. This guy seems all right."

Within minutes, Captain Benton, the 1st Cav Division public information officer, arrived and climbed aboard the already running Huey.

"Just find a place to sit and make yourself comfortable, sir," Williams told the young captain over the intercom.

"Apache Three Eight, this is Red, are you ready to go?"

Apache Three Eight was John Williams's aircraft commander number.

"Yeah, Red, we're loaded and ready to go," Williams replied.

"Okay, great, just follow us out. You know where we're going, right?" Red asked.

"Yeah, I've got a solid on the location," Williams responded.

Finally, Piper thought, as he felt the air hitting his face. By then the sweat was pouring out of his helmet.

The Huey gained airspeed and altitude and headed northeast toward the Cambodian border. Williams had been told to stick with Red until the Pink Team decided to break for fuel. He was then to deliver all the ammo and grenades he was carrying to the Blues at Loc Ninh.

Nobody really knew what to expect, on this second day into Cambodia, as the three-ship team approached the border. S. Sgt. George Slye, cradled the M-60 machine gun in his arms as he scanned the jungle below from his position in the rear of Lieutenant Brewer's low bird. He and Frank Corona, who was sitting in the left front seat as the observer, had flown the same general area the day before.

"I don't think they'll be out smoking and joking today," Slye said to Brewer over the intercom.

"No, I don't think so either," Brewer said to the career soldier whom he put so much trust in.

Slye had made staff sergeant (E-6) in January and still had five years to go on the present hitch. The army was his home and way of life, and all the Vietnam crap was just part of his job.

Ten minutes after crossing the border north of Loc Ninh, Williams watched from his position above Red's Cobra as Brewer's low bird let down over the jungle and began his searching. An hour and a half went by with nothing but the usual conversation between the low bird and the Cobra, with a few spot reports thrown in about trails showing light recent use. Art Docktor's thoughts were on going home in two months, to Fargo, North Dakota, where it actually got cold in the winter.

"Hey, Piper, what do you think?" Doc asked, forgetting that Piper couldn't read his thoughts.

"What do I think about what, you dumb shit! Are you sitting over there daydreaming again?" Piper asked with a deep southern accent. He was trying to ignore one hell of a hangover.

"About snow; if we could get a couple of days of snow over here, we could win this damn war without ever firing a shot. Those little rice-eating, slant-eyed bastards would find their balls frozen and dropping off after the first day."

"Don't hold your breath, soldier," Captain Benton said over the intercom.

"Well, we can always dream, Captain," Art Docktor shot back as Piper held his helmet with both hands and shook his head.

Daydreams and thoughts of home were quickly erased when Brewer reported, "I've got a trail running alongside this stream that shows a lot of recent heavy use."

"Okay, just watch your ass down there," Red advised.

Williams could almost make out the trail from where he was. It was following the course of the stream through low grass that didn't provide much cover, for either the enemy or the low bird. From where Williams was, he could see that up ahead the trail entered an area covered with bamboo, then opened up again. Beyond that started thick jungle. Williams watched Brewer's low bird follow the trail as it entered the bamboo, and then noticed that Brewer appeared to be circling the same spot.

"Hey, Red, it looks like the trail keeps going the same way as the stream, but I've got a spot here where it looks like a lot of traffic turned off the trail and headed west through the bamboo. It's real hard to make out the trail, but maybe somebody decided to stash something and come back for it later. I'm going to head west from where I am now and see if I can come up with something."

"Okay, but just watch your butt; that bamboo doesn't give you a lot of cover, and you've got to fly too slow to really see into it," Red said.

Williams watched as the low bird started down the center of the football-field-size grove of bamboo.

"Taking fire, Taking fiiii—," Brewer called from the circling low bird, his last words interrupted in midsentence.

Williams watched in horror as Brewer's low bird rolled violently to its right and tore into the bamboo, the rotor blades sending pieces of bamboo flying into the air like rockets, along with chunks of helicopter and rotor blades. The low bird righted itself before slamming into the ground, in a level, skid-down attitude. Not more than a few seconds later, the low bird exploded in a huge black-and-red ball of flames, which completely engulfed the entire aircraft.

"Apache, Red! Scramble, scramble, scramble. My low bird's down and burning!" Williams heard Red call to the radio operator at Loc Ninh.

"Roger that, Red. The Blues have been scrambled," replied the radio from Loc Ninh.

Williams banked his Huey sharply to the right and started a steep descent to treetop level, and then headed straight toward the thick column of black smoke and flames boiling out of the bamboo. Everyone on board knew that it would take a miracle for anyone to survive a crash such as the one they had just witnessed. All eyes were glued to the crash scene as the Huey passed over. It looked hopeless. Then Art Docktor yelled over the intercom, "I saw Slye; he's outside the low bird, and he's got his M-60. I think he's alive!"

At the same time, everyone on board the Huey heard the unmistakable sounds of bullets impacting the aircraft. Williams banked the Huey hard left, away from the crash scene, and half turning in his seat, glancing over his right shoulder asked, "Is everyone okay back there?"

"Yeah, we're okay, but what about Slye?" Captain Benton asked.

"We're going to go get him. Now listen up, the only place I can put this thing down is about twenty yards from the low bird, at the edge of the bamboo. We'll try to get to Slye first, and then check out the low bird. Mahler will stay with the bird, and keep it running. Take as much ammo as you can run with. Everyone got the picture?" Williams asked.

Everyone indicated that they understood, and started grabbing extra ammo.

Dead leaves and grass blew skyward as Williams landed the Huey in the low grass alongside the trail that Brewer had been following prior to entering the bamboo.

Piper and Doctor were first off the helicopter, followed by

Captain Benton and then Williams. Captain Benton took up a kneeling position at the nose of the Huey and began firing at four NVA who were running along the other side of the stream. The four Americans had only moved a few yards toward the low bird when the unmistakable sounds of AK-47s forced them down into the tall grass. Doc rose to his knees and laid down a heavy stream of fire on some of the muzzle flashes he could see at the edge of the bamboo. NVA, some only partially dressed, began running in every direction.

It was obvious that the discovery and assault upon their encampment had come as a complete surprise. The return fire stopped, and Williams said, "Let's go," at the same time jumping to his feet and running forward. Williams felt just a slight bit naked as he had given Lieutenant Mahler his pistol before jumping off the aircraft, but the other three members of his crew were putting out a lot of fire.

Once inside the bamboo they saw what Lieutenant Brewer had stumbled upon. There were tables, chairs, pots filled with steaming rice hanging above small fires. Food, still warm, on the tables, clothes hanging on lines drying, and weapons and ammo everywhere, plus lots of NVA firing at them. The constant chatter of the AK-47s was only broken by the sound of Doc's M-60 and the CAR-15 of Captain Benton. Piper was firing his M-16 on full automatic and going through ammo fast.

"Doc, we're going to need more ammo. I'll go back to the ship and bring back as much as I can carry. I'll try and bring some of those grenades we were hauling to the Blues."

Staying as low as he could possibly get and still run, Williams headed back toward the Huey. As Williams jumped into the back of the Huey, a very wide-eyed Lieutenant Mahler asked, "How's it going?"

"Oh, not too bad. We're just going to need a lot more ammo. See if you can get the Cobra to put down some cover fire for us. Tell them it really doesn't matter where, NVA are everywhere down here."

Within minutes—of course it seemed like hours—Williams returned with a lot of ammo and grenades. Again they rose and laid down a heavy stream of fire. One stubborn NVA, directly in front of the foursome, was holding up their advance forward. Doc would fire, and the NVA would fire. Back and forth it went until Williams couldn't stand it any more. Williams took one of the newly issued baseball-type grenades, pulled the pin, and tossed it. It seemed like years passed and nothing happened.

"Did you remember to pull the pin?" Piper asked.

"What do ya'll think that looks like?" Williams said, holding up a finger that still had the small ring and pin attached.

"No, the other pin on the handle!" Piper exclaimed, holding up a similar grenade to show Williams that the newer grenades had two pins.

"No, I didn't!" Williams said.

When the NVA soldier rose to fire again, Piper tossed his grenade; so did everyone else. Doc and Williams stuck together and tried to move in the straightest possible line toward where they thought Sergeant Slye was lying. As they passed the bunker containing the dead NVA who had held them up for so long, they noticed that in his hand he held the unexploded grenade that Williams had thrown. Apparently he was intending on throwing it back when he died.

Piper and Benton did what they could to provide covering fire. As best they could tell, the NVA were moving out of the area to the west along a trail very visible from ground level but invisible from the air. Benton and Piper were taking fire from five or six different locations. It became obvious that the NVA had left behind a few people whose duty it was to make life as miserable as possible for the crew of Williams's Huey.

"Watch out!" Doc yelled as he fired, almost cutting in half the NVA soldier rising out of the bunker directly in front of them.

"Doc, I think I see Slye," Williams said, pointing to an open area at the edge of the grove of bamboo.

Half crawling and half running, the two made their way to Sergeant Slye, and took up prone positions on each side of him. He was just as Doc had seen him from the air, appearing to be in a prone firing position, with his M-60 in front of him.

"Doc, he's dead!" Williams said in a tone close to a whisper.

Williams and Doc had friends who had been killed, but watching your friends die and the deep hurt that goes with it is something you just don't get used to.

"Lets try and get to the low bird," Williams said in a low voice.

They crawled back into the bamboo, not really knowing what to expect. Every movement produced noise as they made their way carefully toward what was left of the burning low bird. All Doc had on his mind was the hope that they would find that one or both of the guys had managed to get out of the aircraft alive. Then Piper and Captain Benton ran up, firing, before throwing themselves to the ground alongside Williams. A long burst of AK-47 fire cut into the bamboo inches above their heads as another NVA soldier fired from behind a stack of wooden crates, and then turned to run. He took only two steps before being hit by a massive number of bullets. Williams and Piper were the first to crawl forward into position where they could see what was left of the cockpit of the downed low bird. What they saw would make the strongest of men weak at the knees. Lieutenant Brewer and Spec Four Corona were still strapped into the aircraft, burned beyond recognition.

Doc and Benton crawled up as close as the heat from the still-burning helicopter would allow and started throwing dirt on the flames. Williams and Piper joined in until rockets from one of the Cobras started impacting one hundred meters in front of the wrecked low bird.

"Anybody got a smoke grenade?" Williams asked.

"Yeah, I've got a couple," Doc replied.

"Toss me one, quick!" Williams yelled. He rose from his prone position and pulled the pin from the smoke grenade. Running hunched over, Williams stopped and threw the grenade as far as he could. At least now, they'll know where we are for sure he thought to himself, turning to rejoin the others. There was no time to react as the rockets from a Cobra screamed over his head, impacting just beyond where the smoke grenade was disgorging a stream of green smoke. As he dove for cover, Williams felt a sharp pain in his back when a piece of red-hot steel cut through his flight suit and lodged between his shoulder blades.

"Son of a bitch!" Piper yelled as he rolled over on the damp ground, holding his left arm, blood flowing out between his fingers.

Art Doctor crawled over to where Piper was lying. "How bad is it?"

"Ah shit! It ain't that bad, Doc, but it hurts like hell."

"Okay, see if you can find something to wrap around your arm that will put some pressure on it. I'm going to check on Williams," Doc said.

Captain Benton had already reached Williams and was looking at his back when Doc crawled up alongside him.

"He's going to be okay," Benton said. "I think it's just a

flesh wound. I can see a little piece of the metal fragment sticking out of the skin, but I think we should get to a first-aid kit."

"We've got one in the aircraft, sir," Piper said as he rejoined the group.

"What about you, Piper. Are you okay?" Benton asked.

"I'm okay, sir. I don't think they'll be sending me home early because of it."

"Let's get the hell away from here!" Benton yelled as a Cobra's minigun chewed up the bamboo a safe distance away from the foursome.

"Lets get back to the aircraft and check with Mahler. I'll bet he's been shitting his pants having to just sit there and wait," Williams said.

A low bird flew over the foursome and made a tight circle over them as they made their way back to where the wide-eyed Lieutenant Mahler sat at the controls of the Huey. Looking up at the low bird, Williams recognized Mike Reardon as the pilot, and pointed in the direction that they had seen the NVA moving. Mahler had hoped all along that somehow the low-bird crew had managed to escape the inferno, but the looks on the faces of his fellow crew members told him that was not to be the case.

As Williams approached the Huey, Mahler opened his door and leaned out, cupping his hands around his mouth.

"The Blues will be here any second now. What do you want me to do?"

"Just hang in there, Karle. We're not going anyplace just yet."

"Yeah, but the TOC and Red have been yelling at me to get this damn helicopter off the ground, and I told them that I wasn't going anywhere until you guys were back on board."

"Good for you, Mahler. We may have pissed some people off, but we can deal with that later. Right now we have more important things to deal with. If they call back, just stall, but tell Reardon and his high bird, that Brewer and his crew are all line ones so if he sees anything moving, he should shoot it." (Listing someone as a line one indicated that the person was dead, line two indicated that he was wounded.)

Bill McIntosh, better known to his fellow pilots as Mini Mack, was seated in the right seat (copilot) next to Ron Black who was piloting the lead lift ship, of the three-Huey formation full of Blues. Neither of the pilots saw the NVA soldier rise from his bunker at the edge of the tree line and put a full clip of AK-47 bullets into the side and bottom of the Huey as they approached the right rear of Williams's parked Huey, but the master caution light and hydraulics warning lights came on and got their immediate attention as the controls became extremely stiff and hard to move.

"Holy shit! Get on the controls with me, Mack," Black said as he struggled to control the large helicopter.

Mack was thankful that they were only ten feet off the ground, and they wasted no time putting the Huey into the tall grass, with something less than a school-book landing.

"Hey, Ron, didn't we get out of flying Scouts so we wouldn't get all shot up any more?"

"Yeah, I thought it was supposed to be safe in the lift platoon."

"Bart, we just took a bunch of hits from the tree line to our right," Mack called to Bloody Bart in the Cobra covering the insertion of the Blues.

Within seconds, the tree line erupted with explosions as Bartlett's rockets impacted the ground, kicking up billowing clouds of debris. As he sat in the rear open door of his still-idling helicopter, John Williams watched while the other two Hueys landed and disgorged their troops and then departed.

Mahler leaned over the pilot seat and yelled at Williams who was, by then, having Piper pull the small piece of steel out of his back.

"The TOC wants to know if we need a QRF?" (quick-reaction force, usually a company-size strength.)

"Tell them to ask Blue (Lt. Jack Hugele). He's in command now," Williams yelled back.

Mahler was trying to decide whether to shit or wind his watch as he watched, with amazement, as Williams, Doc, Piper, and Benton, loaded down with ammo, ran over to Lieutenant Hugele and joined up with the rest of the Blues. Piper and Doc led the way for the Blues, along with Jorgenson and Cortez, as they headed toward the downed low bird. Once there, Lieutenant Hugele sent some of the Blues to set up a perimeter around the downed aircraft. The rest of the platoon set upon the grisly task of recovering and placing in rubber body bags the remains of the crew.

Nerves were rubbed raw, and the sound, in the distance, of Reardon's torque firing his M-60 from the back of the low bird made everyone more anxious.

Again, the unmistakable sound of an AK-47 close to the western perimeter sent everyone diving for cover. One of the Blues, out of breath, crawled up alongside Blue.

"We've got gooks in bunkers on both sides of the trail about one hundred meters out, sir."

"Okay, have you got a yellow smoke?" Blue asked.

"Yeah, Blue."

"Okay, get back up there and pop a yellow smoke. I'll advise the Cobras to fire two hundred meters west of the smoke, and for God's sake, keep your heads down. I don't want you to move any further up the trail than you are right now."

Blue picked up the radio mike and advised Bill Fuller, Apache Two Four, that the Blues were in contact and that his point man was going to pop smoke. He further requested that Fuller contact the TOC and advise them that he wanted the QRF, ASAP.

Blue was amazed at the amount of equipment hidden under the cover of the bamboo, and he knew it was going to take a bigger force than his platoon to secure the area and, if need be, root the NVA out of their well-concealed bunkers.

"I've got yellow smoke," Fuller said from his vantage point a thousand feet above the blues.

"That's a roger on the yellow smoke, Two Four. We've got gooks in bunkers on each side of the trail, two hundred meters, two-seven-zero degrees from the smoke," Blue said.

Blue knew his job, and so did the rest of his men. They were to secure the downed aircraft and remove the bodies; they were not to engage an obviously larger enemy force unless it became necessary. The crew of the downed low bird were placed in body bags and loaded on Williams's Huey. Because of the condition of the low bird it was decided not to recover it, but to use the sling gear to get Black's Huey slung out.

"How come we didn't take a ride out of here on one of the other lift ships?" Mack asked Black as they helped the other two crew members remove the M-60s from the wounded Huey.

"What do I look like, an RLO (real live officer) or something? How the hell do I know?"

"You dumb shit, you're the aircraft commander, aren't you? You're supposed to take command of the situation," Mac retorted with a laugh.

"In case you haven't noticed, shit-for-brains, we don't have an aircraft to command any more. You got it all shot full of holes!"

"What are you talking about? I didn't do anything. *You* were the one flying this piece of shit."

"All the damn fire came from *your* side of the aircraft, didn't it? You didn't see my side getting punched full of holes."

Ron Black had just gotten in the last word as another burst of AK fire from the western tree line brought the two young pilots back to reality. Mini Mack picked up one of the M-60 machine guns and started toward the tree line where he had last seen the Blues.

"Where in the hell are you going?" Black asked.

"Hell, with you in command the only damn way I'll get back to Tay Ninh is to walk. You're welcome to come along if you'd like, or do you plan on waiting here like a good captain, waiting for your ship to sink?"

The four crew members set up a defensive position at the edge of the tree line and waited for whatever was going to happen next and watched the three body bags loaded on John Williams's Huey. A short time later, three Blues made their way along the tree line to where Black and his crew were kneeling. One of the Blues was suffering from heatstroke, and Black was told that a medevac helicopter would be arriving within a few minutes.

"Hey, Mr. Black, Lieutenant Coons wants you to fly your bird out of here to a more secure area," one of the Blues advised.

"You've got to be shitting me; I'm not going to fly that piece of Swiss cheese anywhere, and you can tell Red that."

"Okay, sir, I'll have Blue pass it along when I get back to him. Will you look after our guy until the medevac arrives?"

"Sure, no problem. We'll take good care of him."

Within minutes, the medevac set down where Mack had tossed a smoke grenade to mark their location. Black and Mack carried and half dragged the stricken Blue out to the medevac and loaded him aboard. Then they turned and sprinted back to the cover of the tree line while their other two crew members covered them and the departure of the medevac Huey with M-60 fire.

A Chinook helicopter was called in to lift Black's Huey out, but on approach, it, too, received fire, so Mini Mack opened up on the NVA position with his M-60 and covered the huge helicopter until the Huey was safely slung out. At that point, everything was put on hold until the QRF arrived, except for Williams being ordered to return to Tay Ninh to get treatment for himself and Piper and return the bodies of the low bird crew. The Blues were extracted two hours later, along with Mack and Black and their crew, leaving the area in the custody of a full company of troops.

The mess hall that evening could have passed for a morgue. Few people were talking, and even fewer were eating; the loss of the low bird brought Apache Troop its first deaths since December 1969. For the newer members of the troop, myself included, it was a great shock as well as a great loss. I found it extremely difficult to accept the fact that the pilot I had eaten breakfast with and spoken with just that morning would never be around again. I went back to my room, and as hard as I tried, I could not get the memory of Lieutenant Brewer's face out of my mind. Until then, the war had been a very scary game played with guns, rockets, and bullets. Now, without warning, it had turned into a very deadly, serious business. For the first time, I think I finally understood what Red, Lieutenant Coons, was trying to beat into us new guys.

I sat down at my makeshift desk and wrote Sonny and Dusty a letter, telling them what had happened. I thought that it might make me feel better, but it didn't. I ended up going back to the mess hall and drinking coffee, just to be around someone, until the place closed down and the cooks ran me off. Two days later, May 4, a memorial service was held in the evening. Colonel Burnett, the squadron commander, whom I'd never seen before, was there with Captain Funk and Captain Voelker the squadron chaplain.

As each of us entered the room, we were handed a piece of paper, folded in half, with a picture of the tomb of the unknown soldier on the front and the names of those who had been killed on the inside. On a long table at the front of the room were three sets of black boots and three flight helmets. The chaplain gave a very nice talk about people he probably had never met, speaking of them as if he had met them every day. I wondered how many times a week he had to give the exact same speech about other soldiers. Then I became angry when I noticed that someone had spelled Frank Corona's name wrong on the paper we were all handed. I wanted very much to stand up and yell, "If you knew these guys so well, why the hell couldn't you spell their names right!" Instead, I just sat there as everyone else did, just wanting it to end; we all wanted to mourn in our own way.

Later, small groups of men formed at different places around the company area. Some just to talk, some to drink, and I suspect, some to continue to mourn. Everyone was saddened by the loss of Brewer, Corona, and Slye. I wanted to cry, but nobody else was. I wanted to rip the head off the stupid son of a bitch who misspelled Corona's name, but nobody said anything. I wanted to ask why someone who really knew the crew wasn't up there speaking about them. Inside I was crying and yelling, but nothing was being said aloud.

Sometime during the night, during one of the thousand times I saw Brewer's face and remembered how we had sat and talked just before his last flight, I finally figured out why nobody had said anything or showed much emotion. Most of them had already gone through this before, and they knew how to let go. They had learned how not to dwell on something that could never be undone. I understood that they also knew that, for us new guys, it wouldn't be the last time we spent an evening filled with sorrow, missing someone we had become close to or hardly even knew.

Despite our feelings of loss, we knew that life would go on, but what us new guys had really not yet fully understood, was that the dying would also go on.

I finally fell asleep wondering why, after spending two million dollars training us to be helicopter pilots, the army hadn't even mentioned how to cope with the loss of friends and a fellow pilot. I wanted so very much to ask someone if he felt the same way I did, but I was afraid of the reaction I might receive. I decided that if everyone else was going to clam up, then I guess I'd better do the same.

CHAPTER FOURTEEN

Things were really heating up, not just for Apache Troop, but for all the other units operating within Cambodia. The NVA weren't about to sit back and let all the supplies that they had worked so hard to get down from the North fall into the hands of the enemy. During the next five days, they managed to down two more of our low birds but without doing any serious injury to the crews. Rumors started floating around the troop about our moving out of Tay Ninh to a place called Song Be (pronounced Song Bay) where a fire support base called Buttons was located. Our AO (area of operation) had moved to the northeast, so flying back to Tay Ninh every night was very time consuming.

I flew with Bill Fuller for the next few days. He had arrived in country only a few days after Lieutenant Coons, back in September 1969, and I quickly learned that the very quiet cowboy from Wyoming really knew how to fly and teach. He was always very friendly, but in a very professional way, and he never seemed to become close to anyone. He never treated flying as something that was fun to do, but rather as a job that needed doing. On the few occasions that he smiled, he did it with his eyes.

With the hours we were now flying, I found it increasingly difficult to sit down at night to write letters. When I got back to my room, all I wanted to do was sleep. I thought that it might be easier to speak into a microphone for a few minutes a night than to try to write all the words down, so I used the small reel-to-reel tape recorder that I had bought at the PX. Even that didn't work out all that well, and I started taking the recorder with me so that during our downtime, sitting under the rubber trees, I might get something on tape.

Bill Fuller, whenever possible, liked to have Mike Reardon

as his low-bird pilot. They made one hell of a team, with Fuller so serious and Reardon full of piss and vinegar and able to read trails as if they were the Hollywood freeway.

Reardon and I were sitting under a rubber tree at Loc Ninh, taking a break between missions. I was again flying front seat with Fuller, and we had already flown one mission and then returned to Loc Ninh to refuel and rearm.

"Where the hell are your little friends this morning, Boyle?" Reardon asked, referring to the two little Vietnamese boys who were usually seen following me around.

"Hell, they know when it's lunch time, don't you? It's only 9:00 A.M.," I said.

Williams was sitting directly across from me, on an empty C-ration box that had been opened to form a makeshift ground cover. With a tree as a back support, John Williams looked as though he should be holding a tall frosted glass with a sprig of mint sticking out of it.

"Why are ya' all feeding those kids anyway?" William asked.

" 'Cuz they're hungry and poor," I answered.

"Shit, I was so poor when I was a kid, if I didn't wake up with a hard-on, I didn't have nothing to play with!" Williams said, without cracking a smile.

"Yeah, right," I said, as Reardon rolled around in the dirt, laughing his ass off.

"Okay, you guys, time to hit the road again," Fuller said as he walked up to where we were sitting.

"What's up?" Reardon asked.

"Somebody captured an NVA or VC, and he gave them a location where he thinks we might be able to find some of his buddies."

For once, the information that had been received proved to be correct. After searching for hours, Reardon finally started finding bunkers and equipment.

I reached down and turned on my tape recorder and placed the microphone up inside my helmet so it would pick up the conversations between both aircraft. I wasn't sure just how well it would work, but thought it would be worth a try.

Mike Reardon was an unbelievably calm low-bird pilot. Under normal circumstances, when a low bird was being shot at, the call was, "Taking fire," followed by red smoke to mark the approximate location of the source of the fire. In Reardon's case, the call was, "Hey, Two Four, I've got some gook down here taking shots at me. It sounds like an AK, but I can't tell for sure, and I can't seem to find him."

We had been searching for the better part of the day in an area along a large river south of the Cambodian city of Mimot. Keeping track of where we were was made very easy by the twisting river's blue line on the map. Knowing that I was with one of the most experienced and respected pilots in the troop, I felt very much at ease flying in the front seat of the Cobra. With Reardon flying the low bird, we had an unbeatable team.

"Two Four, we just had a dude run into a hootch down here. It's got a real heavy roof on it, and I can't see what's inside. Do you think you could help me out and blow the damn roof off?" Reardon requested.

"Sure," Fuller responded, "Just give me a mark."

As Reardon went back in to toss out a smoke, he said, "Two Four, we're taking fire from the doorway, from more than just one dude."

"Okay, hold out to the north. I'll be in, hot, from the east. I've got the best view of the target from that direction."

I looked down at the tape recorder and saw that it was still running as Fuller began firing rockets into the column of smoke rising out of the trees. When he had finished, I let go with a long burst from the minigun, as we pulled out of the dive. The gun had fired until I let up on the trigger, which meant that it had not jammed and that, in itself, was unusual.

"You're cleared back in," Fuller advised Reardon.

"Two Four, we've got something strange down here," Reardon advised as he circled the smoking ruins of what had been a small building. We've got a total of eight dead, three by the door and five lying on bamboo tables. Looks to me like some sort of aid station or hospital."

I was expecting some sort of adverse reaction to Reardon's assessment of the target, but Fuller just said, "Okay, let's go get some fuel."

If anything more was said about the target's being a hospital, I never heard it. My spot reports reflected Reardon's speculation, and that was the end of it.

After refueling, we returned to the same area and started working our way down the west edge of the river. Mike Reardon didn't miss much, so I was constantly writing down spot reports, page after page. I just hoped that someone, somewhere, was making good use of all the information.

While we had been rearming the Cobra back at Loc Ninh,

I had a chance to check the tape recorder and found it was working better than I had expected. The one big drawback was the small amount of time I was able to record on each side of the tape on the very small reel-to-reel recorder.

It was getting late in the afternoon when we rounded a sharp bend in the river and discovered ten very large rafts made of huge logs lashed together with rope. They reminded me of the log rafts near a lumber mill, but these rafts were loaded with crates and fifty-five-gallon drums. As we rounded the bend in the river, numerous people were seen jumping off the rafts into the tall brush along the edge of the river.

The rafts had been secured to the bank by long ropes, which were tied to trees.

Reardon immediately began receiving small-arms fire from all along the bank adjacent to the rafts.

Fuller told Reardon to get clear of the area and we would put down some fire with the minigun. That announcement was great news to me. I was getting real tired of writing.

"Jerry, see that big tree right at the edge of the water?" Fuller asked.

"Yea, I've got it."

"Okay, start at the tree and work the shoreline to the east."

The *brrr* of the minigun was like music to me. After hours of doing nothing, I was finally allowed to get involved. Even more exciting, was knowing that all the conversation and gunfire was being recorded on my tape.

The first burst was short, then I let loose a long burst that covered both the shoreline and the edge of the rafts. I stopped firing as Fuller pulled out of his dive, and at the same time, Reardon was cleared back into the target to see what he could find.

"Two Four, I'm still getting shot at by someone out on the rafts, but I can't find him."

"Okay, Mike, get clear again, and I'll put some rockets down there."

The Cobra bucked as Fuller launched six pairs of rockets toward the loaded rafts. With amazement, I watched as the rockets impacted the rafts and numerous secondary explosions took place and fires started. As we pulled out of our dive, Reardon advised, in the calmest of voices for the circumstances, "Two Four, there is a dude who just jumped off the rafts and is trying to climb up the bank."

Fuller immediately banked the Cobra over into a very steep and sharp turn. Without asking, I pressed the trigger on the minigun as the glowing cross hairs of the gunsight centered on the NVA soldier trying to climb the slippery, muddy riverbank. His legs were moving as if he were on a fast treadmill, but the rest of his body was going nowhere as his feet slipped in the mud. As the burst from the minigun chewed up the mud around him, all motion stopped, and he and the AK-47 he was carrying slipped backward in the mud and slid into the river. There was no yelling or celebration, only Reardon's acknowledgment that we could add one more to the body count for the day.

Because of the size of the target, Fuller switched to the VHF radio and called the air force to see if they could assist.

Chip Wolfe, with the call sign of Rash One One, answered the call. We had worked with Chip in the past and knew he would take care of the target if possible.

He arrived in his twin-engine OV-10 within minutes, and Reardon showed him the rafts and where he had been taking fire. Chip was an air force forward air controller (FAC). When he found a target, he would call in a flight of three jets from Bien Hoa to bomb the target.

I wanted to stay around and watch all the action, but Reardon had advised Fuller that he was having a hard time seeing things on the ground as it was getting late in the day and there wasn't enough light.

For almost the entire flight back to Tay Ninh, I was on the radio calling in all the different targets we had engaged on our last flight. We had damaged or destroyed a lot of equipment, and there were eleven NVA soldiers who wouldn't be shooting at anyone again, or as Mike Reardon put it, "They would now be eating their rice from the roots up."

That night, Carl Rosapepe and I sat in my room and listened to all the action on the tape recording. Although some of the conversation was covered up by other radio traffic, most of the conversation between Fuller and Reardon was loud and clear, along with the sound of the minigun and rockets being fired. More than anything, the tape revealed elation, fear, anger, and anticipation in the voices on the tape, plus the unbelievable amount of radio chatter that we were all subjected to from three different radios. Later that night, I mailed the tape to Sonny and Dusty Jones, in Texas, and asked them to save it for me.

The following morning, Captain Funk's tour of duty in Vietnam ended, and he was replaced by Maj. William Harris. As I was an infrequent visitor to the officers club, I missed out on all the informal good-byes that took place the night before, and

I was already flying when he departed the troop in the morning. Rumors were flying all over the place about our new CO. Having already spent almost seven years in the army, I was well aware of how accurate rumors could be, so I decided to just take a wait-and-see attitude.

On the night of May 13, 1970, we were all briefed on an operation that would take place the following morning. A Huey that had been flying support for another unit had been reported missing two days prior. On the morning of May 13, the crew chief from the missing helicopter had walked into a fire support base called Kantum. He said he had been E & Eing (escape and evade) for two days and nights. He reported that his ship had been shot down but landed safely in a large clearing. Immediately upon landing, they were captured by regular NVA soldiers. He also advised that one crew member had injured his ankle during the landing, and because of his inability to walk very well had been shot on the spot. When the crew chief saw that, he just took off, running. He said he never looked back and had been running ever since.

I was assigned to fly with Jimmy Mills. Our low-bird pilot would be Bob Everest, the same pilot who had been shot down the month before, the one I had led back to the Huey. Bob had asked to be transferred out of Scouts into the lift platoon, but his request had been denied or put on hold because of the pilot shortage in the troop, especially in the Scout Platoon. The entire platoon had been assigned the one mission of trying to find the captured U.S. Huey crew. The Blue Platoon, headed by Lt. Jack Hugele, was to be inserted into the area shortly after dawn. A Pink Team would cover the insertion and then scout the area. Mills and I were scheduled to relieve the first Pink Team and continue scouting out in front of the Blue Platoon.

The flight from Tay Ninh to Kantum took only twenty minutes. Everest was a quiet type of guy, so there wasn't a lot of radio chatter on the way up. I used the time to make sure my tape recorder was working, and started the tape to Sonny and Dusty by telling them where we were headed and what we were going to be doing. Then I turned the recorder off and began locating spots on the map that I could easily pick out from the air. Because everyone was going to be flying in the same general area all day, I turned in the seat and pushed the intercom button.

"Hey, Jimmy, do I have to write down spots today?" He just looked away with a disgusted look on his face and said, "We record spots anytime we fly."

Jimmy Mills was getting the short-timer's attitude that affected everyone when they got within a couple months of going home. I could tell from the tone of his voice that he would rather be someplace else that bright, clear morning. Only a few thunderstorms were visible off to the west as we neared the area where the Blues had been inserted.

We had flown directly over Kantum and then turned west. The area was very beautiful. Long thin rows of jungle acted as yard markers for wide bands of tall grass that resembled huge football fields. It was in one of these fields, in front of us, that the Blues had been inserted. Jimmy was talking to Blue and arranging for them to pop smoke so we could get an exact fix on their location. I was busy trying to keep an eye on Everest and keep us on the map at the same time. With Everest in the low bird was Kenny Walls, who was the observer, and Larry Geiger, who was renowned as the best torque in the troop. I didn't know Walls very well and had only spoken with Geiger a couple of times. Geiger had introduced me to his aunt when she came up to Tay Ninh from Saigon where she had something to do with the Red Cross. Walls was looking forward to getting back to the EM club at the end of the day because it was his nineteenth birthday. Any excuse to get drunk was immediately seized upon by everyone.

Blue had his point man pop smoke, and Mills advised Everest that he could let down and start working north from the yellow smoke that was billowing up from the tall elephant grass. I reached down and turned on my tape recorder, hoping that I could get a little conversation between Mills and Lieutenant Hugele, who was on the ground, and the low bird. If I was lucky, I might even get something out of Ron Black who was flying a Huey a thousand feet above us.

Our orbit, above the low bird, took us over a thin tree line that ran east and west and was about three hundred yards out in front of the Blues. The tree line was only about two hundred yards long and two hundred feet wide. The first time our orbit took us over the west end of the row of trees, I thought I caught a reflection from something shiny. I didn't say anything to Mills as I thought it might just be a puddle of water reflecting the sun. The second time over the same spot, I waited for the reflection to appear. When it did, I felt it might *not* be water, so I brought it to Mills's attention. Although Mills didn't see the reflection, he advised Everest to check it out when the low bird reached that point. Just then Everest was working his way along the thin tree line from east to west. I had seen the reflection at its far west end.

As Everest approached that point, he called Mills on the radio, "I've got some pieces of aluminum down here. Can't tell what they're from though."

"Okay, check it out and let me know what you think," Mills responded.

Everest made a few more tight circles over the aluminum and then resumed the normal, larger circles.

"Two Seven (Mills's AC number), I've got a bunch of three-by-five bunkers down here," Everest advised.

"Okay, Bo. Watch your ass down there," Mills said.

Mills then called Blue and advised him of the bunkers.

Everest was just about to complete his first large circle after reporting the bunkers, when the radio crackled with a barely audible, "Taking fire." My eyes were glued to the low bird as it came out of its turn and headed due north, away from the area, which was the normal procedure. Mills pushed the nose of the Cobra over into a steep dive and began firing rockets where the low bird had just been. Besides holding a straight course north, Everest was also descending. I never took my eyes off the low bird as he descended. I assumed he had lost his engine and was making an autorotation, but there was no slowing, and the little helicopter slammed into the ground and immediately exploded in a huge black-and-red fireball.

Mills was still in his dive, firing rockets, as I stepped on the intercom button and said, almost crying, "Our low bird just crashed and exploded!"

"Oh God," Mills exclaimed, "Blue, Blue, our low bird was just shot down, he's two hundred meters north of the tree line in front of you."

"Okay, Two Seven, we're on our way."

I was shocked. It was impossible for anyone to have survived the crash and explosion. We circled the crash, but couldn't see anything except smoke and fire. So intense was the heat that the low bird's ammo and grenades were cooking off, adding white, red, and green smoke to the black smoke provided by the burning fuel.

Out of breath, Lieutenant Hugele's voice broke through the shock of the moment, "Two Seven, Two Seven, we're in contact. We are taking fire from the western end of the tree line. I think our point killed the gook who shot down your low bird, but we've got a lot more down here."

"Okay, Blue, have your point pop smoke and tell me where you want me to put it from the smoke."

The radio was now going nuts with traffic. Two more Pink Teams were enroute, two more Hueys, in addition to Ron Black who was now hovering over the burning low bird.

"Two Seven, we just took a bunch of hits through the belly," Ron Black called as the Huey he was flying accelerated away from the burning helicopter.

"What about your low-bird crew?" Blue asked.

"Doesn't look very good, Blue; I think they're all gone," Mills said.

"There isn't anyone living down there," Black said.

I hit the mike button and asked Black how he was doing and how bad was his aircraft hit, thinking that Mills might have missed what was said about Black taking hits.

"We're okay so far. I think they may have hit the fuel cell though."

"I've got yellow smoke, Blue," Mills said.

"Roger that, Two Seven. The bad guys are one hundred meters on a heading of three zero zero from the smoke."

"Okay, Blue. I'm in hot from east to west. Tell your folks to keep their heads down."

I didn't ask, I just put the cross hairs of the gun sight on the target area and squeezed the trigger on the minigun. I'd been firing only about four seconds when Mills began firing rockets, which automatically shut off the minigun. It also automatically jammed the minigun, and it couldn't be cleared until we landed somewhere. The 40mm grenade launcher was not the best weapon to use for close-in support of ground troops, so our turret was out of action, and all I could do was observe. The traffic on the radio was unreal, everyone was trying to talk at the same time on all three radios.

"Two Seven, you were taking a lot of fire on that last pass. Are you okay?"

"Yeah, Blue. We're okay so far," Mills said. My ass came up off the seat as Mills pushed the nose of the Cobra over into a steep dive. Without anything to fight with or shoot, and no low bird to watch out for, I had nothing to do but be scared. More scared than I'd ever been in my life.

Glen Senkowski, in another Huey, showed up over the crash site and immediately came under heavy fire, taking numerous hits. Sweat was pouring out of my helmet; I was so scared I didn't know what to do. I had never witnessed anything like this before, nor had I experienced the wide range of emotions that seemed to be engulfing me. All I wanted to do was get the hell out of there.

"Two Seven, this is Blue. We're going to need the QRF (quick reaction force) down here, and just as fast as you can get them here."

"I think they're already on their way, Blue, but I'll check," Mills reported.

I was amazed at the fact that Jimmy Mills could keep track of everything that was being said, all of it by very excited voices, on three different radios, still fly the aircraft, and shoot the weapons, all at the same time. It became very apparent why the front-seat pilot of a Cobra usually flew in that position for from five to six months before being moved to the back-seat. It took that long before he had learned enough to be trusted with command of the aircraft, and competent enough to take responsibility for the low bird. Had I been in the backseat on this terrible day, I would have been very tempted to fly to Bangkok and get on the first commercial flight home.

We were about out of ammo when Zeroth and Fuller each showed up, accompanied by their low birds. Mills briefed them on where the Blues were and where we had been taking fire from. We then made two more rocket runs on the area where Blue was taking all the fire from. Each time, Blue would say, "Two Seven, you were taking a lot of fire on that pass!"

On our last pass, Bill Fuller followed behind us in our dive as Jimmy fired the last of our rockets. I kept my fingers crossed that whoever was shooting at us was shaking just as much as I was. As we pulled out, Fuller started firing to cover us, much the same as the Cobra does when the low bird takes fire. It's designed to make whoever is firing duck for cover.

Not a word was spoken between Mills and myself as we flew back to Kantum to refuel and rearm—there just wasn't anything left to say. What bothered me most was the realization that I had been more than just scared, I had been terrified. I wondered if feeling that way made me a coward, but there just wasn't any-one to ask. Nobody discussed their inner feelings or fears.

After we had refueled, we moved the helicopter to the rearm area. I was able to locate a sergeant who really knew a great deal about miniguns.

"Hey, Sarge, do you think you could give me a hand with this gun; it's all jammed up?"

Within fifteen minutes, this very young sergeant had completely disassembled the minigun, cleared the jam, located a cracked part in the gun, and then reassembled it.

"It'll be okay for one firing, sir. You'll have to get that part I showed you replaced when you get back to your base; I don't have any spares with me."

"Thanks a lot, Sarge. I'm not sure if we have any spare parts either, but I'll check."

While the sergeant had been working on the gun, which required the Cobra's battery to be on, I had put on my helmet and listened to the massive volume of radio traffic that was still going on back at the crash site. Bill Fuller (Apache Two Four) had pretty much taken command of the situation, and the Blues had finally reached the downed low bird after having to fight every inch of the way. They had also recovered the weapon that they believed was used to shoot down Everest. It was a Chicom hand-held drum-fed 9mm machine gun. The NVA soldier had emptied one entire drum into Everest's aircraft, and when the point man for the Blues had approached, he had apparently slammed a new drum into the machine gun. As the Blues neared his position, he stood up, pointed the machine gun at the closest Blue, and fired. The machine gun jammed, only one round fired, missing the Blue. The Blue, carrying a 12-gauge shotgun, killed the NVA with a single blast. It was later found that the gun had jammed because the NVA had failed to clean the cosmoline out of the drum, which is used to protect parts during storage for long periods of time.

Mills and I stayed at Kantum and waited to be called back, but the call never came. We returned to Tay Ninh after the operation had been completed and all the troops were off the ground and out of the area. Back at Tay Ninh, instead of the planned birthday party, the troop, and especially the Scout Platoon, was in a state of shock. In twelve days the Scout Platoon had lost six men and had two low birds totally destroyed.

The only guy who I felt I could really talk to was Rosey (Carl Rosapepe), and he was a welcome sight when he walked into my room.

"Pretty shitty day, huh?" he said as he sat down in front of the fan. "God, that feels good. I've got to get to the PX and get me a fan."

"Yeah, that fan is about the only thing that lets me sleep at night; I don't know how you do it without one," I said. "Rosey, do me a favor will you?" I asked, with my eyes looking at the floor.

"Sure, what do you need?"

"Stay here and listen to the tape I made today," I said, sounding very guilty.

"You had your tape going during that mess up there today?"

"Yeah, I did. I turned it on just as the low bird was letting down, and I didn't turn it off until we left the area to go refuel."

"Holy shit, I've got to hear this. Hell, you don't have to ask me to stay; you know damn well I want to hear it."

"Well, I got a little scared up there today, and if the tape picked up everything that was said, I'm sure you'll be able to tell when you hear my voice. I just don't want someone thinking I'm some sort of chicken, and I know you won't laugh at me."

I took the small recorder out of my helmet bag and rewound the tape, then pushed the play button. Everything was there, loud and clear, and it was as if I were watching a rerun of my worst nightmare. Everest's voice was loud and clear when he described the bunkers he was observing as he made his orbit over them. Then there were forty seconds of nothing but the sound of the Cobra, and then, "Taking Fire," the last words spoken before the aircraft impacted the ground and exploded. Rosapepe sat with his eyes glued to the tape recorder, as if he were watching on TV everything that was taking place on the tape. Up until Everest was shot down, radio traffic had been very light, with a few exchanges between Mills and Blue. After the crash, the traffic was chaotic. The tape had picked up everything. Some conversations I didn't even remember until I heard them on the tape. After we had finished listening, the mood in my room was as if we both had just attended a funeral. The other voices on the tape did prove one thing to me, I wasn't the only one flying around that terrible day who was scared. Scared or not, they all continued to fight and do their jobs as best they could. I wondered whether, if I was ever put in that position, I'd be able to keep my cool as everyone else had.

After Rosey left and went back to his room, I just lay on my bunk with the events of the day replaying in my mind over and over until I finally fell asleep. Once again the tape was addressed to Sonny and Dusty with the request not to erase it, but to save it for me. The following morning was no different than any other morning. For some reason, I expected something to be different, but it wasn't. Apache troop just had three people fewer in the mess hall for breakfast. Nothing else had changed.

CHAPTER FIFTEEN

By the third week of May 1970, most of the FNGs were beginning to feel like seasoned veterans. Flight times were becoming unreal, with ten to fourteen hours of flight time each day becoming normal. It never ceases to amaze me the positions a person can sleep in if he is tired enough. Everyone in the troop was tired to the bone. I had started taking an air mattress with me, which I'd deflate and stuff in my helmet bag. When I thought we were going to be on the ground long enough, I'd blow the damn thing up and lie down wherever I could find some shade. In most cases, the only shade available was under the parked helicopter.

Our area of operations in Cambodia had moved east. A fire support base named David had been built just north of a small village named O Rang. David sat on the top of one of the many grass-covered rolling hills. If you have hills, you also have valleys, and each of the small valleys usually had a very narrow stream with a line of thick trees on each side of the water. Wild game was everywhere you looked. Wild pigs, deer, elephants, flocks of wild peacocks. Mixed in with all the wild game, beautiful waterfalls, and the rolling, green grass-covered hills that reminded me of a golf course, were some of the toughest NVA regulars Apache Troop had ever run up against. Unlike the VC, who would hit and run with guerrilla tactics, these guys were pissed off, well armed, and determined to kick our ass. They were also very hard to find, unless they wanted to be found.

The NVA, for years, had had a free run of Cambodia, and it had become a huge storage area for all their war supplies. Most of these storage areas were very close to the border, but still well hidden. As in the past, it was the job of the "Pink Team" (Cobra and Scout bird) to go out and attempt to locate these storage areas or caches. Firebase David was at an elevation of approximately 2500 feet and located five miles north of the border. The border itself was easy to pick out because it was a river, with very thick jungle on each side. Within a half mile of the river on the Cambodian side, the terrain sloped steeply upward. The thick jungle continued up the slope until it reached the top where the rolling hills started. This is where our effort was concentrated, because it was the only area that provided the cover needed to hide large stores of equipment.

Each morning we would take off from Tay Ninh and fly northeast to either Song Be (Fire Support Base Buttons) or to a small dirt airstrip, located halfway between Song Be and David, called Fire Support Base Snuffy. We would refuel at either location and then continue up to David. During the day, when we needed to refuel and rearm we would return to Snuffy.

It was on one of these refuel and rearm trips to Snuffy that I saw Lieutenant Coons laugh, the first time I could ever remember that happening, at least with me. He never let up, always on my ass to learn everything possible about the aircraft, tactics and especially emergency procedures. So when we received word to park the aircraft at Snuffy and wait there for an assignment, I figured I'd really be in for the rotten afternoon. It was scorching hot and there was no shade, except for the thin shadow of the sleek Cobra gunship. The dirt runway provided the frosting to the cake. Every time a helicopter or airplane landed or took off, the dirt was blown around and stuck to our sweating bodies like glue.

"Son of a bitch it's hot. I'd give anything for something cold to drink," Coons said as he sat on the open ammo bay door of our Cobra.

Our low-bird pilot had wisely chosen to park his helicopter at the rearm location, I suspect, to remain out of the watchful eye of Red.

"I may be able to help you out, Red, if you'll promise not to jump in my shit today."

"Yeah, Boyle, and just how do you plan on doing that?" Coons replied in his normal tone of voice, something similar to a runner being called out at home plate.

I didn't say anything, I just walked to the nose of the Cobra and opened the hatch and removed a large, green, nylon helmet bag. Actually, there were two helmet bags, one inside the other. The bags were filled with ice, Cokes, and small cans of fruit salad, which for the last week, I had been obtaining from

Mike Cutts in the mess hall. The helmet bags worked great, and the ice would last most of the day if the bag was not opened too many times.

"How about an ice-cold Coke and maybe a little fruit salad, Red?" I asked, thoroughly enjoying the puzzled look of dismay on his face.

He reached out and took the Coke from me, holding the frosty can in his hand and just looking at it.

"Boyle, I want to tell you something. The other day, while you were out flying, I had to take our new CO on an inspection tour. Both of us were very impressed with your room, and now with this ice-bag thing, I'm more convinced than ever that you could make a pigpen into the Waldorf Astoria!" Red said with a loud laugh.

I was floored. I wouldn't have been any happier if the president had walked up and pinned the Congressional Medal of Honor on me. I really didn't know what to say, and what finally came out sounded pretty childish.

"Gee, thanks, Red."

"Well, you may have done yourself more harm than good, Boyle. The Old Man liked your room so much, he wants you to do the same thing to the officers club!" Red said, with a smile, as he opened the can of ice-cold fruit salad.

"Apparently he has no idea how much time and effort went into scrounging up all that stuff I used to do my room. Do you have any idea how long I spent just pulling nails out of rocket boxes and then pounding them straight so I could use them again?"

"Not my problem, Boyle. But you may be saved. Rumor has it that we're moving back to Phuoc Vinh pretty soon."

"Don't suppose they'll let me take my room with me?" I said, not really expecting an answer.

Someone a lot higher up the chain of command than any of our pilots came up with the idea of staying at Song Be instead of returning to our base at Tay Ninh. We were told that we would only be there for one night, and then the following night, we would be allowed to return to Tay Ninh. It was a reasonable idea because it cut the flying distance in half and allowed us to stay around David longer, as it only took about thirty minutes to fly from David to Song Be. The major problem was that whoever the person was that came up with this fantastic idea failed to tell anyone at Song Be about it.

After flying off and on all day, I was ready for something hot to eat and a soft place to lie down. We had landed at Song Be just before dark in a rainstorm. As I was tying down the main rotor blade, my aircraft commander mumbled something and disappeared into the darkness of the flight line. I had absolutely no idea where we were going to be put up or where we were to eat, and as it turned out, neither did anyone else. I stumbled into Rosey and asked him if he knew what was going on.

"Are you kidding; I haven't a clue as to what we are supposed to do or where we are staying.

For almost an hour we walked around the base and were treated like lepers. We tried to get something to eat in another unit's mess hall, and the mess sergeant kicked us out, saying he was only allotted enough food for his unit. We finally found some other troops from our unit who had found shelter in what appeared to be halves of sewer pipes laid side by side. From the ground to the top of the corrugated steel pipe was about five feet. Each section of pipe was about twenty feet long, and there were almost fifty of them, in three rows, making each tunnel sixty feet long. As was always the case, some smart individual from the lift platoon, had the foresight to drag a few cases of C rations into the sewer pipe.

The ground felt cold and damp, so I went on a search to find something we all could sit on. While on my search for dry cardboard, I just happened to stumble upon the back door of one of the mess halls that had refused to give Rosey and me any food. The screen door was locked, and all the lights were out. I was sure someone would hear my survival knife cutting through the screen on the door. It would have been a lot easier had I been able to locate a lock cutter, as the door was padlocked from the outside. When the hole was big enough, I climbed into the mess hall and headed for the rear storage area. There I was able to liberate two loaves of bread, a big chunk of cheese, part of a tube of rolled ham and a number-ten can of applesauce. When I got back to the sewer pipes, I found that someone else had found some cardboard for everyone to lie on, and another Scout had liberated enough candles to light up the place. We didn't exactly have a party, but nobody ended up hungry. The pipes were also crawling with the biggest rats I've ever seen, which prompted some of the guys to try and sleep in their aircraft. Rosey and I returned to our separate Cobras, but after an hour of trying to sleep in the cramped cockpit, compounded by the fact that every time I opened the cockpit for a little air the rain poured in above my head and soaked me, I decided to return to the sewer pipe.

Walking down the flight line, I thought I heard familiar voices coming from the darkness, interrupted by a laugh now and then. As I got closer, I saw that the voices and laughter were coming from John Williams's Huey. I really couldn't tell what they were doing, but whatever it was, they were having a good time doing it. As it turned out, the crew, Williams, Art Docktor, and Morris Piper, had stolen three litters from an aid station and were installing them in the Huey, for a place to sleep for the night. Piper and Doc had also managed to steal enough C rations to feed our entire troop. I think it was the only time I ever envied the crew of what I liked to refer to as a flying Greyhound bus. They were going to have, at least, a chance of getting a good night's sleep, and a dry one at that.

The following night was a rerun of the previous night, right down to the rain and rats. The only difference being that Song Be had been put on alert. Not because of an impending attack by the NVA but because of the attack that was taking place from within the base. The enemy it would appear were the members of Apache Troop. Apparently I had not been the only one out finding ways to make life a little more comfortable. From the look and sounds of the people around, including some of our ranking officers, Song Be had been raped the previous night, and the people were not very happy about it.

I had been walking around the place trying to find some unit's supply room where I might beg, borrow or steal, some batteries for my flashlight. At least we had landed a few hours prior to dark, and that afforded me the time to scope out the place. I finally found a sergeant who directed me to a supply room. As I walked in, I saw a young red-haired spec four who could have been my younger brother, had I had one.

"What can I do for you, sir?" he said with a very Stateside tone in his voice.

"I was hoping that I could talk you out of some batteries for my flashlight so I can find my way around the inside of those damn sewer pipes that we have to try and sleep in."

"Well, sir, I sure can help you out, but I better warn you that if you are in A Troop, you better watch out tonight."

"Why's that, troop?"

"The word is out on you guys. They've told us to post a guard on anything that can't be bolted down," he said as he handed me a small cardboard box with twelve batteries in it.

I sat down in a handmade chair and told this young soldier about the previous night and how miserable it had been. I guess he must have really felt sorry for me. Or maybe it was the fact that I promised to get him a ride in a Cobra. Within an hour, he had introduced me to his mess sergeant and arranged for me to eat in their mess hall. He then found me a bunk that was not being used in his barracks, and showed me where I could take a hot shower. What they used as a hot-water heater was ingenious and very dangerous. They had rigged a fifty-five-gallon drum so that, after they filled it with water and lit a fire under it, the pressure that was built up inside forced the hot water out through a shower head. They then mixed the steaming water with cold water from another fifty-five-gallon drum. I was warned that if for any reason the hot water started to slow down, I was to get the hell away as the drum was probably going to blow up, as it had done a few times in the past. Despite the threat, the warm water felt great as I stood there, still wearing my flight suit, and scrubbed down with soap. I think Bartlett had told me that that was the way real pilots took a shower. When I figured that the flight suit was clean, I took it off and rinsed off the rest of myself, then put it back on. Within a few minutes, the flight suit was completely dry, and I headed for the mess hall. I was very uncomfortable as I ate. I felt that all eyes were on me, and I was probably wrong, but I got out of there as quickly as I could. I thanked the mess sergeant, and then headed for the cot that had been pointed out to me. A rolled-up poncho liner had to make do as a pillow, but that didn't seem to matter as the next thing I knew I was being awakened by the young spec four.

"It's starting to get light outside, sir. I just thought you'd like to know in case you have to go fly or something."

"Thanks a lot, soldier. Do you think your friendly mess sergeant will part with some coffee?" I asked.

"No problem, sir. I'll walk over with you."

After three nights at Song Be, some of us were allowed to return to Tay Ninh for a change of clothes and a good night's sleep. Most of us felt that if Captain Funk had been running the show, he never would have put his troops in the rotten position that most everyone was subjected to. I felt that it probably wasn't a decision made at our new CO's level, but the guys needed someone to blame, and Major Harris got stuck with it. I really felt sorry for the guy, because he had some awful big shoes to fill.

I had been flying with John Bartlett all day, and we were enjoying a break on the grass at FSB David. I was still finding it hard to believe that there was a war going on in the beautiful part of Cambodia or that Arnold Palmer or Bob Hope hadn't made it all into a golf course.

Major Harris walked up to me and asked where Bartlett was.

"I think he's over there by that low bird talking to Reardon, sir."

"Do you know if you've got enough fuel for another mission?" he asked.

"I think so, sir, but we would probably have to stop at Snuffy and put on some more fuel to get back to wherever we're going to spend the night."

Either he didn't notice the sarcastic tone or didn't care.

"Mighty fine, I'll go talk to Bartlett," he said as he took off in the direction of Reardon's low bird.

I could tell by the way Bartlett walked toward the Cobra that he wasn't very happy with whatever Harris had to say.

"You look like someone shit in your mess kit. What the hell's wrong?"

"Well, Boyle, we get to go cover the Old Man on some sort of rescue mission. You know the huge rice cache that was found southwest of here last week, well, the unit that was put in there to guard it is in contact, and they have three wounded that need medevac.

"Why don't they send in a regular medevac ship?" I asked.

"Not enough room. The LZ that they were inserted into is too far from the rice, and they're surrounded by a big bunch of very pissed-off and hungry NVA. They've managed to cut an LZ just big enough for a low bird to get into," Bartlett yelled as he climbed into the rear seat of the cobra.

Major Harris had his own low bird and usually flew by himself. We really never knew for sure where he was or when he would show up, but you could just about bet that if there was some sort of action going on in the AO, he would be around. Harris had decided that because his ship was light on fuel and didn't have a few hundred extra pounds of ammo in the back seat, as the other low birds did, that he would take the mission. Everyone knew that getting in and out of a tight hole in the trees with four people on board, was a kamikaze mission.

"I've got a bad feeling about this one, Bart," I said as we took off over the grass-covered hills and turned southwest toward a sun that was getting ready to set.

"Shit. All he wants is to win a medal or something," Bart said.

"That may be true, but I bet there are a few low-bird pilots back at David who are real glad he decided to take the mission himself."

The situation contained a lot of unknowns. The unit we were going to assist was not one that either of us had worked with before. None of us knew for sure how big the LZ was going to be or if Harris could get into it. The biggest problem for Bart was that his low bird was our commanding officer. Always in the past, the Cobra pilot was in command of the team. Usually the low bird would only be listening to the Cobra, but because none of us knew for sure what to expect, Bart suggested to Harris that we all come up on the frequency being used by the unit on the ground.

"Mighty fine," Harris responded.

"I sure as hell hope so," Bart said over the intercom.

As we approached the area, Bart made contact with the ground unit. My ass immediately started sucking up seat cushion because of all the firing I could hear in the background every time the radio operator on the ground spoke. His voice was excited, out of breath, and a little confused. Compounding the already very tense situation, was the fact that there was little if any daylight getting into the hole that had been cut for the LZ. Muzzle flashes and tracers were clearly visible, and as yet, we didn't know whose was whose.

Harris's voice broke over the radio. "I'm going down for a look." He descended and started a clockwise circle over the intended landing spot. The unit on the ground had really done a great job cutting out the trees for an LZ. It was a lot bigger than any of us had expected, but the actual landing spot was very small. Fallen trees were lying everywhere. I couldn't believe Harris on the radio. Every time the radio operator would say something to Harris, regardless of whether it was to tell him he was taking fire or where they wanted him to land, he would say "Mighty fine." There was no excitement in his voice at all. It was a term we would all become very accustomed to.

"Bart, either this guy has the balls of an elephant, or he's dumber than a tree."

"I'll pick the last one," Bart said.

Harris was doing all the talking, as far as keeping in contact with the people on the ground, and he had decided where he was going to land the small helicopter. He would come in from the south and depart to the south, the lowest trees being on that side. The landing spot was very small and very close to the north tree line, and Major Harris would have to be very careful turning around to keep from sticking the tail rotor into a tree or stump. Normally when a helicopter was going to land in a hot LZ, the borders of that LZ were first shot up by the covering Cobra. Bartlett had already determined that we were there for show only. The fighting was so close and the communications so poor between the troops on the ground that we couldn't take a chance of shooting for fear of hitting our own troops. Muzzle flashes along the eastern edge of the clearing were as clear as flickering streetlights on a cold winter night, and although we were at a thousand feet, I would have preferred to be at ten thousand. A lot of the tracers were coming straight up at us, which made it painfully clear that whoever was doing the shooting was not on our side; Bartlett would not let me shoot back. I told Bart I thought I could hit them without hitting our own troops, but the judgment behind shooting or not shooting was the reason Bartlett was in the backseat and I was still an FNG in the front seat. So I did the next best thing, I got down so low in the seat, behind the armor plate, that Bart had to ask if I was still in the aircraft with him.

The radio operator on the ground advised Major Harris that the three were badly wounded, but he thought they would be able to sit up in the helicopter. He further said that he would have a man on the ground directing him where to land. Harris requested that the landing guide keep an eye on the tip of the rotor blades so he wouldn't hit the trees that would be directly in front of him.

"Apache Two One, this is Apache Six. I'm going in now."

"Roger that," Bart responded.

Bartlett and I watched with amazement as Harris guided the small helicopter down toward the intended landing spot, through what appeared to be a Fourth-of-July fireworks show. Our troops on the ground opened fire with everything they had, apparently trying to cover the descending low bird. In response, the NVA opened up with everything they had.

"Shit, Bart, if they want their damn rice that bad why the hell don't we just let them have it?"

"Yeah, right, Boyle."

We were both surprised to see the cloud of dust come up as Harris set the low bird on the ground at the intended landing spot. Muzzle flashes and crossing lines of tracers continued as

Bart and I circled the small opening in the trees. We could see the soldier who had been watching the rotor blades standing in front of the helicopter, next to the closest tree, firing his rifle at the eastern tree line. It seemed to take forever as people carried the wounded, one at a time, out to the helicopter. Out of the corner of my eye, I saw a stream of smoke come out of the eastern tree line, headed straight for the low bird. Before I could even start to push the mike button, the silence was broken by Major Harris. "Oh, God! An RPG (rocket-propelled grenade) just took off the head of the kid standing in front of me."

Bartlett didn't care if he was talking to the CO or not. I don't think he even thought about it.

"Get the hell out of there, Six. You may not be so lucky if that son of a bitch decides to try again."

It was obvious that the RPG was intended for the helicopter, not the poor soldier standing in front of it. Harris picked the helicopter up to a slight hover and turned around. The dust and debris were more than doubled this time because the extra weight of the wounded caused a more violent downwash from the rotor blades.

"Two One, this is Six. I'm coming out."

"Roger that," Bart replied. "Hold your breath, Boyle, if he doesn't get shot down, I doubt he'll make it over the trees with all that weight."

"What do you mean, hold my breath? I've been holding it ever since we left David."

As the low bird started moving forward, the world around it erupted in explosions and a heavier volume of tracers. This time, a lot of the fire was directed at us. I pleaded with Bartlett to let me fire the minigun.

"No, Boyle, we can't take the chance."

The only way I could have fired was if Bart had armed the weapons system, and that switch was in the backseat. The low bird emerged from the dust and dirt and strained to gain airspeed and altitude, and much to our surprise, accomplished both, clearing the trees to the south with just a little to spare.

The wounded were returned to David and then medevaced by larger helicopter to the hospital at Phuoc Vinh. Very little was made of this action by Major Harris, and I suspect it was because he was the new CO and not well liked by some of the older members of Apache. As for me, it was one of the bravest acts I've ever witnessed, regardless of the motivation which prompted it.

CHAPTER SIXTEEN

Sitting on the cool green grass, just outside the huge pile of dirt that represented the only wall of defense surrounding Firebase David, I listened to the other flight crews. Most of the talk had been about John Williams and his Huey-load of captured items that had been brought back to David the previous day. As they talked about the weapons brought back, from flintlock rifles to modern machine guns, I sat and wrote a letter to Sonny and Dusty. One of the items that Williams had given me was an old Grundig typewriter, which I hoped I would be able to make work, and I wrote about it in my letter.

I decided to walk down by the eastern tree line that ran along the base of the hill that Firebase David sat on and finish my letter where it would be more quiet. Although I had never been there, I had flown over it just about every time we took off, and I was sure there was a small stream in among the trees. As I approached to within twenty-five yards of the tree line, I had to step over an old dead tree. I stopped and sat down on the old log, attempting to act as normal as my pounding heart would allow me. I was sure I had seen someone move, just inside the tree line. I sat on the log with my notepad that contained the first page of my letter and tried to make it as obvious as I could that I was in no way interested or had I seen anything that may have moved in the trees. I sure as hell wasn't going to get any closer, and I didn't want to turn and run. I kept telling myself that if I acted as if nothing was wrong, I'd be left alone. It was obvious to me that if there was actually someone watching me, that they did not want to be seen. If they were NVA and wanted to kill me, I would have already been dead. I sat for, what seemed like hours, but in actuality was only ten to fifteen minutes. While I sat there, I thought of my son, James, and my second child who was due to be born any day now. I wondered if I would make it out of this country to ever see them again and be able to take them fishing. Hell, I almost said out loud, I better think about just making it through this day, and decided that I had acted long enough and it was time to leave. The booming voice of Lieutenant Coons, from the top of the hill, was like receiving an electric shock, and I jumped straight up off the log.

"Come on, Boyle, time to head for home."

I can't describe how happy I was that Coons had called me as it gave me the perfect excuse to get up and leave the area. I also wondered just how high the poor son of a bitch jumped that may have been watching me. I didn't say anything to Coons or anyone else, convincing myself that I had seen nothing, and probably because I was afraid that if a search was made and nothing was found, I'd really be in a bad way with Red. I would later regret my decision.

It was June 11, 1970, and as I climbed into the front seat of Red's Cobra, I figured it was going to be just another late afternoon flight back to Song Be, and the search for a mess hall and a dry sewer pipe to sleep in. I had given up sleeping in the bed that had been provided me by the spec four from supply because the higher ups wanted to keep everyone together where they could be found if needed. A few tents had been put up for Apache Troop use, but there still was not enough room or cots for everyone.

As Red (Lieutenant Coons) and I took off and turned south toward Song Be, we were accompanied by two low birds and John Bartlett in another Cobra.

"Boyle, as soon as we get a little altitude, I want you to send all our spot reports to the TOC at Tay Ninh, and tell them we're off David enroute to Song Be."

Red was talking to Bartlett as I fumbled with my spot reports, getting ready to send them.

"Two One, (Bart's aircraft commander number) how much fuel do you show?" Red asked.

"I've got about six hundred pounds (seventy-five gallons). Why? How much do you have?" Bart asked.

"I'm showing a little over four hundred pounds (fifty gallons), but the fuel pressure gauge just started going nuts. It's bouncing all over the place."

"Probably just a short in the wiring," Bart remarked.

"Boyle! We're at three thousand feet, and we're not going to get any higher; send the damn spots!!"

I wondered for a long time if Red spoke to all the new guys the same way he spoke to me. When I finally got the guts to ask someone, they confirmed that he treated everyone just the same.

I made contact with the TOC and began sending my report. I had shut off the switches to the other radios so I wouldn't have to listen to Bart and Red shoot the shit. I was still sending spot reports as we crossed over the border, a narrow river, back into Vietnam. Red banked our Cobra over into a descending, shallow left turn, making a three-quarter turn until we were flying parallel to the river, but still descending. I didn't give much thought to the course change, thinking that maybe someone had seen something. I noticed that the other aircraft were following us, so I continued sending my spot reports to the TOC.

"Who in the fuck are you talking to, Boyle?" Red screamed at me over the intercom.

"I'm sending the damn spot reports just like you told me to do," I yelled back, not having any idea what had set him off this time.

"Well, while you're at it, you stupid shit, tell them that the engine just quit, and we're going down!"

Bartlett later told me that he was the one that told Red that I was still sending spots and that I had no idea that the engine had quit.

"I was laughing so hard I could hardly talk," Bart said. "There you were sending spot reports, just like you always do, and Coons is screaming at me over the other radio that the engine had just quit. It was the craziest thing I've ever seen."

Red had entered the autorotation so smoothly that without looking at the engine gauges, which I hadn't, it was almost impossible to tell that the engine had quit.

"This is Red Xray, we're going down, scramble, scramble, scramble," I yelled over the radio, to the TOC at Tay Ninh. I then heard the Blues at David acknowledge that they were scrambling. I put all my paperwork on the floor and tightened my shoulder straps as tight as I could possibly make them, then started looking around to see where Red was headed. As far as I could see, we had only two choices, the river or a small clearing next to the river. There was no conversation between Red and myself as he turned right, away from the river, and headed for the clearing. I thought that we would have no trouble getting to the small clearing.

As far as I was concerned, I was with one of the best pilots in Apache Troop. But respect for Red's flying ability did little to stem the increasing flow of sweat pouring out of my helmet. I told myself that the sweat was caused by the air-conditioning not working because of the engine failure. The cigarette that I was sucking on so hard also ceased to function when the copious amounts of sweat caused it, also, to flame out. My confidence drooped considerably when a very tall dead tree appeared in front of us. It had been impossible to see until we had descended below the level of the top of the tree. I think we both saw it at the same time. Red's only comment was, "Oh shit!" as he pulled back on the cyclic and up on the collective. The Cobra immediately gained altitude, enough to clear the top of the tree, but in so doing, it almost came to a stop, with very little rotor RPM left. Red had used the rotor RPM to clear the tree. That RPM is designed to cushion the landing during an autorotation; now we had used that up. We fell straight down, in a level attitude, for fifty feet before we hit the ground with a bone-jarring crash. My left arm slammed into the top of the armor-plated seat. My left knee had made contact with something under the instrument panel, and my back and shoulders hurt like hell. I immediately undid my seat belt and slid down in the seat to avoid the main rotor blade, in the event it flexed down low enough to come through the cockpit.

"Are you okay, Boyle?" Red asked over the intercom.

"Yeah, I'm okay," I said after a second or two.

"Well, where the fuck are you anyway?" Red yelled. "I can't see you."

"I'll be right up, as soon as I get myself untangled from the damn gunsight."

"Jesus Christ, Boyle, quit screwing around and get the hell out of this thing."

Red didn't have to ask me twice. I opened the cockpit canopy and dove out onto the damp ground. I didn't wait for any instructions, I just headed for the brush that was fifty feet in front of the nose. The pocket at the bottom of the left leg of my flight suit kept banging into my leg as I ran, and it hurt. I stopped and unzipped the pocket and removed the irritant, a small Brownie camera. I turned around and took three pictures and then put the camera away when Red asked me what the hell I was doing. Red was inspecting the crashed Cobra, which looked pretty funny as it sat on its belly with the skids sticking straight out to the sides. Other than the very bent skids, I couldn't see any damage.

As Red climbed up on the Cobra and was removing his personal, hand-held 40mm grenade launcher, I took out my camera again. As I backed up to get more of the area in the picture, I fell backward into a hole.

"Shit!" I yelled. Just what I needed was something else for Red to scream about. When I finally picked my ass up and crawled out of the hole, it dawned on me that the hole strangely resembled a bunker. It *was* a bunker! And as I looked around, I saw more. They appeared to have just been dug.

"Hey, Red, there's a couple of three-by-five bunkers over here."

"Very observant, shithead! Did you also notice that we crashed in a brand-new garden plot?"

My eyes went immediately to the ground. Sure enough, we had landed in someone's garden, and this gardener would like nothing better than to kill us.

I raced back to the left side of the Cobra the minute the firing started. One of the low birds was firing into a stand of bamboo, fifty yards up the hill from our tiny garden plot. Red was right beside me, and I watched with eyes the size of dinner plates as he loaded his weapon. I pulled my Smith & Wesson, .38-caliber pistol out of its holster and looked at it. I knew damn well that six rounds of .38 ammo wasn't going to hold off anybody. Bartlett then rolled in and started shooting rockets into the bamboo, with a devastating effect.

"If they don't get us out of here before dark, our goose is cooked," I said to Red.

He just gave me a look that would freeze hell, but said nothing. All I could think about was the fact that I didn't think I'd be able to walk all the way from there to Hanoi. Bartlett continued making rocket runs on whoever was in the bamboo. During one of these rocket runs, my thoughts of capture were turned to pure joy as a Huey full of Blues landed next to our Cobra.

Before the skids had even touched the ground, Tony Cortez, Ed Beal, and Kregg Jorgenson were leaping off the skids, followed by other Blues. The last Blues off the helicopter were carrying and throwing off the sling gear needed to hook up the

Cobra so it could be slung out and returned to Tay Ninh. My visions of impending doom immediately turned to elation.

Red didn't have to say it twice, as he hit me in the back, with the palm of his hand. "Let's go, Boyle."

I sprinted to the Huey and dove through the open door. Within seconds we were airborne, and I watched, from my prone position as the jungle became smaller and smaller below us. A feeling of relief swept over me like a slow-moving wave of warm water. Only then did I feel my stomach begin churning up inside me. I prayed that I wouldn't get sick in front of all these other people. I'd never be able to live down the disgrace I thought it would cause. When the feeling had lessened a bit, I rolled over and looked up into the big smiling face of Paul Foti, the aircraft commander, who was leaning over the edge of the left seat.

"Are you okay, you big Irish Mick?" he asked, with genuine concern.

"Hell, if I'd known it was going to be you who was going to pick me up, you big Spaghetti Western Wop, I would have waited around to get captured."

Red and I were flown back to Tay Ninh and dropped off at the hospital, to be checked over for spinal compression we might have received during the very hard landing. Except for an abrasion on my left arm and leg, we both checked out okay. The flight surgeon advised both of us to take the next day off and then go back on flight status.

Even though the water was cold, the shower felt great. As I stood under the water, I thought of watching Williams, Doc, and Piper, taking turns standing in front of their Huey, tipping the large rotor blade down, and showering as the rain water ran off the blade. I wondered if they were doing the same thing that night, up at Song Be. I was glad to be able to sleep in my own room and bed for a change, but felt guilty, knowing that Rosey and some of the others were having to endure another night in damp sewer pipes. My feelings of guilt did not seem to affect my ability to fall asleep the minute my head hit the pillow.

I awoke around 9:00 P.M. to the sounds of gunfire coming from the green-line bunkers. Apparently, someone on guard duty had seen something move through his Starlight Scope and had opened fire. It was not an unusual occurrence at Tay Ninh. I got up, put on my flight suit and shower shoes, and walked over to the mess hall in hopes of finding someone still there.

As usual, Mike Cutts was working on getting things ready for the coming breakfast meal.

"Hey, Mike, how about letting me in," I yelled through the rear screen door.

"Mr. Boyle, what are you doing up and about? Last I heard, you were in the hospital."

"Na, they just wanted to look us over and make sure we didn't catch the clap or something while we were visiting a strange country."

Mike opened the door and I made a beeline for the coffee pot.

"Don't drink that stuff, sir; I've got a small pot going on the stove that's only a few hours old."

We sat down and talked for an hour or so about my little romp around the garden in Cambodia. I got up and really took a good look around the mess hall.

"Hey, Mike, how come the mess sergeant has never really tried to clean up this place and make it into a real mess hall?"

"Heck, I don't know. He keeps telling me that the mess officer won't go to bat for him, and that's the only way to get things changed is with his help."

"Who is the mess officer, and where can I find him? I've got a few ideas I want to talk over with him."

"I think the Old Man sent him up to David to sort of act as a liaison officer or something, and I don't know his name. It won't make any difference, sir; nobody gives a damn about the mess section anyway. The only time anybody thinks about us is when they bitch about the food."

"Okay, Mike, well I'm going to try and talk to Harris about changing a few things around here, if he'll let me, but I'll need your help."

"You've got it, sir. All you have to do is ask."

"Okay, troop, I'm out of here and back to bed, now that the guards have killed all the ghosts that they were shooting at. Thanks for the coffee, and I'll see you for breakfast, maybe. Believe it or not I've got the day off."

I didn't get out of bed until 10:00 A.M., and spent the rest of the day trying to buy some cigarettes and film. I was sore all over, and the abrasions hurt like pavement burns.

"Mr. Boyle, wake up," the voice was saying.

I thought I was having a dream, but the shaking of my body was no dream.

"Mr. Boyle, wake up. Major Harris wants everyone in the TOC right away."

"What the hell time is it anyway?" I asked.

"It's 4:00 A.M., sir. Firebase David is under attack, and the Old Man wants all the gun pilots in the TOC."

"Okay, I'll be there in a minute."

I jumped up and threw on my flight suit and boots, then headed for the TOC. I wasn't the first pilot there, nor was I the last to arrive, but we all had one thing in common. We all looked like zombies.

Major Harris walked in and explained that at 2:50 A.M., Fire Support Base David had come under heavy enemy attack. David was receiving mortar fire, B-40s (rockets), and heavy machine-gun fire from all sides. The NVA had penetrated the perimeter wire, at a number of locations, and fighting was going on inside the firebase. Compounding the problem, Harris explained, was the fact that low clouds and fog were hanging over David to within a few feet of the ground, and only fixed-wing aircraft flying over the top were able to assist, by dropping flares.

"I want everything flyable to move up to Song Be and stand by there. Snuffy is also socked in, but if it clears before David, I want you all up there. The liaison officer that I had at David was wounded when the attack started, so my information is coming through brigade. Now go get something to eat and be out of here at first light. I'll see you up there."

I was assigned to fly with John Peele. I felt very much relieved not to have ended up with Lieutenant Coons again. I already felt guilty enough after not saying anything to him about what I had thought I had seen back at David, and I didn't need another day of yelling and screaming. John, on the other hand, was an easygoing southern boy and a good teacher, without all the yelling. He also let me do a lot of the flying from the front seat, which was a lot of fun once you got used to the very sensitive controls.

After sucking down three cups of coffee at the mess hall, I packed my double helmet bags with ice and Cokes, then headed for the flight line.

The flight to Song Be was uneventful, and we were there only long enough to top off the tank and then depart for Snuffy. The clouds and fog had lifted at Snuffy high enough for us to get in there and land. Snuffy was less than fifteen minutes from David, so as soon as we got the word that the ceiling was high enough at David, we could be there quickly. Medevac helicopters arrived shortly after we landed, as they, too, were waiting for the weather to clear. Their mere presence indicated that there were a lot of wounded up at David. Their flight crews stayed close to the aircraft, knowing that the word to take off could come at any minute.

A radio operator from Apache was sitting in the door of one of the Hueys, monitoring a hand-held radio. He would be the one to tell us it was time to take off. He was also the one passing on all the info that he was able to pick up about what was going on at David. So far, all we knew for sure was that the NVA had been driven outside the firebase, but that the fighting was still raging just outside the barbed wire.

"What do you think we'll run into up there, John?" I asked Mr. Peele.

"I don't know for sure, but when something like this has happened in the past, the gooks usually pull out just before it gets light. With all this fog and low clouds, they may stick around longer."

"Man, wouldn't it be great if we could catch a bunch of those dinks out in the open running around."

John just gave me a funny look and reminded me that even if we were to find some people out in the open, I could bet my ass that there would be a lot of other people standing behind antiaircraft guns, who would not be out in the open. My enthusiasm drained away as quickly as taking a piss after drinking a six-pack of beer. The word *antiaircraft* always had a chilling effect on me as I had seen, too many times, what antiaircraft weapons could do to a helicopter. Being only thirty-six inches wide, a Cobra was hard to hit. On the other hand, since the Cobra was that narrow, everything inside it had to be packed into a more confined space. When the Cobra was hit, you just knew something was going to quit working.

Major Harris flew in and landed close to the Huey where the radio operator had stationed himself. There was a brief discussion, and then Harris walked over to where most of the flight crews were sitting.

"Things have slowed down a bit up at David. Looks like they've decided to pull back into the trees, but they are continuing to drop mortars on the place. Our job, as soon as we can get up there, will be to locate the mortars and put an end to their little game. Brigade tells me that there are dead gooks all over our parking lot up there, so be careful, there could also be a lot of unexploded ammo."

As Harris started to walk away, I got up from where I had been sitting and followed him.

"Excuse me, sir. May I speak with you a minute?"

"Sure, Mr. Boyle, what can I do for you?"

"Do you know yet what's going to happen to your liaison man who was wounded up at David?"

"Not for sure, but I get the feeling that he will be going home. Why, was he a friend of yours?"

"That's not why I asked, sir. I was told that he was the mess officer for the troop, and if you need another mess officer, I want the job."

"That's an unusual request, Mr. Boyle. Usually officers try everything under the sun to keep from being assigned to that job. Why in God's name would you want it? It doesn't do a thing for your OER (officer efficiency report), and everyone will always be bitching at you?"

"That's the point, sir. I was a mess sergeant in the reserves, and I think I can get the mess hall squared away to where the troops won't be bitching—at least not as much as before. All I ask is that you give me a free hand and don't ask a lot of questions, and I think I can get the job done."

"Mighty fine, Mr. Boyle. You're my new mess officer, and I wish you all the luck in the world. With the move that is planned, you're going to need a lot of it. I'll have your orders cut as soon as I get back to Tay Ninh. Just remember you asked for the job."

"Yes, sir, and I hope you remember that, sir, when you write my next OER," I said, laughing.

Major Harris just walked away, shaking his head. Every officer in the troop was assigned an extra duty, some were good and some not; mess officer was one that everyone tried to avoid. With the hours we were flying, I knew this new duty was going to make for a very long day if I was going to do it right.

"Let's go! There's holes in the clouds over David," someone yelled. Everyone came to life and headed for their aircraft.

The medevac Hueys were first off the ground. Watching them leave, I thought back to flight school when I had thought about flying medevac helicopters—until I saw my first Cobra at Fort Wolters. Now I was very glad not to be in the pilot's seat of one of those departing Hueys. The medevacs were the real unsung heroes of Vietnam. Everywhere they went, it was to pick up a wounded GI, and the same people that had shot him would be shooting at the medevac.

Our first fuel load was spent looking for holes in the clouds big enough to let us work with the low bird. It turned out to be impossible to work our usual mission and still keep the low bird in sight, so we returned to Snuffy and refueled. We then went back to David, dropped down through a large hole and landed on the grassy hillside. David had not received any enemy fire for over two hours, and it was considered safe for us to land. Viewed through the breaks in the clouds, David had not looked very different from the way it had before the attacks. But upon landing, it became very obvious that one hell of a fight had gone on there. Dead NVA bodies lay everywhere I looked. Some were in full uniform; others were wearing black pajamas. But all were barefooted. Some were missing arms or legs or both. One, lying very close to where we had landed, had almost been blown in half. I later learned that he had been carrying extra ammo on his chest. When he was hit, that ammo exploded. In all, there were twenty-eight NVA bodies on the ground where we usually parked our Cobras. The people inside David had suffered twenty-six wounded and no deaths, which amazed me, considering the number of NVA who had actually gotten inside the firebase.

The flight crews were walking around our parking lot *very* carefully. The grass that had looked as clean as a putting green the day before was now covered with debris, from pieces of toilet paper to parts of bodies. As I walked toward the closest bunker, where a group of flight crews had gathered, I looked down at one of the enemy soldiers who was lying on his back. Even after being a cop for eight years, I never got used to seeing dead people. Eyes wide open, the soldier was staring up at me. At first I thought that he might still be alive, but the eyes told the story—they had a dull, gray, unseeing look about them. I couldn't recall ever seeing a dead person with eyes open, and it was a chilling sight.

I sat down on a sandbag and listened as others asked questions of some of the troopers who had been up all night. In Vietnam, everyone got very tired of listening to war stories, but at David the storytellers were surrounded by the proof of which they spoke. A young sergeant described how he was setting up his M-60 machine gun shortly after the first NVA had set off a trip flare in the barbed wire in front of the bunkers.

"Bullets began hitting the sandbags all around me, but they weren't coming from the wire in front of me. I turned around and here's this gook standing on top of the aid station, firing an AK at me. I swung around and got off one good long burst and blew him off the top of the bunker. That was the first time I realized that they were inside the wire."

Others had similar stories, but through the laughter, you could sense one underlying feeling that was not so readily mentioned, or easily hidden, they all felt very lucky to be alive.

By noon, the weather had cleared enough for us to work with the low bird. The NVA were gone, but they had left a lot of equipment behind. In reality, they were not really gone, just gone from our sight. Everyone expected a replay as soon as the low clouds and fog returned.

Every morning was the same drill. We would take off from Song Be, fly to Snuffy, and wait for the low clouds to lift around David. We did a lot of treetop flying, trying to get to David every morning, as nobody liked sitting around Snuffy. But for some reason the NVA never did launch another big attack. They just sat back, and as soon as it got dark, dropped a few mortar rounds on David to keep everyone awake and on their toes.

Eight days after David had been attacked, I was once again sitting at Snuffy with John Peele, waiting for the low clouds to lift a little higher so we could make it up to David.

"Hey, John, why don't we trade in this shitty dust and dirt for some cool green grass?" I was anxious to get out of Snuffy, away from the bugs, heat, and red-clay dirt and dust.

"I guess we could give it a try; we can always come back if we can't make it. Go over and tell the low bird we're leaving."

We took off and headed north toward where the landscape would abruptly climb two thousand feet, although we could not see it through the fog and clouds. With the low bird off to our left side, we shot across the tops of the trees at less than one hundred feet, with the bottom of the clouds just above us. As we crossed the river that marked the border, we started gaining altitude, trying to maintain clearance between the trees and the clouds. My feet felt it first, a bump and then a vibration.

"What the hell was that?" I said over the intercom.

"I think we've just been hit," Peele said in his usually calm voice.

"I thought maybe we had hit something with the skids."

"Nope, something hit us. I just got a master caution on the hydraulics. We're going back to Snuffy. Tell the low bird to follow us."

I told the low bird what was going on, and then called the TOC and told them we were returning to Snuffy and what the problem was. The Cobra has a backup hydraulic system for the collective, but it only allowed for three movements of that control, and after that it was frozen in that position and impossible to move. I knew, without asking that we were going to have to make a running landing at Snuffy, something that we had practiced in flight school many times.

"Do you want me to call Snuffy and let them know what's going on?" I asked.

"Na, I'll let them know," Peele said.

We got lined up on the runway, about a mile out, after making a very wide sweeping turn, so we could land from the south. John greased the Cobra onto the dirt runway as if he had done it every day, and we came to a jerky stop about a third of the way down. As we climbed out, we were met by a very angry lieutenant, from the firebase, who demanded that we move the damn helicopter. John tried to explain that we could not move it until our maintenance people showed up and fixed the problem. This lieutenant didn't give a rat's ass that we had just made one very beautiful emergency landing. His only concern was clearing the runway so that the resupply C-130s could land.

"I'll give you thirty minutes to get your damn helicopter clear of the runway, or I'll have it dragged off!" the lieutenant roared at Peele, hands on his hips, white foam forming in the corners of his mouth, with his face just inches away from John's.

I couldn't take any more of this pompous jerk RLO and much to John Peele's surprise, I walked up and nudged John out of the way. I took John's position and moved my face even closer to the lieutenant. "Good morning, sir." I said, in the same loud tone of voice the lieutenant had been using.

"Who's this guy?" the lieutenant asked, looking at John.

"He's my copilot, sir."

"I'm also the turret operator, sir, and if I might add, a pretty good one. I'd just like to point out that our emergency landing in no way affected the operation of the minigun."

"What in the hell does that have to do with anything?" the lieutenant screamed into my face as if he were a drill instructor and I was a new recruit.

"It means, sir, that Mr. Peele and I are responsible for this aircraft, and unless you provide us with a written release, taking full responsibility for this aircraft, the only thing your equipment will be dragging off this runway will be your dead ass!"

If looks could kill, I would have been vaporized on the spot, as it was, all I heard was a lot of throat clearing from John and our low-bird pilot, standing behind me.

"Don't you realize I outrank you, mister?"

"Yes, sir, I do, but we were talking about a broken helicopter, not body odor."

Without saying another word, the lieutenant turned and stormed back toward the firebase compound.

"Holy shit, Boyle! That stupid bastard is going to hang your ass!" the low-bird pilot exclaimed.

"Bullshit!" Peele said. "Boyle was right, and I'll be right behind you, Boyle. Especially when they stand you up in front of the firing squad!"

The situation became a little more tense when we noticed a couple of C-130s doing large circles over Snuffy. Peele climbed into the Cobra and contacted maintenance and told them to hurry as we were blocking the runway and had a problem with some officer from Snuffy. Within the hour, maintenance showed up and replaced the hydraulic line that had been severed, and we were able to move off the runway and then give the aircraft a good check. Nothing more was seen or heard of the jerk lieutenant, but Major Harris showed up just as the repairs were being completed. He informed us that he wanted us to pull another mission before going back to base. We had hoped that we could go straight back to Tay Ninh, where maintenance could give the helicopter a proper inspection. That would also mean that we would get a good night's sleep and some good food.

But, once again we headed north toward David. And, once again, I felt three solid bangs.

"Piss on it!" Peele yelled over the intercom. "We're going back."

We landed at rearm at the north end of the runway at Snuffy, and a quick inspection showed three bullet holes in the horizontal stabilizer.

"That's it. God doesn't want us to fly anymore today; we're going home," Peele said.

CHAPTER SEVENTEEN

June 29 is a day most people in Apache Troop won't forget as it was the day we pulled out of Cambodia and returned to Tay Ninh. Trailing different colored smoke from the doors of the low birds, each team that returned made a low pass down the flight line. Everyone was in the greatest of moods, and those who, two months before, thought that Tay Ninh was hell on earth, now thought it was the greatest place to be. Not counting the States, of course.

Covering the withdrawal of men and long lines of equipment, I had flown convoy cover with John Bartlett the previous day. Because we had no low bird with us to look out for, it was a pretty relaxed and enjoyable assignment. When the convoy of trucks, tanks, and other vehicles reached the border, we were released to return to Tay Ninh. Bartlett and I were very happy to be getting out of Cambodia, not just for that day but, hopefully, forever. Saying that our spirits were high would be an understatement. I reached into my helmet bag and dug out a small 8mm movie camera that I had purchased at the PX and started filming the traffic on the road we were following and the numerous Buddhist temples and anything else of interest.

"Hey, Bart, this is really great," I said over the intercom.

"What the hell are you doing up there anyway?" Bart responded.

"I'm filming all the action. Hell, for once I don't have to take any spot reports, and I can just sit back and enjoy the ride."

Good old Bloody Bart decided that he would really give the folks back home something to talk about. He dropped the Cobra down to within ten feet of the road and pulled in all the power our worn-out Cobra could muster up. Through my view finder the cars and motorcycles were flashing by beneath us. We were barely clearing the roof of some of the small shops that occasionally appeared on either side of the road, and I was having a hell of a great time. As we rounded a curve, a large tree on the left side of the road came into the viewfinder. Bartlett banked right, for clearance, but another tree came into the viewfinder on the right. So close was this second tree that I later swore that I could see bugs leaping off the leaves in a vain attempt to save their lives. All of a sudden, there was a loud *bam* and then a burring sound as the main rotors tore through the foliage of the tree.

"Holy shithouse mouse, Bart! Watch where the hell you are going!" I yelled over the seat. There was a long silence while we both waited to see if we had done any real damage. No warning lights!

"Did you get it on film?" he yelled back, laughing.

"Yeah, I got it, you crazy shithead."

We flew all the way back to Tay Ninh, with the helicopter flying as if we were driving a car on square tires. Bartlett had knocked the main rotor system so far out of balance that we could hardly talk without sounding like a couple of Donald Ducks. Somewhere during this part of the flight I decided that most of the other pilots were correct about Bartlett. He truly was nuts, insane, crazy, loved to fly, ate rats, and was not much different from the average Apache Troop pilot.

The following day, our official last day in Cambodia, I flew with Jimmy Mills, another ho-hum day of flying along the border but not into Cambodia. Our low bird had advised us that he had prepared all of his smokes for the low pass we were going to make as we approached Tay Ninh. A few miles north of the runway, both aircraft went into a dive and headed straight for the base. Out both sides of our low bird streamed bright colored smoke. The red, yellow, and green smoke, billowing from the rear door openings and trailing far behind the small observation helicopter, was breathtakingly beautiful. I wished that I had not used up the last of my film with Bartlett the day before.

"Okay, you break left, and I'll go right when we get over the runway," Mills advised the lowbird.

We were going about as fast as we could go, close to 190 mph.

"Okay, break!" Mills advised the lowbird.

The nose of our diving Cobra came up just a little as I felt the armrest under my right arm slide forward just a little.

"I can't pull out!" Mills yelled over the intercom. I immediately looked down at the pistol-grip cyclic control next to my right hand. The armrest was pushed up against the control, making it impossible for Mills to pull it back. As I tried to dislodge the armrest, I glanced forward out the front of the windshield. We were diving straight at a wire fence at the south end of our short helicopter runway!

I tore at the small armrest, envisioning the deadly crash that was about to take place. Finally I got a good grip on the armrest and ripped it out of its narrow slot. The back pressure Jimmy had on the cyclic caused the Cobra to shoot damn near straight up, missing by what looked like inches the wire fence at the end of the small runway.

"What the fuck was wrong up there?" Mills screamed over the intercom.

"Sorry, Jimmy. The armrest slid up against the cyclic," I said as the sweat flooded down my face. I tried not to talk because everything I said came out sounding like some sort of squeaky toy.

"Shit, that was close! I thought we had bought the farm!" Jimmy sighed.

I didn't ever tell Jimmy Mills that the armrest had slid forward because I had stuck a couple of extra packs of cigarettes behind it. When Jimmy put the Cobra into the dive, the armrest had shifted forward allowing the cigarettes to fall between the armrest and the bulkhead, jamming the armrest up against the cyclic. Never again did I ever put anything close to the controls.

As it was still early in the afternoon and there were still a lot of aircraft out flying, I made a mad dash for the PX and bought more movie film. When I got back to the flight line, I climbed up into our makeshift control tower and was able to film the arriving flights of Cobras, low birds, and Hueys as they made their smoky low passes over the base. On the ground, the Blues were standing on the flight line popping dozens of smoke grenades, not to mention the popping of other kinds of cans. After all the aircraft were safely on the ground, the officers club began rocking with pilots who were intent on getting very drunk. Everyone was also celebrating the promotion of Jimmy Mills and John Peele to the rank of Chief Warrant Officer (CW2) and Red (Norm Coons) to the rank of captain. Besides, the next day was a day off for everyone.

I spent most of the early evening just sitting in the mess hall talking to Mike Cutts and some of the other cooks and listening to western music that Mike had brought with him from the States. I listened to one song over and over, "Heaven Below" by Eddie Arnold, because the lyrics mentioned Texas, and returning home, and seeing runway lights far below the airplane. It was as if the song had been written about the way I was feeling. When it came time to close up the mess hall, Mike gave me the record even though I had nothing to play it on. The lyrics of the song playing over and over in my mind, I went back to my room and wrote letters. For a lot of the pilots and crews, the escape mode was to get drunk; mine was to write down what I was feeling and, depending upon the particular circumstances, send it to the people I thought might understand. Sometimes the return letters from my wife were few and far between, and it really began to eat away at me. I began to rely on letters from Sonny and Dusty more and more, and those of other friends who wrote to me. I spent a lot of time in the evening writing letters and began to feel that I was withdrawing into my own little world, away from the other members of the troop.

The feelings of withdrawal were short-lived when we began the move out of Tay Ninh. Half of the troop was moved to Song Be, and the other half to Phuoc Vinh. As the new mess officer, it was my responsibility to see that everything was packed up and shipped to Phuoc Vinh and then set up in a mess hall similar to the one at Tay Ninh. One advantage to being the mess officer was that I was able to pack up a lot of the junk I had gathered and move it with the mess hall equipment.

Shifts were set up so that a pilot only had to spend three days at Song Be before returning to Phuoc Vinh for three days. But I remained at Phuoc Vinh for almost a week, getting the mess hall set up. I could see how easy it would be to get used to living in an area that had a good mess hall and PX and the other comforts that were nonexistent up at Song Be. I requested that I be put back in the normal pilot rotation, not because I missed all the action, but because I was beginning to feel guilty.

When I arrived at Song Be, the only real change I noticed was that the engineer company had poured three large cement slabs that were to be the floor for our new mess hall. I was really disappointed when I learned that tents were to be erected over the slabs, instead of buildings. The army figured that we wouldn't be there very long so tents were good enough. I had learned never to assume anything about the army. I decided to treat our mess hall as if it might still be there in ten years. I guess the thing that really bothered me the most was how the other 95 percent of the army lived, not more than ninety miles south of Song Be. They had real mess halls, with silverware and china plates. Real coffee cups, not Styrofoam. Air-conditioned rooms, real beds, and clean white sheets, and hot and cold running water. Hell, I thought, we were the ones that should have that stuff. We were the ones getting shot at, shot down, and too frequently, getting killed. Those "straps" (a slang term used to describe someone who stayed in the rear, away from the fighting, and wrote phony war stories home) wouldn't have lasted a day if they'd ever been subjected to the mud, rats, cold food, incoming mortars and rockets every night, and then had to go out and get shot at during the day. I made up my mind, that if ever given the chance, we were going to have just as much comfort as the straps had, and I really didn't care how I got it.

Every day Song Be changed just a little. Construction of the sewer pipes that we were to soon call home progressed, and our new troop area began to take shape. The pipes were not round, but had a semiflattened lower half. Plywood floors were to be built and installed, leaving about five and a half feet from the floor to the highest point of the pipe, which meant walking bent over any time you were moving around inside them. Plywood caps would then be constructed and placed over the open ends of each pipe, with a small door at each end. The pipes would then be covered with thick sheets of rubber and *that* would be covered with dirt and bags of sand. While construction by the engineer company went on, we were still forced to fend for ourselves and sleep wherever we could find a place. Some tents had been provided for the members of Apache Troop, but they afforded no protection against the nightly mortar and rocket attacks that our two-month excursion into Cambodia had been designed to stop but had not.

On one of my stays back at Phouc Vinh, I was forced to go see the flight surgeon because of a hemorrhoid problem. His office was quite comfortable because of the air conditioner sitting in his window. After the exam, he asked, "What type helicopter do you fly, Mr. Boyle?"

"A Cobra, sir. Why? Does it make a difference?"

"Well, I'll just bet you a beer that you fly around all day long with the air duct under the seat pointed right straight up at your ass, am I right?" he asked with a big smile on his face.

"I guess I owe you a beer, sir."

"You'll just have to turn it off, or you're going to have some real problems. And even if you turn it off, for the rest of your life you're going to have to be careful. Speaking of air conditioners, do you know anyone who would like to buy mine? I'm going home next month, and I've got to sell mine before I go. I've got a small refrigerator that I've got to get rid of also."

"I want them," I said without hesitation. We settled on a price of three hundred dollars, and he promised to give me a call just before he left so that I could come down and get them. All I had to do was figure out where I was going to come up with three hundred dollars. I had just spent every cent I had in the PX buying a combination AM/FM radio and turntable, and two used speakers from a friend of Mike Cutts who was going home in a few days.

I worked in the mess hall the rest of the day and temporarily hooked up my new sound system. Compared to what we had been listening to, it sounded like we were in a concert hall. By eleven that night I had just about worn out the record that Cutts had given me, but it still sounded great. Finally Rosey (Carl Rosapepe) walked into the mess hall, looking for a late-night snack.

"Hey, Boyle, where were you hiding all day?"

"I was out buying furniture for our new home."

"Whose new home."

"Yours and mine—you know, our brand-new sewer pipe at Song Be. We're going to have the most modern, up-to-date sewer pipe the army has to offer."

"Yeah, well I'll believe it when I see it. What, pray tell, do you consider modern and up-to-date?"

"That all depends on you and your wallet, and if you have an extra $150 that you can contribute to the cause."

"Depends on what you've got in mind," Rosey said with a lot of skepticism.

I explained what I had arranged with the flight surgeon, and showed him the new radio equipment while we sat and ate some fresh-baked apple turnovers.

"Sounds great to me, but I'll have to wait for our next pay period."

"No problem; we can't get the stuff for another couple of weeks anyway, and I may have a TV lined up by then, too."

"Holy shit, Boyle, how do you plan on getting all this crap from here up to Song Be, and what's the Old Man (our commanding officer) going to say about it?"

"Where there's a will, there's a way. Just don't worry about it. As far as the Old Man goes, he can't say much. Hell, we won't have anything that all these straps around here and back at Bien Hoa don't already have."

"Yeah, but Song Be is a firebase. People just don't have that stuff on a firebase."

"Well, consider us trend setters, because we're going to have it and probably more."

On July 16, while flying with Bill Fuller, a radio call came in from the Song Be TOC (tactical operations center).

"Apache Two Four, we've got a message for your Xray (front-seat pilot)."

Fuller had to tell the TOC to stand by as we were in the middle of blowing the roofs off some bunkers that the low bird had located.

"You ready to write, Boyle?" Fuller asked.

"Yeah, I'm ready."

"This is Two Four, ready to copy," Fuller told the TOC.

"Two Four Xray, the Red Cross advises that you are the father of a new baby boy. Mother and son doing fine. Over."

"Two Four copied, and thanks a lot!"

"Well, congrats, Mr. Boyle. Looks like the drinks are on you tonight," Fuller said, laughing.

I was overjoyed but felt a little strange getting a message as important as that while trying to blow someone else away. I was also concerned about where I was going to come up with the money to pay for all the booze that I knew the guys were capable of putting away in one night. As it turned out, they let me off the hook with only one round and then showed me where there was a MARS station (Military Amateur Radio Service). I had heard of MARS but really didn't know too much about it. As I found out in a hurry, it was a place that someone like me could call home. Contact was made between an amateur radio operator in Vietnam and another amateur in the States. The amateur in the States then placed a telephone call, collect, to my home, and through a special hookup, I could speak to my wife just as if on a regular phone, with the exception of our having to say "Over" when each party was through speaking. As it turned out, the radio operator in the States was at Sen. Barry Goldwater's ranch in Arizona, so my wife only had to pay for a long-distance call between Arizona and California. I later found out that, as a service to the troops in Vietnam, Senator Goldwater had numerous amateur radio operators on duty at his ranch. I kept the conversation short as there were other GIs waiting to call, but I did find out that my new son's name was Kevin Lee and that everyone was doing fine. I went back to the room that the supply sergeant let me use and started writing letters to everyone telling them of my new son. I was very proud.

Once the engineers really got going on our new home at Song Be and made clear that there was little doubt that it was really going to happen, instead of just being a strong rumor, people began selecting their sewer pipes. And people began making plans for an officers club and the NCO club. Apache Troop couldn't operate effectively without beer. Official segregation reared its ugly head in the form of an unofficial order that warrant officers had to room with other warrant officers; the same went for commissioned officers. No one ever saw anything in writing, but that's the way it turned out. Major Harris took the heat for the order, but I suspect that it came from higher up the chain of command. As far as the officers themselves were concerned, it was all bullshit. Commissioned or warrant, enlisted or NCO, we were all a team, regardless of rank. Up until that point there had never been a problem about rank between any of the members of Apache. There were occasional difficulties between individual members, but that seldom had anything to do with rank. Within a week, the order was forgotten or ignored.

The official name of the fire support base was Buttons and it was located next to the small village of Song Be. The fire support base was actually bigger than the village. It had a runway capable of handling a C-130 cargo plane, and all the equipment necessary for making an instrument approach. Apache Troop's area was on the far western side of the base. I suspected that we were put there because any attack on the base would most likely come from the west. In addition the distant location would keep our large group of disruptive individualists and America's own kamikaze pilots away from the rest of the troops who were used to acting in the traditional army manner. We didn't mind our reputation a bit; in fact, we were very proud of it, even if it did give our officers headaches and gray hair. We just did what ever it took to accomplish the mission.

None of us had any delusions about the NVA and Viet Cong. We knew that our two-month trek into Cambodia had put a big dent in the amount of supplies the enemy had available. But we also all knew that the incursion would not stop them from replacing all that had been captured or destroyed or keep them from crossing the border into Vietnam. At the same time, rumors ran wild about the 1st Cav being pulled out of Nam and sent home, or at least back to the area around Saigon. The term Vietnamization could be heard on the radio every day and in all the news broadcast. All that meant to us was that more and more of the dying was supposed to be done by the Vietnamese. None of us believed that South Vietnam would ever be in a position to defend itself, but that's what the politicians wanted the public to believe.

In an attempt to keep the NVA in Cambodia, most of our missions were along the border. We knew that, at the most, we would only be able to piss them off and slow them down. Of course when it came to pissing people off, whether it was the US or NVA, nobody could do it better than Apache Troop. We had found a small bridge, close to the border, that the low bird advised showed signs of being used a lot. Everyday we shot up the bridge to the point that it became unusable. The following morning, the bridge would be completely rebuilt and show signs of having been used during the night. On at least three occasions, we even had the air force come in and destroy it, and still the damn thing was up the next morning. So it became an unloading point for Cobras on their way back to Song Be with unfired rockets onboard. That bridge showed me just how much resolve the NVA had, and it was an uncomfortable feeling.

We were finally given the go-ahead to start moving our personal belongings into our sewer pipes. Rosey and I had selected one that was the closest to the green line (base perimeter) and second in from the south end of that row of pipes. The engineers had done a great job putting all the pipes together and waterproofing them, but one problem became obvious as soon as we moved it. The plywood floors could not fully close off the interior from the area beneath the floor because of the pipe's corrugations. Along each edge of the floor were small half-moon openings that the rats loved to use to gain entrance inside the pipes. It didn't help any when some of the troops decided that the openings were a lot more handy than a trash container. Within a week, our area was alive with huge rats, which prompted the army to place traps and poison around all of the sewer pipes. Rosey suggested that we nickname ourselves "The Song Be Sewer Rats," but the name never caught on.

As the troops began moving their personal items into the sewer pipes, another problem became apparent—the wiring to each of the pipes was not much bigger than a regular extension cord so power blackouts became a nightly occurrence when anyone plugged in a fan or tried to heat up some food on a hot plate. We had enough generators to power a small city, and yet we kept blowing fuzes. Nobody bitched too much about it though, as we were all really happy about finally having a place where we could sleep and stay dry, and relatively safe from mortars and rockets.

Because of the electricity problem, I didn't get too excited when the flight surgeon sent up a message saying that he only had a week left at Phuoc Vinh, and I'd better get my butt down there and pick up the refrigerator and air conditioner. I did manage to get back to Phuoc Vinh to help with the arrangements to move the equipment for the mess hall up to Song Be, and I sent the refrigerator up in a shipment of mess-hall equipment, along with my radio gear and a well-built clothes dresser one of the troops going back to the States had made. The air conditioner was going to have to wait until I could find a way to fly it up.

Everything went great setting up our new home. Although our sewerpipe was designed for four people, Rosey and I were the only two assigned to it. The refrigerator was small and didn't draw much juice, so we got by without blowing any fuzes. But I had doubts about what was going to happen when I plugged in the air conditioner. But first I had to get it from Phuoc Vinh to Song Be without the Old Man finding out. He was already mad about all the personal electrical equipment that had the lights going out four or five times a night.

"How's it going, Mike," I said to the assistant maintenance officer as I walked into the large tent that acted as a hangar.

"Not bad, but I bet you've got a problem."

"Hell I didn't know it showed that much."

"Not really, Jerry. It's just that nobody comes by maintenance unless they have a problem."

"It's really not a problem; it's just that I have a piece of equipment down at Phuoc Vinh that I'd really like to get up here, preferably at night. I just thought that you might be making a trip down there tomorrow afternoon and returning after dark."

"Well you just might be in luck. I got word about an hour ago that they have in some parts that I need bad, and the Old Man has approved the flight. I'll be leaving in about an hour. Can you go today?"

"Let me check, and I'll get back to you," I said as I hot-footed it out the door. I found Rosey and told him what was going on, and then got Captain Coons' permission to go, telling him that we were just going to the PX and would be returning within a couple of hours. Mike King enjoyed having the company on the flight down to Phuoc Vinh, and Rosey enjoyed being able to fly a Huey again. The difference between flying a Cobra and a Huey was like driving a sports car and then getting behind the wheel of a Greyhound bus. Both were fun to fly but completely different in feel.

The flight surgeon had already left his office, and it took over thirty minutes to locate him. Removing the large air conditioner took another thirty minutes, and then came the hard part. We had no ground transportation, so we had to carry the air conditioner, wrapped in a blanket, for what seemed like forever, before reaching Mike King's Huey. When Mike saw our secret cargo, he just started laughing.

"Shit, Boyle, we can't hardly turn on a fan without blowing a fuse, what makes you think you're going to be able to run that thing?"

"Hell, Mike, there's got to be something wrong with the wiring or something. We've got six huge diesel generators, and we can't power a few fans and light bulbs. I plan on talking to the kid who takes care of the generators to see if he can't help me out."

We landed in complete darkness back at Song Be, and then waited until Mike had gone through the engine cool-down, shut-down procedures and the blades had quit turning.

"You see anybody we should be concerned about, Rosey?" I asked.

"Na, nobody. Looks pretty quiet."

"Okay, lets get this heavy piece of crap to our room before someone asks what's under the blanket, and you, Mike, mums the word okay?"

"Don't worry about me; it's the Old Man I'd be sweating if

I were you two. But if you do get it working, I expect an invite."

"Any time, Mike. And thanks for helping us out."

We started trying to carry this awkward piece of equipment toward the troop area where our sewer pipe was located. We tried every possible way of carrying the damn thing, and there just wasn't any graceful way. We were within one hundred yards of the safety of our room when a strangely familiar voice boomed out of the darkness.

"Mr. Boyle and Mr. Rosapepe, I presume. And what do we have here under the blanket?"

My heart went into my throat like a pheasant taking flight. It was our commanding officer, Major Harris.

"Just a piece of furniture for our room, sir," I managed to stutter in a very unconvincing tone of voice.

"My information, Mr. Boyle, is that your piece of furniture is somewhat related to the air-conditioner family," he said sarcastically as he pulled the blanket off our prize possession.

"I think this will make a very nice table for you and Mr. Rosapepe because you sure as shit aren't going to be able to run the damn thing up here. I hope you had to pay a hell of a lot of money for your new table. You two deserve it!" he said as he stomped off toward his own sewer pipe.

"Do you think he was angry?" Rosey asked with a huge grin on his face.

"Ah, hell. He probably just got a Dear John letter from his wife. What ya say we get the hell out of here before he comes back with the MPs," I suggested.

I had planned far enough ahead to have already cut an opening in the back wall, big enough to fit our new toy. After sliding it into the opening, we stacked boxes and old lumber between the AC and the ground to support all its weight. As we walked back inside our pipe, I bent down and picked up our one and only extension cord.

"Hey, wait—you're not going to plug that thing in are you?" Rosey asked. Terror was written on his face.

"I've got to give it a try. Don't you want to know if it's going to cool down this place?"

"Yeah, but I just don't want to be cooling my heels in Long Binh jail."

The cord from the air conditioner was plugged into our extension cord and I reached over and turned the knob to on. The light bulb in our room dimmed slightly and then stayed steady.

"All right!" I exclaimed, until I noticed that all we were getting was hot air.

Rosey grabbed his flashlight and looked at the face of the air conditioner. "It's on vent," he said, handing me the flashlight.

I looked at the dial and turned it to "cool." Immediately the plywood wall that supported the device began to shake and rattle and the conditioner began making moaning sounds, then everything went black. A chorus of moans erupted from the troop area, which was common every time we had a power failure. What was not common was the high-pitched, murderous yelling and screaming of the Old Man's voice.

"Boyle! If you plugged that damn thing in, I'm going to have your ass hung so high you'll die from lack of oxygen."

"Rosey, quick unplug the damn thing and throw something over it, I'll try and stall him," I yelled as Rosey began to exit the back door.

I damn near ran into the Old Man as I sprinted out the door. I didn't wait for him to ask the question.

"Sir, I only plugged in our hot plate to try and heat up some C rats. We missed chow because it's so late."

"Yeah, right, Mr. Boyle. I'll believe that when you start to grow wings. If it ever happens again, the only thing you'll be flying will be kites and weather balloons. Do you copy me, Mr. Boyle?"

"Got a solid copy, sir."

I stood at attention and watched Major Harris storm back across to the eastern row of sewer pipes. I didn't know if his anger was just for show, or if he really was pissed off.

"Psssst, Boyle? Is he gone?" Rosey whispered from the dark opening of our pipe.

"Yeah, he's gone. But you can bet your ass he'll be right back over here if the power goes out again."

"You're going to get both our asses court-martialed if you keep screwing around with the Old Man," Rosey said.

"We've got to figure a way to get some heavier wire run to our hootch. I'm going to see if I can find out who's in charge of the generators."

The line of generators had been placed in a row, running east and west at the north end of our troop area, a barrier between the helicopters and the sewer pipes. Near them, I could make out the outline of a person sitting on a toolbox in the darkness.

"How's it going, troop?" I asked from twenty yards away so as not to startle him.

"Okay, I guess, sir. Is there something I can do for you?"

"Got any objections if I sit down and ask you a few questions about the generators?"

"What aboot the generators, sir?"

"First of all, soldier, where the hell are you from? My mother use to say 'aboot' instead of 'about,' and she was from Canada."

"Me too, sir. British Columbia. After my dad died we moved to Oregon. After I got out of high school, I got drafted. I guess I could have gone back to Prince George, but I decided to give you Yanks a hand."

"You can give this Yank a big hand. How come we keep going off line every time we turn on anything?"

"Sir, they used the wrong-size cable. It's enough to run lights to each of those things you guys like to call home, but that's about all. Nobody said anything about you guys bringing everything except the kitchen sink."

"But we did bring the kitchen sink, and a hell of a lot more. What's your name soldier?"

"PFC Heffner, sir."

"Yeah, I can see that on your uniform. What's your first name?"

"Lindsay, sir, but the guys call me Slime."

"Why the hell do they call you, Slime?"

"Oh, it's a nickname I picked up when I was working for the forest service in Oregon during summer vacations. It stuck with me. Hell, I don't mind."

"Okay, Slime. How do you and I get enough power to my hootch to run a refrigerator, radio, air conditioner, and maybe a TV?"

"You've got all that stuff in that little culvert?" Slime asked.

"Yep, sure do. Only problem is, we need more power. And that's where you come in. Got any good ideas?"

"I could run a heavier cable down to your hootch, sir."

"Is there any way it could be done so that it wouldn't be noticed by anyone?"

"I guess I could dig a small ditch and bury it."

"Sounds great, when could you get started and how much will it cost me?"

"I'm off during the day, sir, and I could start on it tomorrow.

As far as payment, I don't need any money, but I can't buy Scotch and you can. How aboot a couple bottles of Scotch?"

"It's a deal. I'll get someone to bring it up from Phuoc Vinh, but it may be a couple of days. Is that okay?"

"I'll take your word for it, seeing as how you're half Canadian."

I had started to walk back toward my sewer-pipe hootch when Slime called out, "How will I know which culvert is yours, sir?"

"It's the only one with an air conditioner sticking out through the back wall."

"Okay, sir. I'll take care of it."

When I told Rosey what I had done, he just sat there, on his fold-out army cot with his head between his hands, and moaned. He knew, as did I, that it was very much against regulations to give hard liquor to an enlisted man.

The power had come back on, but our small fan was doing little more than making it very difficult for the bugs to fly in a straight line. I knew I had finally become a real member of Apache Troop when I could derive entertainment from sitting and watching huge bugs do loops and rolls, and cheer when they got slammed into the wall by a gust from the fan. It was unbelievable how many bugs one forty-watt light bulb could attract, but if we closed the doors at each end, the pipe became a sauna. If we opened them up, we got eaten alive.

"Just wait, Rosey. With any luck, tomorrow night we will be cool again."

"I'll believe it when I feel it," Rosey said.

The following morning I was assigned to fly with Rick Zeroth. More and more, the area of our operations was shifting away from the border to the northwest, to an area north and east of Song Be. LRRP (long-range recon patrol) teams were being used a lot more to try and monitor enemy movement. It was one of the most dangerous assignments of the Vietnam War. Those soldiers were all volunteers, in the best physical shape of anyone around and, in my opinion, had balls the size of elephants. A small group of them, usually four or five men, would be inserted by helicopter into a selected area, which usually had been reconed by one of our low birds some days prior. Usually the patrol area had been assigned because of something the low-bird pilot had reported seeing. The LRRPs' mission wasn't to engage the enemy but to observe what was going on and report back what they saw. A LRRP patrol required persons who could remain motionless and silent, sometimes for hours, while bugs nibbled at their bodies and sweat poured into their eyes. Too often, they were discovered and had to fight their way back to a pickup location, frequently the same LZ where they had been dropped off. Finding the same LZ in the daylight was usually not a problem; finding it in heavy rain or at night was next to impossible.

Zeroth had been assigned to cover the insertion of a LRRP team into an area northeast of Song Be. Another LRRP team, many miles to the southeast of Song Be had reported observing a small group of NVA headed north, with what appeared to be an American prisoner, the previous day. All they could tell for sure in the dim light was that he was tall and appeared to be Anglo.

The insertion of the team went off without a hitch. The Huey that dropped them off didn't even come to a hover or a full stop. The team was out the doors and had disappeared into the tall grass in a blink. All three helicopters, the Huey, our low bird, and us, were also out of the area in a flash. It was very important not to draw attention to the clearing.

"Did you confirm that the field we used is the one the TOC gave us, Boyle?" Zeroth asked.

"Yeah, Zero. It's the same one. I'm just really glad I'm not going with them. That walk in the jungle stuff is for shit."

We started to head back toward Song Be with our low bird beside us, only we began to climb much higher than usual.

"Hey, Zero, why are we getting up so high?" I asked.

"Just watch and listen and try and remember. A lot of lives may depend on what we do next, and yours may be one of them."

Zeroth climbed to around five thousand feet, and then turned back toward where we had just dropped off the LRRP team. First, he called the team and received a whispered response that they were okay and taking up their positions. Zero then called Song Be radar and advised them that he had just inserted a LRRP team and needed to mark its position. Once Song Be had located us on their radar screen, Zero flew back over the LZ and gave Song Be radar a "mark." When Zero called "mark," Song Be drew a small circle on the radar screen and labeled it with the LRRP's team number. Zeroth then explained to me that should the team ever get into contact at night or in heavy rain, Song Be radar would be able to talk the pickup Huey right back to the exact same place where the team had been dropped off.

"Boyle, don't ever forget what I just showed you. You would never find that team at night without it."

"I won't forget," I said.

We finished the day early and returned to Song Be around 3:00 P.M. I was really happy because Zeroth had let me do most of the flying after we dropped off the LRRP team. I had been in Vietnam five months, and I hoped Zeroth's letting me fly all day was a prelude to my becoming an aircraft commander and moving into the backseat. I also couldn't wait to get back to my sewer pipe and see if the new wiring had been installed.

As we landed, I saw Rosey standing on the flight line talking to a pilot who had arrived during the last week. I had told Zeroth about the air conditioner and what I hoped would be waiting when we landed. He was nice enough to let me out of the normal afterflight duties of an Xray.

Nothing appeared different from the outside of the sewer pipe, but when we got inside and back to the air conditioner, a large switch box on the wall told the story. I opened the back door and saw a large black electrical cable exiting the ground and running up the back wall and through a hole into the sewer pipe.

I reached out and took hold of the large metal handle on the box and pushed it to the "on" position. Then I went over to the air conditioner and turned the knob from "off " to "cool." With a soft hum, the AC came to life, and Rosey and I went nuts. The joy wouldn't have been any greater had a *Playboy* bunny walked through the door. Immediately the temperature within our hootch began to drop. Ten minutes later, the temperature was still going down.

"Shit, I never thought I could ever actually get cold in this part of the world. Why don't you turn it down a bit?" Rosey asked.

I turned the temperature knob until I heard the compressor kick off. Over the soft hum of the fan motor, I heard water running. I opened the back door and saw a steady stream of water coming from a hose at the bottom of the air conditioner. Before we turned on the AC, the humidity in our room must have been close to a 100 percent.

"Well, Boyle, now we have another problem."

"Make it a small one, Rosey; I don't need any more right now."

"I suggest we find ourselves some blankets because it's still colder than a well-diggers ass in Alaska, and you've got it turned all the way down."

"Okay, I'll see what I can come up with."

Not really knowing what I was looking for, I started walking across the large firebase. I kept thinking about the poncho liners that each of us were issued and used as a blanket when needed, but they were hard to come by. As soon as I saw the small field hospital, the answer came to mind. Hell, hospitals always have blankets, now how do I go about getting a few? I thought to myself. I walked around the hospital until I noticed two GIs standing by a row of conex containers (a smaller version of the metal containers used for shipping cargo overseas and usually seen at a seaport, they had double doors at one end.)

"How's it going?" I said as I got closer.

"Not bad, sir. How's it with you today?"

"I've got a small problem you might be able to help me with. I'm looking for about four extra blankets."

"Hell, sir, that's not a problem, follow me."

The young medic led me around the conex container he was standing alongside, to another row of containers. He opened a door. Inside were cardboard boxes full of new blankets, each stamped "US."

"How many did you say, sir?"

"Four will be just great. Now what can I do for you two?" I asked as he handed me the blankets.

"What type aircraft do you fly, sir?"

"Cobras."

"Any chance on getting a ride one of these days?"

"That's a pretty stiff order to fill, but I'll work on it. I probably won't be able to do it until I become an aircraft commander, and that may be over a month away."

"That's okay, sir. We'll still be here. If you need anything else, just let us know."

"Well, now that you mention it, if you guys should stumble across a couple of hospital beds and mattresses, I and my roommate could sure use them," I said, more as a joke than anything else.

"Where's your hootch, sir? We'll drop off the blankets so

you don't have to carry them across the company area. I'm not really sure if we're authorized to give these out or not."

I thanked them after telling them how to find our hootch, and walked back across the firebase to the Apache Troop area. As I opened the door to my hootch, a blast of cold air hit me.

"Man, that sure feels great," I said when I saw Rosey sitting on his cot reading a book.

"How did you make out? Any luck?"

"No problem. Our blankets should be delivered any moment now."

Shortly after sundown a covered, one-ton truck pulled up at the rear of our hootch, and the two medics emerged to carry the blankets up to our door.

"Can you and your roommate give us a hand, sir?"

"Sure. Hey, Rosey! Lend a hand," I said over my shoulder as I walked through the mud to the small truck.

The two medics in the back of the truck handed Rosey and me a metal-frame spring bed. Our mouths fell open with surprise. Not only had the troops brought two beds, but two six-inch-thick mattresses. The legs were folded down and the beds slid into place as our canvas cots were drop-kicked to the other end of the hootch. The two medics left with the promise of a Cobra ride just as soon as I could arrange it. Rosey and I just sat on our new beds and smiled at each other for what seemed like an hour. I hadn't felt anything as comfortable as that bed since leaving the States.

When Rosey had finished reading his book and turned out the light, I lay on my bunk, staring into the darkness, listening to the soft hum of the air conditioner. I was thinking about how funny it seemed that a soft bed and a light bulb could end up being so important. Important only because we had become used to them in the past. But that was no longer the case. That night I got the best night's sleep I could remember having at Song Be, and probably for the entire time I had been in Vietnam.

CHAPTER EIGHTEEN

So far, the day had gone like so many other days, nothing worth writing home about. I was assigned to fly with Bloody Bart Bartlett, and we were taking a long break just after lunch. I had been using the time to check on construction of our new mess hall. The large tents had been erected over the concrete slabs, and the first of the field cookstoves had begun to arrive, by truck convoy, from Phuoc Vinh. I had just walked to the rear door of what was going to be the cook tent when Bartlett ran up.

"Come on, Boyle, we've got LRRPs in contact," Bartlett yelled as he turned and sprinted toward our parked Cobra. From where I was standing, I could see the entire flight line and the revetments that were under construction. To protect the parked aircraft against incoming mortars and rockets, the revetments were shaped like the number 7 and arranged in rows of approximately ten. A number of people were running toward the flight line. One of them was Ron Glass, a Huey pilot.

Seldom did we tie down the rotor blades except at night, so there was nothing for me to do when I reached Bartlett's Cobra but to climb in, put on my seat and shoulder belts, and try to catch my breath.

"I've got to quit smoking, Bart," I tried to yell to Bartlett. My voice sounded like a squeaky toy for a cat.

"Maybe you should drink more beer, Boyle," Bartlett said with a smile but not looking up from gauges he was monitoring during the start cycle.

"Yeah, that's just what I need to do, fly every morning with a hangover. Then I could kill two birds with one stone—cough and puke at the same time."

The word "contact" had an electrifying effect on us. The

respiration increased as did the heart rate, and everything shifted into passing gear. Ron Glass was first to take off, followed
by Bartlett and myself, and our low bird. Bartlett explained
that we were going to be backing up Fuller and Reardon, another Pink Team that was diverting from the area they had
been searching to where the LRRPs were in contact. The Blue
Platoon had been alerted and the reaction force was standing
by its assigned Hueys.

"Fly this thing, Boyle, and hand me back your map. I'll
mark the location where the LRRPs are. If you remember
where we got the deer the other day, it's just to the northeast."

I took control of the Cobra, and not having to watch the low
bird, as it was right alongside of us, the thought of the deer
filled my mind. The incident had occurred a few days prior,
when our low-bird pilot, Joe Schlein, called Bartlett.

"Hey, Bart, I've got a deer down here. Feel like eating venison tonight?"

"Sounds great to me, but don't take any chances over it."

"Bart, tell him to make sure it's not too big." I was thinking
back to Cambodia when the low bird had shot a deer the size
of an elk, and the aircraft couldn't lift it. Game of all kinds
was always being found by the low birds during their search
for the NVA and VC. The only real rules of engagement concerning animals were directed at elephants and water buffalo.
Unless we were shot at by someone riding one, elephants were
strictly protected under the threat of court-martial. Water buffalo could only be shot if they had packs on their backs or
showed pack marks indicating that they were being used for
transportation by the enemy. A week didn't go by that we
didn't find a group of wild pigs, but nobody in the troop was
too hot about eating wild pig. On the other hand, nobody
turned down a good piece of fresh venison and the drunken
barbecue that went along with it. The barbecue was a way for
the troop to get together, to ignore the officer–enlisted distinc-
tion, and to just have a good time.

"Boyle, here's your map," Bartlett said, jarring me out of
thoughts of roast venison.

A mile or so in front of us, Ron Glass's Huey began a wide
sweeping circle as I was monitoring the conversation between
the LRRPs and Bill Fuller's Cobra. The LRRPs had been in an
on-and-off running fight with an enemy force of unknown size
for an hour. The LRRPs had reached the pickup location, an
area of low brush and tall grass approximately three hundred

yards wide, with tree lines on the south, east, and west sides. Until then, Fuller had been powerless to help the LRRPs because they were too close to the Viet Cong. Now with the LRRPs out in the tall grass, Fuller was able to put down rockets and minigun fire along the tree line occupied by the VC.

"Two One, Two Four," Fuller called to Bartlett. Bartlett didn't answer.

"Two One, this is Two Four. How do you copy?" Still there was no answer. I looked in the small rearview mirror that was located about halfway up the right edge of the windshield. Bartlett had his helmet off and was working on the plug. I called Fuller and told him that something was wrong with Bartlett's helmet, and it was obvious that he couldn't hear or transmit.

"Okay, Two One Xray, when he gets it fixed, tell him I could use some help on the western tree line.

"Two Four, Two One Xray, I've got a solid on that. I see where you've been putting the rockets down," I said.

One more look in the rearview mirror showed a pilot going nuts with frustration. Bartlett was trying to tell me something, but with all the traffic on the radio and the cockpit noise, I couldn't make out anything. I ripped off my helmet, and Bartlett yelled, "What the hell is going on? Something is wrong with my helmet or the radio; I can't hear a word."

"Here, try my helmet and see if it cures the problem," I yelled as I undid my seat belts so I could twist around in the seat and hand Bartlett my helmet. My helmet didn't work in the backseat either, which only added to Bart's frustration. I called Fuller and suggested I just try to relay to Bartlett all the information he gave me. Fuller agreed, and at first I tried writing the information on the right side of the cockpit canopy, with my grease pencil. That took too much time and sent Bartlett into a frenzy of shouting over the engine noise. Finally I got the message to Bart that he should work over the western tree line and help cover Apache Three Three (Ron Glass) as Ron made his approach into the pickup area.

Ron made his approach to the LZ from the south, using the cover of the thick jungle until he was over the pickup area. Bartlett followed Fuller, firing rockets into the western tree line as we made our pass from north to south. Out the left side of my canopy and two hundred feet below us, I could see the LRRPs scrambling on to Ron's Huey. Then I felt the G-force as Bartlett pulled out of his rocket-firing run and started a climbing left turn, away from the VC keeping the Huey on our left side, the same as we did when covering our low bird.

"We're coming out hot!" Ron called, to let the covering Cobras know that he was taking off and that the door gunners on his aircraft would be firing. Bartlett had just completed his turn back to the north in order to follow Fuller on another rocket run. I watched as the usual dirt and debris were kicked up by the rotor wash of Ron's Huey as it lifted off the ground and started forward in a climbing right turn to the east, away from the tree line where the VC were entrenched. Ron had just cleared the tops of the trees on his right and started over them when his voice crackled over the radio.

"Going down. Three Three going down."

My heart stopped, and I'm sure everyone else who heard his voice had the same feeling. I watched Ron's Huey do a violent 360-degree spin to the right and descend into the trees. Pieces of rotor blades and tree limbs flew in every direction, and it was difficult to tell which was which.

"Please God, don't let there be a fire this time," I whispered out loud. Then I held my breath and waited. There was no fire.

I didn't have to ask anyone what had happened as I had seen the pieces of tail rotor go flying, even before Ron got off his radio call. With no tail rotor to counteract the torque of the engine, the helicopter wanted to spin in the direction opposite to that of the main rotor blades. Ron Glass had no choice but to roll the throttle off—which would stop the spinning—and attempt an autorotation. His reaction had to have been automatic as everything happened in the blink of an eye, and at that altitude, he had no time to think. As Red always said, "when an emergency occurs, your reaction has to be instinctive and automatic; you won't have time to think about what you should do. You just do it."

Over the engine noise and radio traffic, the muffled sound of Bartlett's voice could be heard screaming, "Goddamn it, Boyle, what's going on?"

When I looked in the rearview mirror, Bartlett looked like a red-faced pogo stick, jumping up and down as far as his seat belt would allow. Not being able to hear anything was driving him nuts. Bartlett didn't understand that I couldn't hear what he was saying unless I took my helmet off; if I took my helmet off, I couldn't hear what was being said over the radio. Fuller directed his and our low bird to go in and check out the crash scene from where they had been holding, out to the south, clear of all the shooting. He then told me to advise Bartlett to follow him and fire when he fired. I shouted the instructions to Bartlett and watched in the rearview mirror as he indicated that he had understood. The low birds reported that the Huey had landed almost upright, and everyone appeared to be okay, and that the crew and LRRPs were taking up defensive positions around the downed helicopter. Fuller then advised me and the low birds that the Blues were on their way to secure the Huey, and I shouted that information back to Bartlett. The next voice I heard was unmistakably that of Captain Coons (Red). The voice that could raise the dead and cause a 50 percent hearing loss if you happened to be within a half mile when he called your name, and he was calling me.

"Two One Xray, advise Two One to take that broken dick helicopter back to base and get it repaired, now! I'm on station and will relieve you. How copy?"

"I've got you loud and clear, Red. I'll advise my backseat."

"Leave your low bird here, I didn't bring one."

I pulled my helmet off again and turned as far to the right as I could, without taking off my seat belts.

"Red wants us to go back to Song Be and get whatever is wrong fixed."

"Right now?" Bart asked.

"Yep, right now."

"Son of a bitch!" Bart yelled at the top of his voice as he turned the Cobra south, toward home.

It took almost the entire flight back to Song Be for the bright red color to leave Bart's face, and I shared his frustration. Nobody liked being ordered to leave a situation like that one just because a piece of equipment failed to work correctly. But I was just happy that Bart wasn't able to hear Red's voice, and the way in which he ordered us back to Song Be. He had sounded like a teacher scolding a couple of school kids caught fighting on the playground. I'm sure that, had Bartlett been able to hear Red, he would have given some very serious thought to finally taking that big shit under Red's pillow as he had threatened to do so many times in the past.

Without incident, the Blue Platoon landed and rigged the Huey so it could be slung out by another helicopter, and everyone was back at Song Be before dark.

For the next few weeks, I put as much effort as I could into learning everything I could from each of the pilots I flew with. I knew from the way I was being allowed to fly from the front seat and make noncritical decisions that I would probably be making aircraft commander soon if I stayed out of trouble. It didn't help a lot knowing that Mills, Peele, Zeroth, Fuller, and Red, would be going home in about a month. Not only were *we* losing a lot of Cobra pilots, but pilots and men from all the other platoons were also leaving. Losing so much combat experience at one time was scary because, with the exception of Bartlett and Thomas, all the Cobra Xrays would be brand new, along with the Cobra aircraft commanders.

Red and I were about thirty miles north of Song Be after completing the last recon flight of the day, and for the first time ever, Red was allowing me to fly. I called Song Be approach control and advised them we were enroute and of our approximate location. Red was on the other radio talking to the TOC, but I knew he was keeping an eye and ear on everything I was doing. He had a habit of lulling the pilot in the front seat into feeling comfortable, and then simulating some sort of emergency. I was waiting for whatever he had in mind.

"Boyle, the TOC told me that I've got to go down to Phuoc Vinh and take care of some business. Brown wants to fly down with me so he can check out the PX. Is that okay with you?"

"Sure, Red, that's fine with me. I'm down to my last twenty bucks anyway, and I can always have Brown pick me up a carton of cigarettes."

"That's fine, Boyle, we'll refuel and then Brown can trade places with you."

After we had refueled, Red hovered over to the area nearest the TOC, and I got out. Dave Brown was waiting as I climbed down the left side and jumped to the ground.

"Hey, Dave, you wouldn't pick me up a carton of Benson & Hedges or Salem's would you?" I asked holding out a ten dollar bill of MPC (military payment certificates), which we called "funny money."

"I'll see what I can get," Brown said. He seemed not too happy about flying with Red.

"I sure hope you've got your emergency procedures down pat. Nobody volunteers to fly with Red unless he has an IQ of at least two hundred or is just plain nuts."

"Brown! Get your fat ass in here. It's going to be dark pretty soon," Red yelled, causing us both to jump.

To get away from the rotor wash, I walked about one hundred feet, then turned and watched as they took off to the south toward Phuoc Vinh. Brown was assigned to the Scout Platoon, but knowing Red as I did, I didn't think that would stop him from messing with Brown's mind a little. I watched the departing Cobra for a couple of minutes and then headed toward the TOC to drop off my paperwork. The usually busy TOC was quiet. Rick Zeroth was talking to First Sergeant Sparacino, so I dropped off my SOI (a book the size of a small pocket notebook, which contained the secret codes for that day) and left. I walked toward my hootch and a bed I looked forward to stretching out on, and the feel of cool air for a change. I felt a little self-conscious, as a big smile came to my face because of something Red had said to me during one of our refueling stops at Firebase Snuffy.

"You know, Boyle, I was thinking, all you would have to do is add a bathroom to your hootch and you could probably rent it out to visiting dignitaries."

I had almost reached my door when the siren mounted on the top of the TOC came to life with its blood-chilling wail, and jarred me out of my daydream. I had not heard any explosions, which ruled out incoming mortars or rockets. Only one other thing caused the siren to go off, and that was a downed aircraft. I turned and ran back toward the TOC. As I reached the door, I was almost run over as Rick Zeroth bolted out, helmet in hand.

"Follow me, Boyle; you're my X ray," Zeroth yelled as we sprinted toward the flight line and Zeroth's waiting Cobra. I couldn't recall ever seeing Rick Zeroth—Apache Two Niner—ever being so excited. He was the most laid-back pilot in the troop. In front of us I could see Rick's crew chief swinging the large rotor blade to indicate that it had been untied. The crew chief had either been very close to the Cobra when the siren had gone off, or he ran a hell of a lot faster than Rick or I. All along the flight line, I could hear turbine engines coming to life as the Blue Platoon members scrambled onto their Hueys.

Rick had our engine turning over before I was halfway into the front seat.

"Who's down?" I yelled over the whine of the turbine engine as it spooled up in RPM.

"It's Red. He's been shot down."

"Bullshit, he just took off for Phuoc Vinh not more than ten minutes ago," I said, thinking somebody had a wire crossed.

"He called the TOC, not more than two minutes after you

walked out, and said he was taking fire and going down," Zeroth yelled back at me.

The Cobra lifted off the ground and immediately turned south. Provided you were flying in the daylight, the route to Phuoc Vinh was easily followed because of a narrow dirt road that ran between the two locations. I estimated that we had about forty-five minutes before it was dark. We climbed until we reached three thousand feet, looking for the black plume of smoke we expected to mark the crash site. We made a half-dozen 360-degree circles as we continued south but didn't see anything.

We descended to fifteen hundred feet and started searching, not really knowing if we were even close to where he had gone down. Our search was complicated by the fact that the people native to the area were lighting their evening cook fires. We checked a hundred small fires, and both Rick and I were becoming increasingly frustrated. Looking down at my map, I tried to guess just how far Red would have traveled in ten minutes. "If we don't find them in the next five or ten minutes, they'll be out here all night. Then what do we do?"

"I wish I knew," Zero sighed.

"Zero, let's try looking further to the east. I'm guessing we're close to the distance Red would have gone, but I think we're too far west."

"At this point I'm ready to try anything. It's damn near dark, and if we don't find them soon we can probably kiss them good-bye."

As we turned toward the east, the evening sky was full of flashing, red aircraft lights. In an attempt to find Red before dark, Apache Troop had put everything in the air that could fly. As we moved east over an old rubber plantation, we descended even lower. The long lines of trees had long since been cut down, and only a few dead ones remained.

"We've got him; we've found Red's ship," came the excited voice of one of the Huey pilots, who was flying with his load of Blues on board. I guess that at least twenty people all said *"where?"* at the exact same time, over the radio. The pilot of the Huey gave the exact location and advised he was landing next to the crash site. By then I could no longer make out the detail on my map without the use of my flashlight, so I just watched for the lights of the Huey that would be descending lower than the rest.

"There, Zero—about two miles in front of us and a tad off to our left," I yelled into my microphone.

"Easy on the ears. You trying to sound like Red, or what?" Zero yelled back at me.

"Sorry," I said.

What I saw next was almost as bad as seeing a helicopter burn. Red's Cobra was in a huge open area of low grass and a few scattered, dead rubber trees. I had never before seen a helicopter so totally destroyed. It looked like a giant had taken a Cobra, completely disassembled it, and then just tossed all the parts into the air and let them fall. The cockpit was upside down, and the Plexiglas canopies smashed almost flat. The main rotor blades, still attached to the rotor mast and transmission, were ten feet away from the helicopter. Just behind the exhaust pipe, the tail boom had been severed from the aircraft and was lying thirty to forty feet behind the cockpit. The left wing and rocket pods had been torn off and lay ten feet from the helicopter. Rockets lay everywhere. The landing skids were torn completely away and lay on the ground like twisted plumbing pipe.

"We need a medevac ASAP. Red's cut up pretty bad, and his Xray is in very bad shape with a lot of broken bones. He's still trapped inside. And see if they'll send a nurse along," came the excited voice of the pilot on the ground.

"Okay, we've got a solid on that," was the reply from the radio operator back at the TOC.

We circled the crash site for what seemed like hours, until we could no longer see anything on the ground. I wanted to land to see if I could help in some way, even though I knew that there were more than enough people down there to do whatever was necessary. Knowing that didn't ease the frustration I was feeling, and my heart sunk when Zero called the TOC and requested permission to return to base because of darkness.

"Two Nine, advise the other aircraft, except the Blues, to return to base. I don't want you guys running into each other out there," boomed the unmistakable voice of Major Harris.

As was always the case, when making a night-landing approach into Song Be, as soon as we turned on the landing light, single tracers would be observed coming up from the areas just outside the base. We guessed it was the ARVN soldiers taking potshots at us and not the VC as nobody had ever been caught, and the area was controlled by the ARVNs.

I waited around the TOC until the word came down that both

Red and Dave Brown had been medevaced out of the crash site to the hospital. Little information was passed on to us about the crew's condition that night. I spent most of that evening on my bunk thinking about all the "what ifs," especially why I wasn't seated in the front seat instead of Dave Brown. I knew, first-hand, how well Red could fly and wondered how the helicopter ended up so totally destroyed. I thought of how the newer pilots disliked Red, as I did at first, and how the longer a pilot knew Red, the more respect he had for Red's judgment and knowledge. It was just Red's way of teaching that caused ill feelings. Once a new pilot had demonstrated that he knew the way things should be done, or at least was attempting to learn, Red lightened up a little. We also learned that no matter how friendly he might seem, you never let down your guard while flying with Red. If you did, he'd find some way to bite you in the ass with an emergency procedure.

In the morning, the initial reports indicated that Red had suffered a lot of upper body cuts from the Plexiglas. It was believed that Dave Brown had a broken hip, leg, and arm, along with numerous cuts from the broken cockpit canopy, and possibly a compressed spine, and a concussion. Red had less than a month to go before leaving Vietnam for the States—or as most of us called it, "Going back to the World." I wondered if Red would even return to the unit. My question was answered in less than a week when Red returned to Song Be. I never saw Dave Brown again as he was medevaced back to the States because of his injuries. Although still officially the platoon leader, Red had changed. He was more quiet than before, staying close to the TOC. He seldom flew.

The mess hall had finally become fully operational, and with the new mess hall came a new mess sergeant who explained to me that he was only temporarily assigned to our unit. My new mess sergeant was a short black man in his late thirties and obviously not real happy about being assigned to a unit with Apache Troop's reputation. I somehow got the feeling that he missed all the good things that were more easily available to a unit closer to Saigon. On the other hand, he had one hell of a sense of humor and was an excellent teacher. One of the first things he did was to teach me how to make Raisin Jack booze; at least he told me how to do it. He either forgot to tell me, or I failed to remember, to let the pressure off of the four, five-gallon cans I had brewing behind the cookstoves. At three o'clock one morning, they exploded and covered everything in the cook tent with a mixture of garbage, the smell of which would have made a maggot puke. After hours of cleaning, most of which was left up to me, we sat and laughed about it all. I found conversations with my new mess sergeant very interesting. The more we spoke, the more I grew to like and respect him. We shared one very important dislike, we both hated to see food served to the troops out of those damn marmite cans. Getting served a spoonful of food out of one of those cans had the same effect on the person being served as food being piled on the plate straight out of a garbage can.

"Mess Sergeant, where could we come up with a steam table?" I asked during one of our nightly meetings.

"Are you really serious, sir?" he asked with a look of disbelief.

"Sure, why not a steam table? Hell, if the straps in the rear can have steam tables to keep their food warm, why shouldn't we be able to have one?"

"Because we're on a firebase, sir, and they just don't have steam tables on a firebase."

"Is there a rule or law or army regulation that says we can't have one?"

"No, sir, not that I'm aware of. I'll check with a few of my friends back at Phuoc Vinh and see what I can find out, sir."

I almost said, "Mighty fine," and then bit my tongue in the nick of time.

"Okay, Sergeant, see what you can dig up for me."

"Oh, by the way, sir, do you like strawberries?"

"Sure as hell do. Doesn't everybody?"

"Why don't you grab a can out of the fridge on your way out, they sent up a lot more than I'll ever use."

"We don't have any ice cream to go along with the berries, do we?"

"Got plenty of that, too. Grab a carton out of the freezer. I just don't understand how we can have ice cream and all the fresh milk we can drink, and I can't get a light bulb to save my ass."

"I'll take care of the light bulbs, Mess Sergeant. You just find me a steam table."

That night Rosapepe, Jim Thomas, Larry Lilly, our new roommate, Jeff Cromar, and I pigged out on strawberries and ice cream until we couldn't eat any more. The box of cookies that I had just received from Sonny and Dusty was also vaporized within minutes of the box being opened.

Within a few days, the mess sergeant had informed me that he had possibly located a steam table. Obtaining the steam table might present a few minor problems; the table in question was being used by another unit, but they were being sent home. If everything went as it usually did, the mess hall would be unused for a day or so before the new unit took over.

"Just exactly where is this steam table, Mess Sergeant?"

"Bien Hoa, sir."

"Holy shit, man, that's like downtown. How the hell are we going to get it out of a mess hall without someone asking a lot of questions?"

"We would have to do it at night, sir."

"I'm going to have to give this little mission some serious thought, Mess Sergeant. Do you know how much time we have before the unit moves out?"

"I'm not real sure, sir. I got the impression that it would only be a few days, though."

"Okay, when you talk to your friend, ask him to find out if there is a helipad close to where this act of grand theft is going to take place."

"Right, sir. I'm going to Phuoc Vinh in the morning on the mail bird, and I'll try and find out then."

I knew where to find my fat little Italian buddy, Paul Foti. At that time of night he would always be watching the movies, especially if they were spaghetti westerns, which they usually were. I couldn't break him away from the entertainment, so I invited him for strawberries and ice cream later.

When Foti showed up at my hootch, I packed his stomach with strawberries and ice cream followed by the last of my chocolate-chip cookies. Then I explained what we needed his helicopter for. I emphasized that the secret mission would greatly increase the quality of the food being served in our mess hall.

"Will it mean we get more pasta?"

"Foti, if you do this for me, I'll make sure you get all the pasta you can eat."

"Okay, I'll do it, but I'll have to figure a way to get it by my platoon leader."

"Hell, just tell him you're going to combine a maintenance flight with going to the PX, that should cover the time we need."

Two nights later as we approached the helipad on the edge of Bien Hoa, my palms were sweating. As far as anyone knew, we were all at the PX in Phuoc Vinh; if we went down for any reason, nobody would know where the hell we were. As we touched down, the mess sergeant, clutching a small tool bag, and three cooks jumped from the Huey and disappeared into the dimly lighted base.

It seemed like forever before one of the cooks reappeared, carrying a stack of inserts for the steam table. It was Mike Cutts, and he had a huge smile on his face. He didn't say a word as he slid the inserts into the back of the Huey. As he turned to leave, he came up to my side of the Huey and gave me the thumbs-up signal. It helped a little, but Foti and I still felt like Bonnie and Clyde sitting outside a bank being held up.

"Holy shit, what's that? Foti asked, pointing at the small group of cooks carrying the steam table, minus its legs.

I jumped out of the still running helicopter, climbed into the back, grabbed the rear jump seat and folded it upright to make room for the wide and long steam table. As the table was slid in, I backed slowly out the other door, holding as much of the weight as I could, and jumped onto the wooden helipad. The steam table kept on coming until it protruded out each side of the Huey by at least three feet.

"Is that it, Mike?" I yelled at Cutts.

"No, sir, we still have some glass and a few gas bottles left to get."

"Well hurry up, before we get our asses thrown in Long Binh jail."

"Three large gas bottles, which resembled welding tanks, were loaded on the Huey, along with the glass front and top of the table.

"Let's get the hell out of here quick," I said to Foti, after I plugged in my helmet.

As Foti piloted the Huey back to Song Be, I looked over my shoulder at what, at first glance, appeared to be a pile of shiny stainless-steel junk. I wished that I had gone along with the raiding party of cooks so I could have seen what all the equipment looked like when it was assembled.

"Mike, I'll get Foti to drop you off at rearm so you can pick up the mule (a small four-wheeled vehicle used to carry cargo), then just meet us where Foti parks this thing."

"No problem, sir."

The rear opening of the mess hall cook tent was less than one hundred yards from where we parked. The transfer of the stolen steam table from the flight line to the cook tent was made without our being detected, even though the quiet night air was filled with our laughter.

"How long will it take to get all this set up and running, Sergeant?" I asked.

"If everything goes right, sir, a couple of hours."

"Okay, I've got to fly first light. I'm going to go get some sleep, and I'll be back at 4:00 A.M. I can't wait to get this thing in operation and see the expression on the Old Man's face when he walks in for breakfast. Tell your troops to keep quiet about how we really got this thing. If anyone asks, just tell them it was issued as part of the new mess hall."

"Right, sir. See you in the morning."

When I walked into the mess hall, shortly after 5:00 A.M., I couldn't believe the transformation that had taken place. I saw a beautiful stainless-steel-and-glass masterpiece, that had to be over twelve feet long. On the front side was the typical rack, used to slide a tray along. On the back side were the stainless inserts, resting in a shallow bath of near boiling water. The inserts held slices of French toast, hot syrup, bacon, scrambled eggs, and fried potatoes. Everything was hot, but most of all it was appealing to look at.

"Sir, I need to speak to you a minute."

"Sergeant, this looks better than I ever dreamed. I hope there's nothing wrong."

"No, sir, but we now have stainless trays and silverware to use instead of the paper plates and plastic utensils. The problem is that we don't have the facilities or personnel to wash all that stuff after every meal, and not enough trays for the entire troop. I forgot about that when we snatched everything last night."

"I was wondering what was in all those extra boxes you were carrying last night. Let's just stick to the paper plates for right now. Maybe we can come up with a better idea later."

"Sounds good to me, sir. The cooks weren't looking forward to washing all that stuff."

I knew that Major Harris would be one of the first to enter the serving tent, which also served as the mess hall for the enlisted members of the troop. I worried a bit about his reaction to the miracle that had taken place. About that time, the mess sergeant retreated to the cover of the cook tent and left me and Mike Cutts and the other servers to take the heat.

"Don't worry, Mike, it will be okay," I said, trying to sound more sure of myself than I was.

"Oh, I'm not worried, sir. I was just following orders, but what's your excuse?" Mike said with a big grin.

"Attention!" someone yelled as Major Harris walked through the side opening in the tent. "As you were," Major Harris quickly stated. I was standing at the far end of the steam table from where he was picking up his plate. I watched for some reaction, but saw none. The sly son of a bitch went down the serving line as if nothing had changed at all. When he got to where I was standing, he looked me directly in the eye, and I thought I saw the slightest glimmer of a smile.

"Would you please join me at my table, Mr. Boyle?"

"Yes, sir, I'd be happy to."

I grabbed a cup of coffee and walked the short distance to the officers mess tent. I had no idea what to expect, but was prepared for the worst.

"Have a seat, Mr. Boyle."

It seemed like forever before he said anything. Other officers entering the tent, and sensing something was up, avoided his table. I began thinking back to my old police interrogation days, the routine where you let a suspect just sit and stew, without saying anything. Finally, he broke the silence.

"It would appear that we have a new addition to our mess hall, Mr. Boyle."

"Yes, sir." I sounded like a bullfrog being run over by a truck.

"I don't recall seeing a steam table on our list of issued equipment. Could I have missed that item, Mr. Boyle?"

"No, sir, I don't think you missed it, sir. It just seemed to appear overnight, and I decided to put it to it's best use, sir."

"Well, Mr. Boyle, because that piece of equipment is not on our assigned equipment list, it might present a problem when the IG (inspector general) comes by for his semiannual inspection."

"Yes, sir, I'm aware of that. But as we are always given advance notice of his inspection, I can assure you that the steam table can disappear as easily as it appeared."

"That will be all, Mr. Boyle. I'm sure you have a lot to do."

"Yes, sir. Thank you, sir," I said as I stood up and hotfooted it toward the exit of the tent.

"Mr. Boyle!" Major Harris's voice boomed across the tent.

"Sir?" I said, and wheeled around to face him.

"Mighty fine, Mr. Boyle. Mighty fine job, and the breakfast is mighty tasty also," he said with a broad smile.

"Thank you, sir, thank you very much. I'm sure the other cooks will be very pleased!"

CHAPTER NINETEEN

I didn't think anything was out of the ordinary when Jim Thomas walked into our hootch one night and sat down on Rosey's bunk. Jim had just returned from the in-country instructor pilot (IP) school, and now was the troop check pilot. I was usually a little nervous around Jim; he always had a big smile on his face, but he had eyes that I felt could see right through me.

"Say, Boyle, guess what I'm going to do tomorrow?" Jim said.

"What do I get if I guess right?"

"Either way, win or lose, you get to take a check ride with me."

"You've got to be shitting me?"

"No, it's true. I get the pleasure of finding out just how much you've forgotten about how to fly. You haven't had a check ride since Cobra school, and it's time."

"You're full of crap up to your armpits, Thomas. I took a check ride every time I flew with Red, and he's a hell of a lot tougher than you."

"Don't give me any of your shit, Boyle. This is a by-the-book, official-type check ride. So quit your bitching and be out on the flight line tomorrow morning after breakfast."

"Yes, sir, Mister check pilot, sir!"

A check ride is something that every pilot, military or civilian, has to go through at intervals determined by the type of flying that is being done. I've never met a pilot who looked forward to a check ride, even one given by a friend. Thomas was probably one of the best of our Cobra pilots, and we were proud of him, even if we didn't show it. The next morning, I met Thomas on the flight line, and he reviewed what we were going to do. I flew the Cobra from the rear seat and everything went well. I was impressed with how professional he was and how well he handled the Cobra from the front seat. We went through emergency procedures, the proper responses to conditions such as engine failure and stuck tail rotor pedal, as well as running landings and other procedures. We then flew back to Song Be, and I figured that the check ride was over until Thomas told me to land at the refuel area.

"Hey, Jim, we don't need fuel. Why are we going there?"

"We still have to do hovering autorotations, and I want the flattest surface I can get."

"Okay, you're the boss."

We landed at refuel and did a few hovering autorotations. These simulate the engine failing at a hover. A hovering autorotation is normally performed with the nose pointing into the wind, standing still, and at about three feet off the ground. The throttle is then rolled off and the student is graded on how well he can hold the heading he had and how soft the helicopter touches down on the ground. Simply put, it's an exercise in coordination. After three such maneuvers, Thomas told me to back the helicopter straight back until we came to the edge of the blacktop of the refuel area. Something in his voice just didn't sound right, and I looked at the rearview mirror that was located in the front cockpit. All I saw was a face full of smile, and I knew for sure that he had something in mind that he wasn't telling me. I started backing up very slowly, holding the altitude at three feet and got a death grip on the throttle. Within seconds I felt the twist-grip throttle, which my left hand was grasping tightly, begin to jerk, as Thomas attempted to roll the throttle to the ground-idle position. He couldn't budge it an inch as he attempted to give me a surprise hovering autorotation while the damn helicopter was moving backwards.

"Let up on the throttle, Boyle," Thomas yelled over the intercom.

"Eat my shorts, asshole. I'm not doing one going backwards."

"Okay, Boyle, I've got the controls."

Thomas just shook his head and laughed as he took control of the Cobra and moved it back to our original starting point. He then demonstrated how to perform the maneuver, which I couldn't remember ever doing before. As it turned out, it was easier than I had thought, and after I had shown that I could do it, we returned to our own flight line and parked the Cobra.

After the check ride, which I passed, I flew with Zero. I was being allowed to fly more and more from the rear seat. Each day, Rick Zeroth would perform his own little test to see just how well I could run a mission from the backseat. I felt very much at ease with him. Although he was very quiet, it didn't take his Xray pilots long to learn that he was very smart.

We took off one morning early, without a low bird, and flew up to Firebase Snuffy. There Zero explained to me that we were going to spend the morning finding out just how accurate I was with all the weapon systems on the Cobra. It was obvious that he was giving me some sort of test, but Zero didn't make me feel that way. He just explained that we were going to pick out things we could use as targets and see how close I could come to hitting them. We landed at the rearm and refuel area at the northeast corner of the firebase, then shut down. While loading the pods full of rockets, Zero explained that we would be going out to a free-fire box (an area known to be free of civilians and friendly troops, in which permission to fire was not required). There we would just pick out anything that could be used as a target.

I was really excited as I hovered the heavy Cobra out to the north end of the dirt runway and pointed the nose south.

"Snuffy Control, Apache Two Niner is taking the active for a south departure." Snuffy didn't have a control tower, just a radio operator who looked for and kept track of the inbound and outbound traffic. It was the pilot's responsibility to keep himself clear of other aircraft.

"Roger Two Niner. No reported traffic. Cleared to depart."

To me, flying the Cobra from the rear seat was like flying a World War II P-51 Mustang, a lifelong dream, only this one just happened to have rotor blades. Some nights I found myself in that state between being half-awake and half-asleep, wishing that the NVA had helicopters similar to the Cobra, so we could have dogfights. But that was part of the war reserved only for the air force. Then the reality of such thoughts would set in, and the realization that someone always lost, and it wasn't always the bad guys. Being able to look over each shoulder at the short stubby wings with pods full of rockets beneath them, gives the pilot a feeling of awesome power. The more I flew the Cobra, the more I learned what it could do, and as the nickname Snake implies, learned that if you didn't treat it right, it would very quickly bite you in the ass, with little or no warning and when you least expected it.

Just trying to get the Cobra to hover out to the runway was a real job; in an attempt to see how well I would handle the situation, Zero had made sure the Cobra was overloaded. Snuffy's elevation was close to two thousand feet, but with the very high air temperature, the air density was very thin and the helicopter much more difficult to control. The schoolbook technique for takeoffs just wouldn't work under the prevailing circumstances. Without overtorquing the engine, the highest I could get the Cobra to hover was about one foot off the runway. I had simulated the same set of circumstances with Jim Thomas when he had given me my check ride, but now it was for real. In an attempt to get down the runway and leave the cloud of dirt and dust behind us, I eased the cyclic forward, which started the Cobra moving forward. To take off, I had to hold the Cobra off the ground without overtorquing the engine and other parts and get the aircraft moving down the runway until it reached "translational lift," that point where the helicopter is no longer hovering due to the ground-effect air cushion, but is flying like an airplane (approximately fifteen to twenty mph). Just being able to see where I was going was a real challenge, but eventually the Cobra gave a shudder and the cloud of dirt was left behind us; we were now flying, no longer in a hover. I waited until the airspeed had built up to sixty mph, and eased back on the cyclic, which produced an immediate climb. The smile on my face had to have been the size of a freeway billboard when Zero said, "That was pretty good, Boyle. Now call the TOC and tell them we're off Snuffy, and where we're going. Then call Snuffy and tell them where we'll be so they'll know not to shoot any artillery that way, or at least to let us know if they have to shoot."

I would have remembered to call the TOC, but I'm sure I wouldn't have thought about the outgoing artillery rounds from Snuffy.

After looking around the free-fire area (sometimes referred to as a gook box), Zero picked out a large tree in the middle of some low-lying brush.

"Okay, Boyle, let's assume that tree is our low bird. I want you to circle it just as if we were covering a low bird. You pick the altitude and the distance that you feel is the best for you, and we'll see what happens. When you're ready, let me know."

"Okay, Zero. I'm ready."

Before I had time to think about anything else, Zero said, "Your low bird just called, taking fire."

I banked the Cobra hard over to the left and pointed the nose at the lonely tree. Immediately I realized that the dive was too steep, and we were closing on the target too fast, close to two hundred mph. I felt like fresh dogshit when Zero said, "Well, Boyle, are you going to shoot or not?"

"I'm trying, but nothing's happening."

"Okay, pull out, and we'll talk about it."

I pulled back on the cyclic and watched as the nose of the Cobra rose and the G-force pushed me down into the seat. I also noticed that, even though the Cobra was in a climbing attitude, we continued to descend for a time before we actually started to gain altitude again. Zero didn't yell and scream but very quietly pointed out a few mistakes, but mistakes that could have been fatal to both the Cobra and the low bird. First, I was too close in to the target, which is why the dive I'd made had to be so steep to see the target. Second, I had not armed the weapons system and could not fire anything. Third, I had pulled out of my dive too low. He went on to explain that whenever the low bird is working, the weapons system must be armed.

"The whole idea of getting off some rockets quickly is not necessarily to kill anybody; you just want them to quit shooting at the low bird. You also want to keep your orbit around the low bird far enough out that your firing run is not a steep dive but a shallow dive. That way, you have time to fire more rockets, and when you pull out of your dive, you won't start mushing in toward those damn trees the way you just did. You also will avoid putting a real strain on my body, and numerous moving parts of this helicopter. One last thing you should remember, when you pull out of your rocket run, don't try climbing immediately. Let your speed take you away from the target, then climb. That way you'll be exposed for the least amount of time to whomever you were shooting at. Does all that sound right to you?"

"Sounds great; I just can't believe I forgot to arm the system."

"We've all done it at one time or another. The secret is to just stay calm. Whatever you do, don't get excited on the radio. If you sound excited, you're going to get everyone who hears you excited. Then all you have is a bunch of people yelling over the radio, and everything turns to shit in a real hurry. Now, let's go back. This time we'll do it right."

My first attempt at hitting the tree with two rockets was not a success. Zeroth pointed out that the aircraft had to be in trim in order for the rockets to go where I was trying to point them otherwise the rockets would curve off to the left or right, depending on which way the helicopter was out of trim. Of course, all that had been taught to me in Cobra school, but that seemed light-years in the past. By the fourth or fifth attempt, I was getting better.

That night I cracked the Cobra manuals and studied the graphs that showed how much a Cobra continued to descend after pulling out of a dive even though it was in a level attitude. What I read was a real eye-opener, and I showed it to Rosey.

"Look at this, Rosey. The book says that if you exceed two hundred mph in a steep dive, the helicopter can descend as much as five hundred feet before the descent stops, even though the Cobra is in level flight."

"Yeah, but we don't usually get going that fast, at least I haven't."

"I did today, and those trees were coming up at me pretty fast, even after I pulled out. I don't think I made a very good impression on Zero."

"You're just lucky it wasn't Red. He'd still be yelling at you."

"Did someone mention my name?" boomed the voice that could jar the faces loose from Mount Rushmore.

Red walked through our door and sat down on Rosey's bunk.

Red just sat there and looked around the hootch, sort of shaking his head, as his eyes did a close inspection of our somewhat unusual decor. He had never been in our sewer-pipe hootch before, but I'm sure he had heard about it.

"You two plan on opening a whorehouse or something? Maybe a massage parlor?"

"Just trying to get comfortable before we have to move again."

As he stood up and started for the door, Red said, "Rosapepe, you're flying with the new AC tomorrow, so try and keep him out of trouble."

"Yeah, and who might that be? I don't recall that we got anybody new in."

"We didn't, but Zero seems to think your roommate is ready. Congratulations, Mr. Boyle; you're now an aircraft commander!"

Rosey and I just sat there and stared at each other, me because I couldn't think of anything to say, and Rosapepe because he couldn't think of a way to get out of flying with me in the morning.

"I'll be right back, Rosey, don't try and hide!"

I felt like skipping, but instead, I walked across to the mess hall. As usual, I found the mess sergeant working on the books by the light of a very small and dim light bulb.

"Mess sergeant, I just made AC, and I want to celebrate. You wouldn't spring loose more of those strawberries and maybe some ice cream?"

"Sir, that's great news, and you don't have to ask my permission. This is your mess hall as much as it's mine."

"Thanks a lot, Sarge, it's just that some years back, I traded a bunch of bacon for coffee without asking. The next morning, when the mess officer found out, I got my butt in a heap of trouble."

"No problem, sir. We've got more than you and all the other pilots could possibly eat, but I still haven't seen any of those light bulbs you promised."

"I'm really sorry, sarge. I'll put it at the top of the list. I've got to go talk with the engineers tomorrow. Maybe I can work some sort of trade."

"Okay, Rosey, time to party," I said as I walked into the hootch with a gallon of ice cream under one arm and a number-ten can of strawberries under the other.

"The hell with ice cream, I need some beer. If I've got to fly with you tomorrow, I want to get drunk tonight."

"Is that any way to be talking to a superior officer? Have you forgotten that you're just an FNG Xray, and I'll be telling you what to do tomorrow?"

"Have you forgotten that I'll be spending the whole damn day trying to keep you out of trouble and most likely from getting lost?"

Bill Fuller was about to go on R & R to Australia. He would have only a few days left in troop when he returned, and then would be going back to the World. I asked him if I could take over his AC number, Apache Two Four, and he agreed. Bill was highly respected in the troop, but more than that, he had an aura about him that drew people to follow his lead. Everyone would miss his leadership, including the officers who greatly outranked him. I knew that just taking Two Four wouldn't bring me respect or automatically raise me to the same quality of pilot, those only came with experience. At this point, I could only hope it would bring me some of the luck that had always gone with that number.

The following day, for the first time in my life, I tried to do everything by the book. We were assigned to an area just west of Snuffy and spent three fuel loads looking for trouble but didn't find anything worth shooting at. Flying with Rosey was great. He was an expert at reading a map, and the only thing I could teach him, as far as running a mission goes, was how *not* to do things. I was sure, after only one day of flying with him, that he was more qualified than myself and would be making aircraft commander very soon. After looking forward to becoming an aircraft commander for so long, actually doing it was a bit of a letdown. All that changed was the amount of responsibility and the realization that there was no one sitting behind me to ask questions of. The knowledge that the lives of the crew of my low bird, copilot, and the troops I assisted on the ground were now my responsibility was a bit overwhelming.

That night as I lay on my bunk, thoughts raced through my mind about what I had done to get to that point in my life and what I wanted to do with whatever more was left in it. I knew I wanted to stay in the army. With my reserve time, I could retire after nineteen more years with a total of twenty-six years' service. Of course, I knew that I could never put up with all the "yes sir, no sir" stuff for that long. Each day I thought more about my goals until, for a number of reasons that no reasonable and prudent person would understand, I walked into First Sergeant Sparacino's office and asked to extend my tour of duty in Vietnam for six months.

"Have you given this a lot of thought, Mr. Boyle?"

"Probably not as much as I should have, First Sergeant, but yes, I've thought about it."

"You don't have to tell me, but I'd be curious to know why you want to spend six more months in this shithole."

"If I tell you, Sergeant, you're going to have to promise not to try and have me locked up or put me in for a section eight!"

"This is just between you and me, sir, I'm just curious, that's all."

"I'm not so sure that my reasoning is all that great, especially when I try and put it into words, but I guess the biggest reason is that I'm beginning to like it here."

I had expected an adverse reaction, but his dark eyes showed no reaction other than interest.

"I know a lot of guys extend so they can get out as soon as they get back to the States, but I plan on staying in the army. I figure that I've spent almost six months just learning how to become an average combat pilot. I'd like to be a damn good one, and I don't see how that will be possible in the time I have left. Sound a little nutty, First Sergeant?"

Well, sir, everyone has their own reasons. My job is to make sure that before I submit the paperwork for an extension, the person's reasons for extension are valid. I know of people who are on their third and fourth extension. What does your family think about your extending?"

"I've mentioned it in letters to my wife, and she doesn't seem to think it's a bad idea, and that bothers me a little. Things aren't looking too good as far as my marriage goes, and that may have something to do with my decision. I also feel that the longer I'm here, the more I'm going to learn, and the more I learn, the better my chances of survival."

"You could survive very well in the States."

"Sure, but you know what that Stateside Mickey Mouse is like, and besides, I want to be able to pass on to the guys just coming into troop what I've learned rather than have them have to find out the hard way; around here that means going home in a body bag."

"If your request is approved, sir, when do you want to take your thirty-day extension leave?"

"How about December 20?"

"I'll take care of it, sir. Let you know as soon as I get the paperwork back from headquarters. If you do plan on staying in the army, this extension will only help your career. I'm assuming that you want to extend your tour in Apache Troop and not some other unit?"

"You've got that right, First Sergeant. Thanks for the help; I'll talk to you later."

"Good luck, sir."

That night, when I told Rosey what I had done, he suggested that I take a trip to Saigon and find a good shrink to speak with; in his opinion, I had slipped over the edge.

"Look Rosey, we've been here almost six months, and we're just beginning to learn how to stay out of trouble. By the time we leave, just like most of the pilots who will be leaving in a week or so, we will have just learned how to do our job and do it well. Red is on his second tour. Did you know that he was a warrant officer on his first tour? I think one of the reasons he's so hard on us is that he's been through all this before. I want to be as good as he is, but I know it will take me a hell of a lot longer than a year. Besides, what's in the States for us to do, be flight instructors at Wolters or Rucker?"

"I know what you're talking about, Jerry, but I'm going home in April, and nothing you say is going to change my mind."

A few nights later there was a large party in our makeshift officer's club for Capt. Norman "Red" Coons who was leaving to go to Bien Hoa the next day, and from there on the Freedom Bird back to the World. I attended briefly, but after a couple of beers, I retreated to the mess hall. As usual, the mess sergeant was sitting at his desk doing paperwork. I sat down and told him about my extension, and he told me of his seventeen years in the army and of his seven kids and wife. After an hour of talking and listening, I didn't feel that my problems were so big after all. I went over to watch the latest spaghetti western.

Morning brought pouring rain, which only compounded the dampness of everything, inside and out. Even with the air conditioner pulling huge amounts of moisture out of the air in our hootch, it was difficult to keep things dry. While looking for a piece of equipment buried in the bottom of a duffel bag, I came across a pair of jungle boots that had been issued to me when I first arrived in Vietnam. I had not worn the boots because they had flamable nylon webbing and were not authorized to be worn by pilots, so they had been packed away for the last five months. When I pulled them out of the bag, anywhere there was leather had an inch-thick layer of mold. The rain also meant that the hard dirt surface surrounding the hootches, would soon turn into a sea of ankle-deep mud and knee-deep in other places.

As soon as the rain let up, my assignment was to cover the insertion of a LRRP team into an area north and east of Song Be. In order to draw the least amount of attention to the area where the LRRPs were to insert, the insertion would be done without a low bird. Lt. Jeff Cromar, who had moved into the sewer pipe with Rosey and me—ignoring the order about warrant officers and commissioned officers living together—had asked if he could ride along with me on the mission. Cromar had been assigned to the headquarters platoon, but he wanted to be where the action was, not just getting to listen to it on the radio. Frustration had prompted him to put in for the Cobra school that the army ran just outside Saigon, but his class was still a month off and he wanted to fly *now*. Jeff could have passed for my younger brother. He had red hair and freckles, and that glimmer in his eyes signaled mischief. I admired his guts. He could have sat out the war, in relative safety, in that headquarters platoon position, but had requested an assignment that he knew stood a good chance of getting him seriously injured or killed. I also had good reason to believe that he wasn't doing it in order to make his officer efficiency report (OER) look better. That report, done once every six months, was sometimes a powerful incentive to do some very dangerous and stupid things, the kinds of things which could result in someone's needless death, and not always the enemy's.

The LRRP insertion point had been picked by someone far removed from Apache Troop. Apache Troop's role in the operation was strictly a supporting one, but we all felt and acted toward one another as if we were all part of the same unit. I never met anyone who envied the assignment of a LRRP. From my one experience in the jungle, I couldn't imagine a worse assignment, but those troops had had to compete for their positions on the team, and it wasn't easy to win one.

I decided to wait in the mess hall for the rain to lift, and told Jeff to round up his flight gear and be ready to go as soon as the weather broke. The men of the LRRP team had already loaded their equipment on Monte Johnson's Huey and had taken cover from the rain with some of the members of the Blue Platoon. The mess hall was always warm and comfortable, a friendly place to burn time. Mike Cutts had all the tent flaps tied open to allow the cooler outside air to circulate through the cook tent. I really enjoyed just sitting and drinking coffee and listening to stories Mike had to tell of family and friends back in Texas.

The rain began to let up around 11:00 A.M., so I decided to walk back over to the TOC and check in. As I walked in, I damn near ran into Captain Coons.

"How's it feel knowing this is your last day?" I asked.

"Real good, Boyle, but I'll have to spend another day at Bien Hoa before I get out of this shithole."

"Would you give me your home address, and I'll drop you a note and let you know how we all are, from time to time?"

"Sure, no problem."

He pulled a standard-issue notepad out of his pocket and jotted down an address in Enterprise, Alabama, which told me he had been assigned to Fort Rucker.

"Thanks, Red. I'll try to keep you informed as to what's going on around here, but with all the old guys leaving in a couple of weeks, I'm a little worried."

"You'll do all right, Boyle. Just remember the things I've tried to teach you, and with a little luck, you'll do just fine."

Monte Johnson, Apache Three One, walked into the TOC and indicated that the rain had let up enough to where the LRRPs wanted to give it a try.

"You make the call, Monte; you're the one who's going to be landing, not me. Don't you just love that idea?" I smiled.

"I'd rather be riding in the front seat with you than pushing that flying Greyhound bus around the sky, but until Harris will let me transfer, I'll be stuck flying lift."

Like me, Monte had attended Cobra school in Savannah, but upon his arrival in Apache Troop there were no openings in Cobras, and he was assigned to the lift platoon. Born and raised in South Dakota, Monte also looked as if he and I could be related, and I was only two years older.

"Let's give it a try; we can always turn around if it gets too bad," Monte said as he headed out the door of the TOC.

"Okay, I'll be right there."

"Hey, Johnson, stay out of trouble, okay? I need you to run me down to Bien Hoa when you get back," Red's voice boomed.

"No problem, Red," Monte yelled.

My crew chief had done a fantastic job cleaning the Plexiglas cockpit canopy. The water was beading up then quickly rolling off as we departed the Apache Troop flight line. Even though it was still raining, I quickly turned on the ECU ("environmental control unit," i.e., air-conditioning) and followed Monte toward the area where the LRRPs would be put out on the ground. Five miles out of Song Be, I called Monte.

"Apache Three One, Two Four. How copy?"

"Two Four, Three One. Loud and clear. How me?"

"Same, same. What's the call sign for the team you're hauling?"

"Stand by one. Two Four, it's Talon Three Six, and he wants to make two dummy landings before going for the real one."

"That's okay by me; you're the one doing the landings. Oh, by the way, you might want to watch what you say on the radio today, I've got Harris's right-hand man in the front seat."

As I said it, I glanced at the reflection of Cromar's face in the rearview mirror. Clearly visible were the unmistakable words, "You son of a bitch," as they were formed on his lips in slow motion. Monte just laughed; he'd already known who was riding with me.

A dummy insertion was a tactic used by the LRRP teams to keep the enemy from pinpointing a team's exact landing site. Before a mission, Monte's Huey, the lift ship, would first overfly the area at a relatively high altitude to locate a clearing where the team was actually to be dropped off. Then he would locate one or two additional locations where dummy landings would be made, usually within a mile of the actual landing spot. During the mission, the lift ship would approach, usually to a hover, the real landing site, and the LRRPs would be out the door in the blink of an eye. Those troops were so well camouflaged that they just seemed to disappear immediately after leaving the helicopter.

Monte called and indicated the clearing that the LRRPs would really be dropped off in as he flew over it. I then advised Cromar what Rick Zeroth had taught me about using Song Be radar to mark the spot on their scope for later reference, should the team get in trouble in bad weather or after dark. Then I asked him to make the call while I kept an eye on Monte. Everything seemed to go like clockwork. Monte made two dummy landings, and then set up his approach for the real drop-off. Monte dropped the Huey down to treetop level a mile west of the landing zone, after first pointing the nose directly at the clearing. At that altitude, it was impossible for him to see the spot until he was almost over it, and he relied upon me to give him directions and distance.

"Three One, easy right, just a little. Okay, start slowing down; you've got maybe a quarter of a mile. Straight ahead now, not very far."

"I got it, Two Four."

I watched while the nose of the Huey rose as if in a steep climb, and the Huey slowed dramatically, and then stopped at a hover above the tall, waving elephant grass. The LRRPs were out the door and had already disappeared as Monte's

Huey departed the clearing. The entire operation had lasted only seconds, and I couldn't help feeling very thankful that I was where I was and not down there with them in that bug-and-enemy-infested jungle.

I dialed up the frequency that the LRRP team would be using and called for a radio check.

"Talon Three Six, Apache Two Four, how copy, over?"

There was an unusually long wait before I heard the whispered reply, "Apache Two Four, Talon Three Six, we've got you loud and clear. Out."

"Apache Three One, Two Four. I've got a solid contact with Talon Three Six. Guess we can head for home."

"Okay, Two Four. I copy we're heading for base. I'll call and let them know we're enroute."

Any further contact with the team would be made between the team and their base via a repeater station located on top of a mountain just east of Song Be.

"Jeff, are you sure Song Be radar has a solid on the LRRP location?"

"Yeah, they've got it circled, and I told them to leave it until I called them."

"That's great, but I sure hope I don't get the assignment if they ever get in contact out here at night. Can you imagine what it would be like flying around out here in the dark!"

"I hear Monte has already had to pull one team out in the middle of the night and that it wasn't much fun," Jeff said.

Returning to Song Be so early in the afternoon felt unusual. Our normal workday usually ended close to sundown or near dark. Even so, I was still looking forward to getting back in time to say good-bye to Red before he left for the States.

Monte's Huey caught my attention as he made a hard left turn back in the opposite direction. Before I could ask him what was going on, he called me.

"Two Four, are you on the TOC's frequency?"

"No, Three One, I forgot to change over."

"We've got to go back and get the LRRPs; they are in heavy contact."

"I've got a solid copy, Three One. I'm right with you."

My blood pressure must have doubled as I tried to envision what I was going to do once we got back to the pickup area. In the past, I could always rely on the aircraft commander to make the tough decisions, now *I* was the aircraft commander. I dialed up the frequency of the LRRP team and called them and at the same time turned the volume up, expecting a whispered answer.

"Talon Three Six, Apache Two Four. How copy?"

The response was so loud that Cromar and I jumped.

"Two Four, Two Four, I've got you loud and clear," the team leader said. I heard automatic gunfire in the background.

"Can you give me a sitrep (situation report)?"

"Two Four, Three Six. We're just inside the tree line on the east side of the LZ where you dropped us off. We were just setting up to monitor the trail down here when the gooks jumped us."

"Can you pop smoke and then adjust me from there?" One of Red's cardinal rules ran through my mind: always know where the friendlies are before you shoot.

"I can pop smoke okay; our location sure isn't a secret anymore. But they are very close to us."

Every time the team leader spoke, I could hear firing in the background, and yet his voice never indicated panic or fear. The guy seemed so cool that it actually helped me calm down and begin to think clearly.

"Okay, Three Six. Here's what I'd like you to do. Throw a smoke as far toward the gooks as you can get it, then adjust me from that smoke. I'm not going to use rockets. They will just go off in the top of the trees and end up getting everyone hurt. I've got a twenty mike mike (20mm Vulcan cannon), and I think I can work with that and get in closer to you. We'll just have to give it a try and adjust from there."

"Sounds okay to me, Two Four. Stand by for the smoke."

"Monte, how are you on fuel?"

"No problem on fuel. I'm at two thousand, keeping an eye on you."

"Thanks, ol' buddy. Sure hope I don't need you."

A stream of purple smoke began to rise through the tops of the jungle a hundred feet or so in from the clearing where Monte had originally dropped off the LRRP team.

"Three Six, Two Four. I've got purple smoke."

"Roger on the purple smoke, Two Four. We are seventy-five to one hundred feet west of the smoke."

"Three Six, Two Four, I'm going to get set up to make my pass from north to south. I'll put out a very short burst on the first pass, and you let me know what happens, then we'll adjust from there. How copy?"

"Jeff, grab hold of the door handle and hang on until I quit firing."

The AH-1G model Cobra wasn't designed to carry such a large gun as the 20mm cannon. When it was fired, the front canopy door had a tendency to fly open, due to the vibration and the pressure change caused by the muzzle blast. The advantage of the 20mm cannon over the rockets was that it was extremely accurate, and the tracers burned for four thousand feet. When fired, it was like directing a fire hose of explosive bullets.

I reached forward and armed the system and watched as the yellow cross hairs of the gunsight appeared on the clear glass square in front of me.

"Two Four, do you want me to get the turret ready?"

"Hold off on the turret, Jeff, until we see just how close we can get to the LRRPs."

"Three Six, keep your heads down as much as you can. I'm in hot at this time," I advised.

My heart felt like a sledgehammer banging off the inside of my chicken plate as I nosed the Cobra over into a shallow dive. Beyond the yellow cross hairs of the gunsight, purple smoke was rising from the tops of the trees. I adjusted the controls so that the cross hairs were a hundred feet or so to the left of the smoke then fired. What appeared to be a solid stream of red erupted from under the left wing and went straight toward the area in the gunsight.

"Two Four, that was great. It sure got their goddamn attention, but it hit behind them. You are going to have to move in closer toward us." Almost as an afterthought, at least that's how it sounded to me, the team leader said, "You were taking a lot of fire on that pass."

"Three Six, Two Four, try and put a smoke where you want me to shoot, if that's possible."

"Stand by one."

"Jesus, Two Four, I'm glad you said something about the door handle. Does it always shake that bad? It was all I could do to keep the canopy closed."

"As far as I know it does. Every time I sat up there and the 20mm was fired, I had to hang on for dear life."

"Two Four, Three Six, smoke out. Hit the smoke; I say again; hit the smoke."

"Roger, Three Six, I've got yellow smoke, and I'm in hot."

Once again I nosed the Cobra over into a dive, but this time

I put the cross hairs right on the smoke coming up through the trees, and fired. Almost immediately the LRRP team leader called; "Two Four, move it just a little more to the west of the smoke."

I didn't have time to talk, as the trees rushed up at us. I lightly put pressure on the right tail-rotor pedal and watched as the stream of bullets moved, ever so slightly, to the right of the smoke.

"Two Four, that's great, you're right in the middle of them, keep it up, keep it coming!"

It was the first time the team leader's voice had shown any sign of emotion, and I was more than happy that it was a good tone of voice.

"Three Six, Two Four, you're going to have to move toward the LZ as soon as possible. I only carry two hundred rounds for the twenty mike mike, and I'm really not sure how much I've got left."

"We're trying to move right now, Two Four. Is the lift ship ready?"

"We're all just waiting on you, Three Six. Whenever you're ready, he'll be ready. On the next pass, I'm going to put down some minigun fire on the smoke and to the east of it. Maybe that will be enough distraction so you can pick up and get the hell out of there."

"Okay, Two Four. Be advised, I think you got some of the bastards on that last pass, but you're taking a lot of fire on your pullouts."

"Cromar, unlock the turret sight and be ready to fire the minigun at the smoke and to the east of the smoke. Let's see if we can confuse the shit out of the gooks."

"Three Six, I'm in hot with the minigun. I'll be overflying your position and firing back to the east, so watch out for the falling hot brass."

"Got a solid, Two Four."

I held my breath and hoped that the minigun would fire, and if it did fire, wouldn't jam, as was usually the case.

I was about to tell Cromar to start shooting, when the minigun came to life with its deep throaty *brrrrrrring* sound.

"That's great, Two Four, keep it up. We're moving west."

As I pulled out of my dive, Cromar quit firing. The minigun had worked perfectly, and I was overjoyed.

"Well, Jeff, what do you think?"

"Out of sight, Two Four, out of sight!" was all Cromar could manage.

"Two Four, Three Six, we're at the edge of the LZ."

"Three Six, did the bad guys move with you?"

"Negative, negative. As best we can tell, they are still under cover back by the smoke."

"Are you ready for pickup, Three Six?"

"Affirmative, Two Four. We're ready."

"Apache Three One, Two Four. Did you copy Three Six?"

"Affirmative, Two Four, we're ready whenever you are."

"Hold off a bit, Three One. I've got enough room now, and I'm going to put down some rockets and try and hold the gooks where they are. Do you have a pretty good idea where the team is located?"

"I think so, Two Four, but I could use a smoke if they think it will be okay."

"Stand by one, Three One."

"Three Six, Two Four. When the rockets start impacting, pop smoke. I'm in hot at this time, and your lift ship is right behind me."

"Roger, Two Four. We're ready."

I reached forward to the control panel and dialed the rocket selector switch to one pair as I nosed the Cobra over into another dive. This meant that each time I pushed the red rocket button with my thumb, one rocket would be fired from under each wing. Firing rockets was not a lot different from firing a rifle or pistol, but it took a lot of practice to be able to hit what you were shooting at, and I had not had very much practice. The first pair left the underside of the wings with a *whoosh* sound and sailed over the smoke, impacting the trees fifty yards east of the smoke. I pushed the nose over into a steeper dive and pushed the rocket button twice. This time, four rockets streaked away from the Cobra and impacted the trees almost on top of the smoke.

The LRRP team leader called, "Smoke out," and Monte acknowledged with "Roger, Three Six. I've got purple smoke. I'll be inbound from the west."

As I pulled out of my dive, I made a wide, sweeping, climbing turn to my right and saw Monte racing in from the west, low level, toward the LRRP's smoke.

"Which way are you coming out, Three One?" I asked.

"Same way we came in, but on the north side instead of the

south side. My door gunner said he thought we may have taken fire from the southern tree line."

"Okay, I'm in hot again, let me know when you pull pitch (take off)."

As Monte set the Huey down in the blowing grass, I pushed the rocket button four times and watched as eight rockets impacted the trees just east of Monte's location.

"We're coming out hot, Two Four," Monte's voice crackled over the radio.

I was completely out of position to really cover their departure from the clearing. I had not anticipated that they would be so quick. I banked the Cobra sharply over to the left, three or four hundred feet off the trees, and headed north, in the same direction Monte was going. As Monte approached the north edge of the clearing, he banked the Huey sharply to the left and headed due west, at the same time calling; "Two Four, we're taking fire from the northern tree line."

"Roger, Three One," was all I could think to say. We were in a lousy position to shoot. When Monte turned to the west, it had put me at his eight o'clock position (left rear), almost the same altitude and a quarter mile away. All I could do was fire behind him, and that wasn't going to do a hell of a lot of good. I put the cross hairs behind the tail of the Huey, then banked a little to the right to leave some room for safety and pushed the rocket button. Two rockets streaked away from the Cobra, and I hit the button one more time with the same reaction. My heart stopped as all the rockets curved to the left, away from where I had the cross hairs located, and passed directly under Monte's Huey, impacting the tree line to the right of the helicopter. From the angle I was able to view the occurrence, I felt that I had just shot down Monte. I was more than overjoyed when the rockets passed under the Huey, and never so relieved. I was about to call Monte, once I was able to speak, and apologize. I had fired with the Cobra very much out of trim, causing the rockets to follow a natural path, rather than where I had expected them to go.

"Two Four, Three One. That was some really great shooting. The LRRPs also said to tell you thanks a lot."

"You're more than welcome, Three One. I owe you a beer, and the rest of your crew also. Let's go home," I said, my voice breaking very badly.

"Jeff, why don't you try your hand at flying this thing from the front seat. It can be a lot of fun, once you get used to it."

"Sure, Two Four, I've got the aircraft."

Under normal circumstances, we would have landed at refuel, and then moved to the rearm area before parking the Cobra. But I didn't want to miss saying good-bye to Red.

"Three one, are you going to refuel before you take Red to Bien Hoa?"

"No, Two Four, the plan has changed. King is taking him down on the mail run; that's them parked close to the TOC."

"Okay. Thanks, Monte."

I asked Cromar if he'd cool the Cobra down so I could catch Red before he left. My legs felt as if they were made of rubber as I climbed out of the backseat and walked across the flight line to where Red was about to climb into the left front seat of the Huey. He turned and stuck out his hand as I approached him and I shook it. I hoped that he wouldn't notice that my hand was still shaking from the realization that I had just about killed nine of my own, or the fact that I was still lily white in the face.

"You did okay today, Boyle. Were you able to teach Lieutenant Cromar anything?" Red asked with a smile.

"I think maybe just a little, Red. The word must get out pretty fast. Hell, we just landed!" I said, feeling a little confused.

"You forget, Boyle, we monitor all the frequencies back here at the TOC. That little crack about Major Harris may end up getting you a few extra duties!"

Mike King began the start cycle on the Huey as Red climbed into the front seat.

"I wish I could go over today's mission with you, Red, I've got a lot of questions."

"Everything I heard sounded just great, Boyle. Don't worry about it; you'll do just fine."

"But, Red, it's what you didn't hear that I'm worried about."

My last comment went unheard as Red slipped his helmet on and adjusted his shoulder and seat belts. We again shook hands through the open upper half of window in the door, and then I backed up to get away from the rotor wash. I watched Red depart as I had watched him depart the month before, and I hoped to God that he made it to Bien Hoa this time without being shot down. Red and I had never really been friends, but still I knew that I would miss him very much. I felt much like the son whose father hauls him to some unfamiliar and remote location, drops him off, and tells him to find his own way home.

Had I been a soothsayer and had the ability to look into the future and all that it held in store for me and the rest of Apache Troop, I think I would have gotten on the helicopter with Red and gone AWOL. For in five months, I and the rest of Apache Troop would return to Cambodia in support of South Vietnamese troops. During that time, Apache Troop would run up against a battalion-size force of NVA regulars, equipped with sophisticated antiaircraft weapons and eager to fight. We would have ten of our fifteen helicopters crash or be shot down, with many of my friends killed or wounded. But that is another story, still to be told. I survived Vietnam, which I attribute to the tradition, at the time, of not allowing a pilot to become an aircraft commander until he had spent a minimum of five months flying in the front seat and had learned just about everything there was to learn about conducting a combat mission. Lt. Larry Lilly, gave his life because a young, hotshot captain got around that tradition, which action resulted in Larry's death. That hotshot captain still flies helicopters to this date, as a civilian in the Gulf of Mexico; Larry still rests in Cambodia.

I somehow managed to depart Vietnam without being awarded a Purple Heart medal, but as Major Harris once told me, "A Purple Heart does nothing but attest to the accuracy of the enemy."

AFTERWORD

Some of the people mentioned in the book and where they are now.

Paul FUNK, commanding officer of Apache Troop, then a captain, has remained in the army and is now a three-star general, with his headquarters at Fort Hood, Texas, home of the 1st Cavalry Division.

William "Bill" HARRIS, commanding officer of Apache Troop after Captain Funk, retired from the army as a colonel and lives in Nashville, Tennessee.

Carl J. "Rosey" ROSAPEPE Jr. is the chief pilot for a hospital in Roanoke, Virginia.

William "Bill" FULLER flies for the Bureau of Land Management and lives in Phoenix, Arizona.

John PEELE and Jimmy MILLS live and work in Florida.

John WILLIAMS lives in Charlotte, North Carolina, and flies for U.S. Air.

Jim "Magnet Ass" THOMAS retired from the army and lives in Lake Villa, Illinois and flies for American Airlines.

Jack "Blue" HUGELE is a businessman in Houston, Texas.

Charles "Charlie" COCHRAN lives in Florida and works for the government.

John "Bloody Bart" BARTLETT lives in Whitefish, Montana, and works for the railroad.

Ron BLACK lives and flies helicopters in Indonesia.

Ordean IVERSON lives and works in northern Montana.

Mike KING lives and flies helicopters for a hospital in New York.

Bob LONG lives and flies helicopters for a hospital in Arizona.

Mike REARDON, Apache Troop's renowned scout pilot, teaches at Saint Michael's Catholic school in Newark, New Jersey, is a playwright and has written a play entitled *Angeles*. He is a member of the Society for Divine Vocation where he is studying for the priesthood.

Rick "Zero" ZEROTH owns his own business in Moline, Illinois.

Mike CUTTS lives and works in Lavina, Tennessee.

Robert "Bob" COMSTOCK is a police officer in El Paso, Texas.

Francis "Tony" CORTEZ is soon to be promoted to sergeant major and is stationed at Fort Lewis, Washington.

Jack BRACAMONTE Jr. lives in Sacramento, California and works for the state.

Art DOCKTOR lives in Fargo, North Dakota, and is self employed.

Morris PIPER lives and works in Whitehorse, Tennessee.

Kregg JORGENSON is a writer and also works as a U.S. customs officer in the Seattle area.

Jeff CROMAR retired from the army as a colonel and is presently an executive with Bell Helicopters in Forth Worth, Texas.

Richard "Dick" HORNE retired from the army and is the postmaster at Fillmore, California.

Command Sergeant Major Joseph BOOK retired from the Army Reserve and lives in Oxnard, California.

Mike MOYSARD, retired from the San Francisco Police Department and now lives in Midland, Texas.

Roger M. RIEPE lives in Webster, Texas, and is a full-time pilot for the Texas National Guard.

ABOUT THE AUTHOR

Jerry Boyle was born May 28, 1938, in Hollywood, California, and was raised there and in the San Fernando Valley until moving to Ventura, California, in the summer of 1960. He joined an Army Reserve unit there and was a member from 1961 until his discharge in 1967. In 1969, he requested a waiver of age from the army and was accepted into the Warrant Officer Candidate Course and Flight School, a forty-week school. Upon graduation, he requested further training at the army AH-1G Cobra, Attack Helicopter School, at Savannah, Georgia, and was accepted.

Upon graduation from Attack Helicopter School, he was ordered to Vietnam and assigned to A Troop, 1st Squadron, 9th Cavalry, of the 1st Cavalry Division. He spent eighteen months in Vietnam and Cambodia and was awarded the Silver Star, three Distinguished Flying Crosses, five Bronze Stars, two Army Commendation Medals for Valor, and the Vietnamese Cross of Gallantry, among others. The author is currently flying in support of offshore operations and lives with his wife of twenty years, Andrea, in Ojai, California.